Multi-national and intercultural services organisations
and the integration in front of global clients

Nordeuropäische Beiträge
aus den Human- und Gesellschaftswissenschaften

Scandinavian University Studies
in the Humanities and Social Sciences

Herausgegeben von / Edited by Hartmut Schröder

Bd./Vol. 31

PETER LANG
Frankfurt am Main · Berlin · Bern · Bruxelles · New York · Oxford · Wien

Christoph O.-Ph. Freiherr von Gamm

Multi-national and Intercultural Services Organisations and the Integration in Front of Global Clients

PETER LANG
Internationaler Verlag der Wissenschaften

Bibliographic Information published by the Deutsche Nationalbibliothek
The Deutsche Nationalbibliothek lists this publication in the Deutsche Nationalbibliografie; detailed bibliographic data is available in the internet at http://dnb.d-nb.de.

Zugl.: Frankfurt (Oder), Europa-Univ., Diss., 2010

D 521
ISSN 0942-0657
ISBN 978-3-631-61600-0

Internationaler Verlag der Wissenschaften
Frankfurt am Main 2011

www.peterlang.de

Geleitwort

Interkulturelles und interdisziplinäres Lehren und Forschen sind die stets wiederholten Anforderungen an die Universitäten, sowohl an Lehrende als auch Studierende. Wirkliche Erfüllung dieser Vorgaben beinhaltet die Integration der Praxis in die universitäre Landschaft, dass interkulturelle Kommunikation auch die wirtschaftliche Praxis reflektiert und – im günstigsten Fall – umgekehrt. Doch können Hochschullehrer auch erwarten, dass Repräsentanten der Praxis als Kollegen oder Doktoranden sich den Gepflogenheiten wissenschaftlichen Arbeitens anpassen. All diese Erwartungen gehen viel zu selten in Erfüllung, so dass die vorliegende Studie besonders zu begrüßen ist.

Christoph v. Gamm legt eine Arbeit aus der Praxis heraus und für die Praxis vor. Im Rahmen seiner internationalen Tätigkeiten wurde er rasch mit der Notwendigkeit einer gesicherten Methode interkulturellen Arbeitens konfrontiert und bemerkte, dass in den 1970er Jahren an Universitäten entwickelte und sukzessive in die Praxis überführte Herangehensweisen und Einschätzungen (z.B. Hofstede) einer Modifikation in einer veränderten, globalisierten Welt bedurften. Diese Überlegungen bildeten die Grundlage für die vorliegende Dissertation, die von Gamm seit mehreren Jahren vorbereitete und schließlich Ende 2010 verteidigen konnte.

In der nun vorliegenden Endfassung der Studie werden Konsequenzen der Herausforderung der Globalisierung für eine Serviceorganisation mit 90.000 Mitarbeitern weltweit beleuchtet, die von sich selbst annimmt, sie agiere interdisziplinär und sei interkulturell verankert. Wie sehr dabei Anspruch und Wirklichkeit bisweilen auseinander driften, zeigt sich an der Befragung von Führungskräften. Von Gamm zeigt auf, wie business unusual zum regulären Alltag wird und was dies für die Mitarbeiter bedeutet, die sich eben aufgrund der Unmöglichkeit einer langfristigen Verankerung in einem bestimmten Bereich mit Personen und Kulturen auseinander setzen müssen, auf die sie meist nur ungenügend vorbereitet wurden (z.B. seitens der Universität, auch wenn von Gamm höflich genug ist, das nicht zu explizieren). Der Ländervergleich beinhaltet Staaten, die auch in den Medien häufig mit Outsourcing in Verbindung gebracht werden: Indien oder Polen. Die für Capgemini bedeutsamen Länder Rumänien und Chile vervollständigen das Bild und gewähren Einblicke in eine Geschäftskultur, die bislang hinter Schlagworten verschwand.

Christoph von Gamm belässt es nicht bei Kritik, er gibt praxisnah Alternativ- und Modifikationsvorschläge für die eingeführten Theoriemodelle, die er nicht stürzen, sondern an die neuen Verhältnisse anpassen will. Er will keine Revolution, sondern eine Verbesserung durch Diskurs erreichen. Dies zeigt sich insbesondere in der Verknüpfung seiner Untersuchungsergebnisse mit den geschäftlichen Realitäten. So ergibt sich auch für den Leser die rasch nachvollziehbare Feststellung, dass Kulturunterschiede Teil von Wirtschaftsforschung sein müssen. Ansonsten scheitern nicht nur einzelne Aktionen, sondern auch Unternehmen und mit ihnen die Arbeitnehmer, ihre Familien, eventuell sogar größere soziale Bereiche.

Im Ganzen stellt die vorliegende Studie einen wichtigen Beitrag zur Erforschung der Auswirkungen interkulturellen und interdisziplinären Zusammenarbeitens in einer Servicefirma wie Capgemini, die durchaus als branchenrepräsentativ anzusehen ist, dar. Christoph von Gamm stellt die richtigen Fragen an die eigenen und auch universitären Theoretiker und findet Antworten zu Punkten wie Unternehmensstrategie, Outsourcing, kulturellem Verständnis oder Leistungsbereitschaft in einer globalisierten Welt. Es bleibt daher zu wünschen, dass der Autor und seine Arbeit Gehör finden in der Praxis einerseits sowie in der akademischen Forschung und Lehre andererseits.

Frankfurt (Oder), Februar 2011 Prof. Dr. Hartmut Schröder

Abstract – Executive Summary

Intercultural and interdisciplinary collaboration in a large IT services organization do have a significant impact in order to gain economic and market success. By looking into specific factor conditions of outsourcing countries and the effectiveness of offshoring Central European IT services into countries like India, Poland, Romania and Chile, this dissertation does research the collaborative model in working with these countries.

At the same time, by taking a practical field of study, the author did examine in the year 2009 in the Consulting and IT Services Company Capgemini – headquartered in Paris, France and present in more than 40 countries. Here, a census survey of colleagues in senior positions with client proximity in Germany, Switzerland and Austria has been performed and analyzed. Capgemini being setup in an organizational structure-division by "Disciplines" - consulting, technology services and outsourcing from the front to the delivering end, interdisciplinary cooperation even with the same client or in the same market appears to be rather sporadic or opportunistic. Caused by the internationalization of labor - especially in outsourcing - additional tension to the company culture has been generated. This creates frictions – and in the interest of financial and market success, these frictions need be overcome.

Besides investigating the intercultural implications, the thesis proposes an organizational change for Capgemini in order to improve the cooperation both across disciplines as well across different countries. This thesis provides the bridge between the Intercultural Business Communication as a science to building mutual understanding of business strategy, the aims and sales to generate more profit and the art of sales management and creates the balance of interests between buyer and seller.

Intercultural Business Communications is about understanding what other people in other cultures mean and want to convey to each other. Sales Management is about generating the right organisational capabilities in order to make more revenues and profits out of an existing client base and attract and retain new clients whilst selecting the right people and structures in order to excel. Combining both Intercultural Business Communications and Sales in order to excel in an international environment can provide an edge in terms of competitiveness.

Capgemini has been founded 43 years ago and has gone through many metamorphoses in order to get to its current state with providing IT and Business services in the area Consulting, Technology Services and Outsourcing to its clients. With an increasing change in the landscape – moving to a global coverage of its clients and a more centralized purchasing authority, clients increasingly demand for centralized, and coordinated one-stop shopping across different lines of business. This dissertation dissects the following five key questions:

- How to work together in different ecosystems, divisional cultures?
- How to plan accounts, specifically international accounts?
- How to organise sales teams in front of the clients?
- How to win deals, profitably?
- How to collaborate across the Capgemini ecosystem?

The founder of Capgemini – Sogeti, Serge Kampf, did initially setup his business with a key motivation to be independent. This notion of independence perpetrates through the whole company. Independence and teaming between partners – or different group division – all too often have a challenge to be integrated. This dissertation integrates these two conflicting points of view.

This dissertation did depict a snapshot of Capgemini in the years 2009 to mid-2010. Many things have changed since the submission of the dissertation, Capgemini Consulting has separated even more by setting up its own brand with a logo in Bordeaux red instead of blue, Technology Services did integrate stronger and became a global Service line dubbed ―Apps One" and ―Apps Two". However it seemed that the constant lobbying for an integration point at country level in Switzerland especially starts to bear some fruits. Organisations change over time and it is very likely that parts of this dissertation – probably not everything – will be applied in practice.

Foreword

Aristotle investigated the difference between Barbarian and Greek culture, later Marco Polo researched and traded with the Chinese and Humboldt travelled the world. Working with different cultures involves an interchange between self-view, experience of the world and performing trade. In today's academia, this has been treated separately from the original goal of intercultural work: making commerce, making trades and achieving a win-win-situation. At the same time, the foundation for trades, Sales Leadership and Sales Management for many decades has been a „black art" and has been more of a neglected stepchild in science. With the internationalisation of the services industry, a new breed of services sales has come to play: the integrated and international services value proposition which transcends cultures and bridges gaps for a commercial advantage.

With the start of the author's career at Capgemini as a Director, he was surprised to find such a highly fragmented approach towards sales leadership in a big organization, despite the fact that Capgemini in one way or the other serves more than 450 of the Fortune 500 companies plus a large series of government bodies. In many situations, Capgemini is a great challenger and contender towards the big competitors with a great passion of its people to win. Having a a Master's Degree in Software Engineering at TU Munich, the author joined IBM in 1995. After a career inside this company throughout various stages and countries in the professions of corporate communications and sales leadership, whilst becoming an MBA at the Open University and an INSEAD-certified Sales Executive the author joined Capgemini early 2008. Whilst working as a Business Development Director at Capgemini, he became MA in Sales Management in Portsmouth. Hence, this study aims to examine what can become better especially in services organisations such as Capgemini while lowering the efforts, thus taking a scientific approach in winning in a multicultural environment. This dissertation compiles those collected experiences in various disciplines and companies and combines theory and practice.

Acknowledgements

My sincere thanks go to

- All the Capgemini leading employees who voluntarily shared their views and responded to the survey; plus the Capgemini Country Board in Germany/Switzerland headed by Antonio Schnieder in allowing me to do so
- My coach Dr. Isabelle Roux-Chenu who challenged my thoughts especially in the first half of 2010
- My colleagues for Capgemini in Switzerland who were more than helpful to discuss and share their views over time – notably here Karl Bernhardsgrütter, Alex Strobel, Nicole Bartlome, Ursula Brändle and Fabian Dülli – a great team to work with.
- My four managers whom I had during the times of writing and did support me in their each very own and particular way – Eduard Bugelnig, Oliver Schwarz, Lennart Koch and Oliver Schwarz (sic!).
- My partner, Dr. Alexander Wimmer, who has brought me a series of ideas discussing this topic and spending evenings around this theme
- My mother Dr. Eva-Maria von Gamm who questioned my thoughts through her unbiased view of the corporate world, especially around international trade and outsourcing.
- My friend, PD Dr. Florian G. Mildenberger, who ignited my academic stamina to research on those experiences more thoroughly.
- And last but not least to Professor Dr. Hartmut Schröder and Ms. Professor Dr. Dr. Claude-Hélène Meyer for supporting and coaching me on this research.

Zurich, February 2011 Christoph v. Gamm

Table of Contents

1 Introduction

This dissertation examines the impact of intercultural and interdisciplinary collaboration in a large IT services organization in order to gain economic and market success. By looking into specific factor conditions of outsourcing countries and the effectiveness of offshoring Central European IT services of countries like India, Poland, Romania and Chile, the collaborative model working with these countries has been investigated. At the same time, by taking a practical field of study, the author did perform a sales-research-related investigation in 2009 in the Consulting and IT Services company Capgemini – headquartered in Paris, France and present in more than 40 countries. Here, a census survey of colleagues in senior positions with client proximity in Germany, Switzerland and Austria has been performed and analyzed. Capgemini being setup in an organizational structure-division by "Disciplines" - consulting, technology services and outsourcing from the front to the delivering end, interdisciplinary cooperation even with the same client or in the same market appears to be rather sporadic or opportunistic. Due to the internationalization of labor - especially in outsourcing - additional tension to the company culture has been generated. This creates frictions – and in the interest of financial and market success, these frictions needed to be surpassed. Besides investigating the intercultural implications, the thesis proposes an organizational change for Capgemini in order to improve the cooperation both across disciplines as well across different countries. This thesis provides the bridge between the Intercultural Business Communication as a science to building mutual understanding of business strategy, the aims and sales to generate more profit and the art of sales management and creates the balance of interests between buyer and seller.

1.1 Introduction - Insight overview

This dissertation will provide the following insights into the academic world through the following questions:

- How can an integrated sales organization for a multi-disciplined IT services and consulting company help improve sales of all disciplines?

Sales and sales management, (B. Rogers, 2007) being a "boundary-spanning role" as depicted by Rogers, has a strong cultural bridging dimension. This reflects with the idea of Grant (Grant, 1999), to develop the right capabilities from existing resources and to provide and a mutual understanding (Oksaar, 1993) of the respective views in production and interaction skills in cross-cultural situations (Trompenaars & Hampden-Turner, 1995) in order to create a competitive advantage. In order to achieve tangible success, the concepts of Hofstede, Bolten, Ouchi and Trompenaars should be executed together with the concepts of sales management as depicted in the works of Rogers, Ryals, and Lemke and McDonald, and put into the realm of the corporate strategy aspects, as shown by Grant, Porter, Kaplan & Norton. The discipline Intercultural Business Communication is thus the foundation for a culture adapted to the customer sales process, which has a strategic importance for companies.

Tangible knowledge and understanding of cultural characteristics (Schröder, 1998), should be codified in the form of databases by local experts who know each other across borders and adds to the knowledge of intangibles. This implies, however, that the enterprise configuration according to Mintzberg (Mintzberg, 1999) should support in addition to the global control and global "strategic apex", an "octopus-like" set of local brains. The part in between, known as the "middle office" or "support staff", and the so-called "techno structure" should be allocated in a globally cost-optimized way.

- How can intercultural differences not only be used as a lever but also as a beneficial advantage for success?

A good cross-cultural collaboration for a company is particularly well effective if there is a common goal. For example, a common customer base as a revenue source helps connect people while measuring the collaboration through a structured measurement system such as the Balanced Scorecard, shown by Kaplan and Norton (Kaplan & Norton, 2001, p. 149). When measuring this, besides the pure financial perspective like revenues, costs, profit other perspectives such as the customer perspective, the innovation and learning perspective as well as the internal process perspective – all centered around a central mission and vision - should be investigated in order to measure and improve the intercultural collaboration. In a client-orientated environment, the sales leaders in charge should therefore have a common set of targets and goals and the salary and bonus system should be connected with these goals.

Leading indicators such as deal pipeline, certification of employees, both technical and intercultural skills, succession plans in Human Resources, and market share tests should be combined with trailing indicators such as revenue, cost ratio, profits and customer satisfaction in a reasonable and weighted measure.

- How might a concise sales management approach refocus a company?

The key success factors for service organizations in order to realize an international outsourcing are high technical ability, low labor costs, global functioning as ITIL processes and not to different corporate culture to the end customer. Enterprise configurations with customer-related functions should therefore be much more culturally adopted towards the client than client-remote areas, however even a backoffice needs to understand the customer in order to perform. An outsourcing business can only be realized if the transaction costs of bridging this cultural factor does not outweigh the cost advantages of the outsource organization itself. Not every place in the world is equally appropriate for the allocation of resources and workers. As Porter has written in his concept on Porter's Diamond (Porter, 2008), factor conditions and surrounding cultures are essential.

- How making a trade-off between critical resources and the focus onto the right resources generate more sales in less time with less effort?

Within different company divisions different sub-cultures do exist, despite being in the same country or cultural frame. These sub-cultures are being influenced by the divisional or company goals and also vice versa, the people having a different mindset within that sub-culture do frame the company goals accordingly. In essence, it shows with the people surveyed that the presumption is true that the business unit is looking for its culture-matching employees and vice versa. For example, to speak in the dimensions of Hofstede (Hofstede, 2001), long-term orientated risk-takers are more likely to be found in the outsourcing business whereas short term orientated risk averse people with a lower power distance are more likely to be found within the consulting business. Technology Services staff, however, show a higher risk awareness - their software at some point has to work, the consulting Powerpoint slide set however is a patient set of files. However, from a customer who only views a company "Capgemini" looks, these cultural differences – almost like "walls of glass" (Meyer, 2005), requires customer-oriented managers. Those people, often known as Key Account Managers are able to understand all three different disciplines of the company whilst understanding the breadth of their customers as the true source of revenues (Sharma, 1999).

The survey of executives conducted within different regions and divisions shows that these people are willing to share bonuses and financial rewards within a team, if it serves the common success. With the cross-cultural understanding being a core resource for the success of a company, this should therefore not only be measured but financial incentives for promoting business useful behavior - both short and long term – should also be set.

For a federally structured company like Capgemini with its very freedom-loving founding entrepreneur Serge Kampf (Gaston-Breton, 2007) and its structure now being changed towards a "globally integrated enterprise" (Palmisano, 2006), this is a fundamental cultural change. This implies change capabilities and provides a new definition of the intangible core resource "values" (Grant, 1999). This resource must be used in changing values ("Capabilities"), such as the ability to act locally and globally as a core requirement to achieve success. A fundamental discussion about values will therefore be the consequence in this company.

Besides the academic value, the research and the dissertation might provide Capgemini an insight and clearer view on how to improve its business in an attractive marketplace with some but limited effort and make more revenues in less time at higher profit. Besides this specific market, this proposal might serve as a template on how to integrate specific market organizations of Capgemini for the better. A further layout of the introduction chapter is depicted in Figure 1-1.

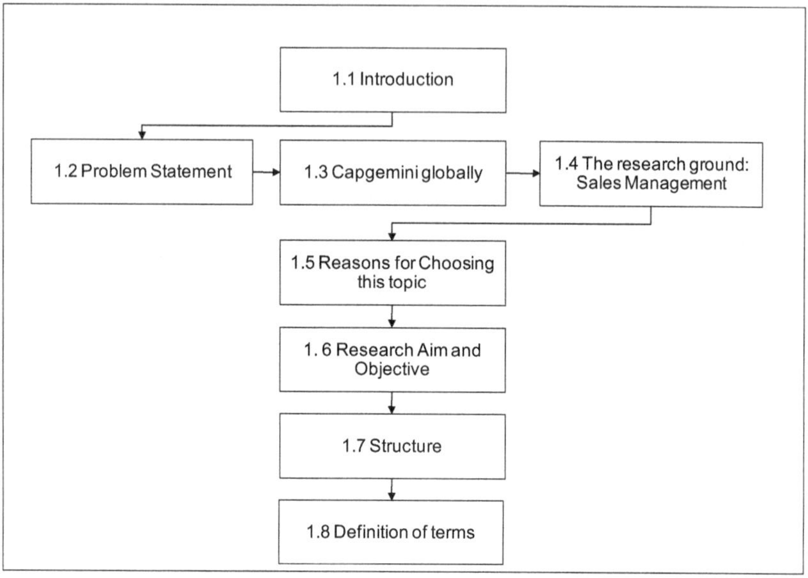

Figure 1-1: Chapter I

1.2 Problem statement

Worldwide, in Europe and in the subject of inspection, Germany and Switzerland, the investigated firm Capgemini is not Number 1 in IT and Business Services. The leader is IBM with EUR 45 bln, and then EDS, T-Systems, Accenture, according to the market researcher IDC (Hedin, 2009, p. 7). However, from an academic perspective, sales is about gaining market share and to displace competition. With Capgemini not being Number 1 in Germany and Switzerland, a question might arise to the business leaders: What does it take to become the leader – what are aspects of business strategy, intercultural and sales management to achieve this ambition?

This dissertation will research using a collaborative enquiry of sales leaders the key factors of winning. It examines what difference might be made with the installation of a controlled and measured professional sales leadership function. As a research subject, Capgemini Group in Germany/Switzerland has been chosen in order to preserve the following academic rules according to Bryman & Bell (Bryman & Bell, 2007, p. 87):

- Originality – It has not been the subject of any larger sales research so far.
- The confines of Capgemini working in the German/Swiss Market are clearly defined and same is the sales function.
- Capgemini as a company and its employees can be and are allowed to be researched - the published work on intercultural business communications, cor-

porate strategy and sales management can be reviewed and put into the context of the company.
- Data from sales leaders of the respective countries can be collected and then be analysed through a primary research.
- Similarly, the data of the economic and socio-political situation of the countries observed can be obtained and compared in an objective way using official and third-party statistics such as from the CIA or the German Foreign Office, the Gartner Group, Forrester and others.
- An analysis of existing practice within Capgemini in terms of the theoretical framework can be established for the study, including comparative organisational practices from competitors such as IBM, CSC or Swisscom IT Services who all frequently publish about their organizational behaviors.
- Conclusions can be drawn and a clear recommendation can be made.

1.3 Research Subject – Capgemini

The subject of research is the IT Services and Consulting company Capgemini, also in comparison with its competitors such as IBM, CSC or Swisscom IT Services.

Capgemini is present in 36 countries and reported 2008 global revenues of € 8.7 billion and employs over 90,000 people worldwide (Capgemini S.A., 2010, p. 16). The global IT Market, according to Hedin (Hedin, 2009, p. 5) amounts to roughly € 800 billion, thus Capgemini has a global market share of around 1.2%.

Capgemini in Central Europe

From a sales side, Capgemini in Central Europe mainly consists of Capgemini Group companies in Germany, Austria and Switzerland. Capgemini in Germany currently employs 2270 employees, Capgemini in Switzerland, once a company of roughly 500 employees, has shrunk by half until 2009. With the dotcom boom and bust in 2001 (Florida, 2002), many of the consulting mandates have been lost and people had to be freed up to the market, and since then, no real sign of recovery has been shown. Capgemini in Central Europe has fallen short of expectations and thus has lost its market share. Still, Capgemini has a good brand name through its global presence and through some strategic and anchor clients. It particular, it is an employer of choice for bright graduates (Manager-Magazin, 2009) in Germany.

As shown in the following chapter, the market for IT services in Germany and Switzerland is both attractive for Capgemini and in Switzerland double as high in relation to GDP than in Germany. Capgemini in Austria has been put out of the inspection set, as the Capgemini business there at that point in time has been in a complete reorganisation and the survey respondents from Austria did not really respond. From a delivery side, additionally, Capgemini does entertain in Central Europe a set of delivery centres, especially in Poland and Romania whose purpose is to deliver services to the sales end countries, like into Switzerland.

1.4 Research Ground: Intercultural Business Communications, Corporate Strategy and Sales Management

Very little literature has been published about the interconnection between corporate strategies per se, sales management practices and intercultural business communications despite the fact that corporate increasingly go international. Therefore, it is worth investigating how those four aspects do go hand in hand in order to achieve corporate success.

Intercultural Business Communications according to Bolten (Bolten, 2007, p. 12) is about investigating the verbal, nonverbal, paraverbal and extraverbal ways of communicating between people of different groups, cultures company enterprise parts or different enterprises and to see what chasms in understanding do exist. With a multinational services organisation, different cultures – both between organisational parts in different countries as well as between different divisions are most likely to exist and be observed.

Corporate strategy according to Grant (Grant, 1999, p. 3) is the "determination of the long-run goals and objectives of an enterprise and the adoption of courses of action and the allocation of resources necessary for carrying out these goals", whilst "gaining competitive advantage... and to enable a company to gain... a sustainable edge over its competitors". In short, corporate strategy is a way to achieve a success and to reach the goal in a comprehensive and cost-effective way, a plan of attack.

Internationalisation of companies according to Rose (Rose, 1977, p. 112) happens mostly because of both defensive and also market-seeking strategic moves. Thus, companies go international because they have reached their natural market ceiling within a certain country or in order to take away market share from a different competitor who has occupied a certain market within that area. Besides this, especially for goods producing companies, scale and scope effects do play a role – the incremental efforts of producing more are rather minimal and therefore a new market might be explored. However, this implies selling internationally and establishing sales and services subsidiaries abroad. Moreover, internationalization might also occur from the producing end, for example by searching for cost and factor advantages.

Sales Management, according to Rogers (Rogers B. , 2007, p. 15), (Piercy & Lane, 2005, p. 565) and Bowman (Bowman, 1990, p. 47) has a key involvement in strategy formulation, provides intelligence to the delivery units about industry and client knowledge, integrates across functions to deliver value, provides marketing and develops infrastructure. In order to understand sales management as a "boundary spanning role", how it is being conducted inside a company and how it helps fuel growth need to be investigated.

For the broader picture, the linkage between corporate strategy as a way to achieve the goal, the intercultural business communication as a fundament that explains how to bridge and differentiates different cultures especially in an internationalised context and the sales management science which formulates concrete techniques and ways how to achieve a sales success is of interest for both scholars and practitioners. It gives a more concrete handle on how to organise sales management systems and sales teams through the knowledge of the intercultural context in order to execute a corporate strategy – i.e. to grow market shares in a certain markets - the most cost effective way. Moreover, it is of essence to find a measurement system on how to measure intercultural behaviour and success and failure to adapt to intercultural differences in order to modify this behaviour from a management perspective over time.

1.5 Reasons for choosing this topic

The main reason why this topic has been chosen is to see how a company can achieve its strategic goal – which is to increase market shares - by improving on its intercultural behaviour in the realms of an internationalised business and by performing better in sales.

Given the global stance vs. the local situation, an opportunity gap there seems to exist just to arrive to a normal European Average market share of Capgemini of 3-5% of the total IT Services Market, estimated in Switzerland to be € 10 bln per annum (OSEC, 2009). This 5% market share gap – meaning € 500 million revenues - at current conversion rates, would imply a six-fold increase of the current revenues.

Given the opportunity gap between the current situation without an interculturally adapted sales management function and a to-be-state with a sales leadership function, the subject of observation "Capgemini in Switzerland" appears to be a good example on how to apply a sales management function.

Purpose of the study

As Rogers (Rogers B. , 2007, p. 22) points out, sales has "always been a boundary-spanning role – representing the company to the customer and representing the customer within the company". Thus, the question is:

Is there a sales management function that enables a) the client to buy from an organization easily and b) the organization to "sell itself" easily? The strategic roles of the sales function is according to Piercy (Piercy N. F., 2001, p. 97) an "involvement in strategy formulation", "intelligence for industry and customer knowledge and analysis", "integration to work across functions to develop value", "internal marketing – of the customer to colleagues" and "infrastructure development".

Sales itself is meant to be the facilitator, the missing link, the packaging of something else – means the organization itself – especially in services needs to be ready to be sold and only might need some adjustments to the clients further, ideally. However, this is often not the case similar to Capgemini. Despite its very strong sales-oriented foundation in 1967 (Gaston-Breton, 2007, p. 22) was – because of a peak demand in services (OSEC, 2009), the organisation had apparently not focused on net new selling – such as in outsourcing, tech services and consulting. For years of highly demand driven economy in IT, Capgemini has been able to be selective in picking up the orders of the clients' needs to sell. However, the economy has changed dramatically.

1.6 Research Aim and objective

The **overall academic objective** is to investigate the influence of intercultural dimensions into sales success. This is investigated by surveying a specific sales population on their behaviour on winning, losing, cooperating in front of the client and behind the scenes in order to win. How this sales population deals with the financial implications of success and failure is also investigated. This key objective is investigated through five main objectives:

- **Primary Objective:** First is to find how a sales management function in an integrated services company can add value by improving the win-rate of deals, by adding knowledge to current engagements and in essence by increasing market share. The hypothesis drawn is that with an integrated sales management function, the company Capgemini might increase its revenues above average as compared to faring with the status quo.
- **Secondary Objective**: Second is how the intercultural aspects of working in a multi-divisional and multinational company can leverage the sales success, especially in working together with international clients. The hypothesis drawn is that a well-functioning intercultural setup helps increase profitability.
- **Third Objective**: Thirdly, it is of importance to see where the gaps of sales effectiveness and cross-collaboration of the entire sales cycle exist. The hypothesis is that the gaps – once closed – helps increase revenues by avoiding slack in execution whilst reducing costs in producing the services.
- **Fourth Objective**: The fourth objective is to find out how such an account management function can be implemented in order to be perceived as value-adding for the rest of the organizations. This also includes sales compensation and payment.
- **Fifth Objective**: The fifth objective is to find out what elements a measurement and scoring model should include in order to yield additional success. Here, the hypothesis is that by measuring the intercultural aspects of the sales and delivery process, gaps can be found and improvement plans can be executed over time.

Plouffe et al (Plouffe, Williams, & Wachner, 2008, p. 81) point out that there is little literature published on services sales research as well as the integration on goods and services into customized "solutions". Therefore, the research subject might be of special interest for academia because of the novelty of the sales research conducted.

Implementing the results and changing the proposals of this study may help Capgemini to achieve more growth, higher revenues and higher profits while providing a superior service experience to its clients. As a result, clients are more competitive themselves.

1.7 Structure

This dissertation comprises eight sections. After the introductory chapter, Chapter two reviews the most recent academic and practical literature on sales management leadership and the construct and considers its theoretical impact on job performance and business outcome. The literature review considers the important aspects of strategy, intercultural management and international enterprises, sales management functions, such as territory and account planning, pursuit planning and performance management and monitoring.

Chapter three discusses the business rationale for outsourcing and considers advantages and disadvantages of a select sample of countries for outsourcing, including the theoretic and practical consideration of implementation aspects in setting up a new organisation.

In Chapter four, challenges to the organisational resources and capabilities of Capgemini and the mapping of theory, and the overall market and practice are discussed as the main subject of research.

Chapters five and six, Methodology and Analysis and Results, consider the practical research aims. Quantitative primary research was undertaken to verify how account management, cross-selling and sales leadership are implemented and how an IT and consulting services organisation be implemented.

Chapter seven takes the relation to the third research aim, mostly makes recommendations for Capgemini in order to improve win-rates and sales richness by implementing a proper sales leadership function. This section also considers the limitations to this research and recommends areas for further study.

Chapter eight is a short thesis-like summary that gives an abstract recommendation on the do's and don'ts in international sales within international enterprises.

1.8 Definition of terms

The following terms are used widely in this dissertation. Since terms can be often misunderstood or misinterpreted, a definition of the four key terms is provided below.

- Consulting, according to Gabler (Gabler Verlag, 2010, p. #Consulting) is defined as the "individual exploration of business issues by interaction with external, independent persons or consulting organisations and an advice-seeking client", sometimes also called "management consulting". Consulting in effect is supposed to help an organization improve its business performance, processes and to analyze existing business plans.

- Technology Services, according to techterms.com (Techterms.com, 2011) "are, not surprisingly, services that involve technology. These include information technology, or IT, services, such as technical support, computer networking, systems administration, and other services. Common Internet services, such as Web hosting, e-mail, and social networking websites also fall under the scope of technology services." Parts of technology services might be seen as a sub-form of consulting. However, as technology services typically provide a functioning service as compared to a pure advice in consulting, there are differences.
- Outsourcing according to Gabler's Wirtschaftslexikon (Gabler Verlag, 2010) consists in the "relocation of value creation activities of an enterprise towards suppliers. Outsourcing thereby comprises a shorting of the value chain [...] of the enterprise. By often taking qualified and specialised suppliers for products and services, the costs of production, development or services can be reduced. By focusing towards core activities, the enterprise can realise cost advantages and own operative and the own strategic market position can be improved", Similarly von Gamm (von Gamm, 2009, p. 59) summarises the term as "subcontracting a process, such as product-design or manufacturing, to a third-party company." IT outsourcing, in particular, is discussed by taking part of a client's organisation and dismantling this part and handing over the service to a second company, called the "outsourcing provider".
- "Offshoring" as Investorwords.com (Investorwords, 2011) describes it as "shifting a business function from one country to another. This can entail moving product manufacturing, service centers or operations". This study looks into the selling impacts of taking the outsourced part to abroad, preferably to a lower-cost country.
- For the purpose of this research, the trademarked term "Rightshoring" will be used as a synonym. Rightshoring has been coined and trademarked by the Capgemini group. Hence (Resourcebridge, 2011), meaning that Offshoring will be only used to a certain and well-chosen extent. Interestingly enough, the word right-shoring has also generated some criticism. In the Urban Dictionary, for example, it was presented in a very vulgar way (Urban Dictionary, 2011), that in essence it would only help the management of the companies to get more executive pay.

2 Literature Review

The literature review focuses on Internationalisation, Corporate Strategy, and Intercultural Business Communications and of course Sales Management. With a sale, many things come together: People communicate, often across boundaries and they follow a strategic impetus. Sales Management in essence is about how to improve a company's situation by increasing its revenues and choosing the right clients. If a business does not do well, a sale is about how to turn around a business. Turnarounds have been discussed widely in literature, starting from Max Weber (Weber, 1904) to the books Peters and Waterman (Peters & Waterman, 1982). However, it is not necessarily always from a sales perspective.

This chapter discusses the following key topics:

- On internationalization, here the writings of Porter (Porter, 2008), Nayak and Jomon (Nayak & Jomon, 2008), Kumar (Kumar, 2008), Hout (Hout, Porter, & Rudden, 1982), Florida (Florida, 2002), Palmisano (Palmisano, 2006) and Segal-Horn (Segal-Horn, 1993) will be taken into account.
- On intercultural works, the works of Hofstede (Hofstede, 2001) and Müller (Müller, 1993), Bolten (Bolten, 2007), several works of Schröder (Schröder, 2008), Schulz von Thun (Schulz von Thun, 2001), Trompenaars (Trompenaars & Hampden-Turner, 1995), Kay (Kay J. , 2004), to name a few will be cited.
- For Market planning, Territory Planning and Account Planning, the works of Rogers (Rogers B. , 2007), Rayner (Rayner & Adam-Smith, 2005) and Cooke (Cooke, 1999) and several others are investigated.
- On Sales Management – what are the key factors of a sales management function using Rogers (Rogers B. , 2007) and Woodburn's (Woodburn, 2001) writings?
- Additionally, the sales process at Capgemini à la Holden (Holden International, 2009), as used amongst others (Capgemini S.A., 2007) will be explained – key factors and advantages will also be depicted.
- What are the SWOT and reputational values an organization needs to have in order to excel in sales? How to manage the people will be taken into consideration using the framework of Rayner and Adam-Smith (Rayner & Adam-Smith, 2005) plus others.
- Using Rogers' frameworks on client value (Ryals & Rogers, 2007) and relationship management – the dependence upon client value and client relationship will be depicted.

The chapter will be structured according to Figure 2-1: Chapter II.

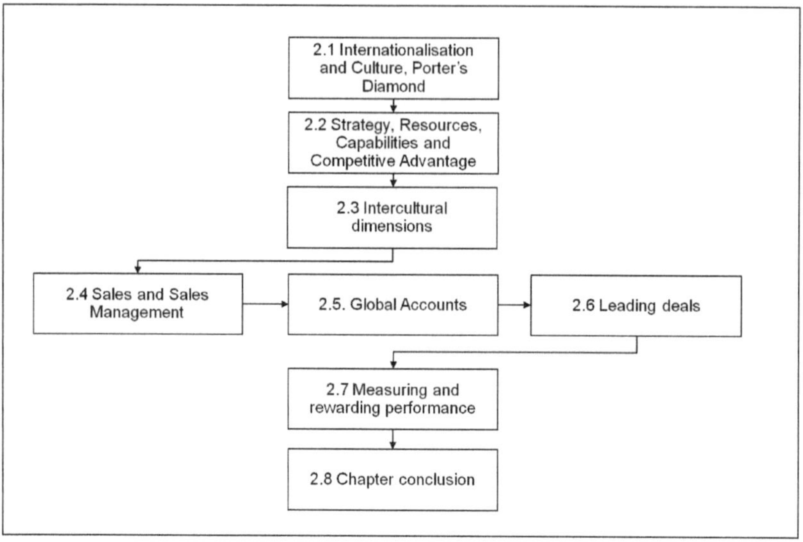

Figure 2-1: Chapter II

2.1 Internationalization of services and Culture

A big theme is that of internationalization, which addresses the questions: why, where and how organizations choose to expand their activities internationally, and how they work together with other international companies. The same is the related theme of standardization versus adoption, which addresses the degree to which organizations structure themselves on a global or local basis.

To emphasize the importance of these themes, some theoretical underpinnings will be outlined in the subsequent paragraphs.

On the topic of internationalizations, one of the first questions any scholar might ask: "Why does an organization choose to operate outside its own country's borders in the first place?" This may sound like a simplistic question; after all people have been trading across borders since the beginning of recorded history. Surely, the easy answer to this is that organizations trade with those in other countries because they seek profit.

But is it so simple? This answer leaves us wondering whether organizations are driven by a strategic mission or whether there are factors that influence international trade and investment that are independent of strategy.

International opportunities for organizations do not exist in isolation from the world's general politics or economic climate. Thus, there are features of this environment that make it more likely for the organizations of one country to deal with organizations in another. If there are, then those making the organization's strategy must become aware of these features. Likewise, are there broader reasons why organizations choose to invest in one country than another?

So the questions that arise are:

- Why do nations trade?
- Why do companies internationalize?
- When do firms expand internationally?
- To what extent do firms internationalize?

2.1.1 Why do nations trade?

Unlike common belief, nations do not necessarily trade but firms and individuals do trade. Nations trade when the nation acts as a buyer of a seller - as part of a firm, but not necessarily as a nation. Since 1450, several theories of trade existed. It started with mercantilism, absolute advantage, and comparative advantage. Later around 1900 the following arose: the theory of factor endowments and the product cycle theory, the stage theories of firms and the international orientation, the internationalization of firms because of market imperfection, the eclectic (OLI theory) (Ohlin, 1933, p. 130), the current best fit and the network theory. In a later stage, Rightshore® is an implementation of the "current best fit" theory.

Simply said, internationalization started to occur when traders realized the need for a trade to be made and the risk of trading would be worth the reward, i.e. that goods were available more cheaply in one part of the world than others. The classical trade theories suggested that nations trade because there are price differences between the same or similar goods in different countries. Murphy writes: "trade makes all parties richer" (Murphy, 2007, p. 147). As a result, people who trade can live from arbitrage and cost differences. The cost differences can be either absolute or comparative. However, most theories built until the early 1900 have been rather looked at the macro side than onto the micro side of the equation. For example: Eli Hecksher (Heckscher, 1919, ed 2006) and Bertil Ohlin (Ohlin, 1933) did attempt to answer this by suggesting that trading occurred because of differences in the endowments or possessions or production factors, such as labor, capital and land. They speculated that countries would specialize in producing those goods which they would have in abundance. Government has been less of a driving factor as often declared by politicians. Findings of modern writers such as those of Nayak & Jomon (Nayak & Jomon, 2008, p. 8) about India's role in the new world order or of Richard Florida about Gay communities (Florida, 2002, p. 56ff) showed that only individuals or herds of individuals who had been given personal motivators and incentives to achieve a certain goal that assembled people more around them. Many industrial assemblies, such as the car industry in Baden-Württemberg or the pharmaceutical industry around Basel with both its founding engineers Daimler, Benz and Hofmann, Roche and Sandoz cannot be explained otherwise. This is similar to the emergence of the Silicon Valley. Thus, it is more a question of why firms and individuals within firms start to internationalize.

2.1.2 Why do corporations internationalize?

One of the most interesting encounters the author had was in 2002 when he was asked by a German-originating Eastern European Business leader why he wants to do business in Eastern Europe: "Have you not been successful in Germany, though?" The author's humble reply was: "Well, indeed I might ask you the same question, as you are also coming from Germany.." In fact, there is some truth in it, as firms internationalize when they have reached a certain ceiling in their local potential within their domestic countries. Thus, the first clear precursor to internationalization is the ability to think beyond one's own country. Therefore, managers might have anticipated the need to internationalize and to seek opportunity abroad. A second set of motive is based upon competition faced by the company, i.e. from international firms. This can be seen in the IT services industry, where Indian players entered the U.S.A in the 1990s and even more from 2000 onwards slowly but surely and did take away market share from the domestic players as Stanley Nollen has noted (Nollen, 2008, p. 69). Robock and Simmonds (Robock & Simmonds, 1989, p. 55) suggest that there is a third motive for managers: Personal career.

In essence, they defined six broad categories:

- Market seeking
- Resource seeking
- Production-efficiency seeking
- Technology Seeking
- Risk avoiding
- Counter-Threatening the firm's competition.

Definitely, these motives seem to change over time. First is what Rose (Rose, 1977, p. 112) points out in 1950: the motives for international expansion seemed to be rather defensive in order to deal with trade barriers, and then in the end of 1950s, the motives became more aggressive to turn towards market and technology seeking. Then, in the 1960s, motives became more defensive again, to set up "overseas manufacturing platforms" in low-wage countries from which to export back home. Internationalization apparently happens in waves. Nowadays, the world has become "uni-polar", as Anup Dash (Dash, 2008) writes. Dash further expanded that now "186 of the top 200 corporations in the world are headquartered in just seven countries (USA, Japan, Germany, France, UK, The Netherlands and Switzerland)". Dash added that these corporations despite all globalization "have been net job-destroyers in recent years, caused by economies of global scale and scope".

It is not enough, however, simply to list the motives of managers and say that these determine the firms' internationalization process. To do so would be like saying that the only thing that matters in decision making on any topic is the individual beliefs of the company's managers.

Perlmutter	Charaterised by	Hout
Ethnocentric	Focus is on a domestic market, overseas markets viewed as of secondary importance. Overseas activities coordinated and developed from home country. Marketing and pricing procedure in foreign market identical to those in home market.	Multi-Domestic
Polycentric	Opposite of ethnocentrism. Organised so as to take advantage of country by country differences. Grouping of quasi-independent subsidiaries	Multi-Domestic
Regiocentric	Organization structured regionally. Within these groupings national boundaries are ignored. Activities standardized for the regional market	Multi-Domestic
Geocentric	Organization becomes viewed as a global entity. Head office establishes universal policies	Global

Table 2-1: Perlmutter's EPRG Framework and Hout's psychic orientations

Perlmutter (Permutter, 1969, p. 9) suggests that the international "orientation of the collective members of the firm" are important to look at, too. He has setup the EPRG framework as shown in "Table 2-1: Perlmutter's EPRG framework and Hout's psychic orientations", combined with the Hout et al. (Hout, Porter, & Rudden, 1982, p. 98) model, as depicted by Plath (Plath, 2001). It distinguishes between four orientations to internationalization – ethnocentrism (home country orientation), polycentrism (host country orientation), regiocentrism (a regional orientation) and geocentrism (a world orientation). The attitudes reflect the goals and philosophy of the organization with respect to its international operations. By consequence, each orientation leads to different manufacturing R&D and product development strategies. These ideas are taken on and paralleled by Thomas Hout and his colleagues (Hout, Porter, & Rudden, 1982, p. 98). They saw that executives' strategic vision had a role to play in explaining the internationalization of companies. Hout, Porter & Rudden adopted a dual classification – *multi-domestic* and *global* companies. The former have expanded internationally in order to compete in a series of domestic markets, by viewing each market-place separately. The companies included here are Unilever, Procter & Gamble, Philips, Ford, and General Motors, which operate in countries separately. In contrast, companies operating in a global marketplace are described by Hout as *global companies*. Managers see here the world as a single entity with products managed on a global basis. Global companies might seek – in order to be effective – to respond to local demand conditions, but try to develop and introduce products with a global character. Examples here are ABB, McDonald's, Toyota, Intel, Michelin, later Ford and more recently the IT Services providers, such as IBM or Capgemini, with the latter being on the move from becoming global from once being multi-domestic.

2.1.3 The internationalization of services

International services are a large and increasing part of the international economy. Yet the ideas are related to international enterprise that have been seen so far have been built upon the experiences of manufacturing industries. So far, little research has been undertaken on the internationalization of services – only since the inception of the Globally Integrated Enterprise by Palmisano (Palmisano, 2006) this has changed. Thus, the specialty of a service compared to a product is discussed first.

Typical features of services are cited in numerous literature, amongst other at Bitner et al (Bitner, Fisk, & Brown, 1993):

- Intangibility – one cannot see, feel or touch them in most of the cases
- Perishability – they cannot be stored
- Simultaneity of Production and Consumption – a service is delivered and used at the same time
- Buyer-supplier interaction – a service involves the customer in its delivery.

Therefore at first sight there are differences between products and services. However, it should be said that services to a more or lesser extent have a "product" component and likewise, all products have a "service" component. As those features of services above are a great flaw in repeating, storing and dislocating production and consumption of services, there is increasingly also the goal to "productize" the services through an "offering", a hybrid between a product and a service.

Depending on the number of variables, some industries that are thought of as service industries may well contain a high degree of production of non-service goods. The distinction can be seen through the separation between "front-office" and "back-office" functions. For example, consulting firms produce large reports; IT service providers operate personal computers and laptops for clients and make them available to run or complete datacenter services; IT development providers develop software code that is then released as a "product" to run properly; banks and insurance companies create financial statements or offer products such as structured vehicles or derivatives yet being in its core a service offering; and advertising agencies produce campaigns. Services also have a locational element. The user may move, or not and the provider may move, or not. This gives the opportunity to name three additional categories of services (Grimwade & Grimwade, 1996, p. 287):

- **Separated Services** – The user does not move, the provider does not move. Some examples are advertising, accounting, help desk services, systems monitoring, and backoffice of the programming

- **Demander-located services** – The user does not move, provider does move. Examples are consultancy, and custom software development (in parts)
- **Provider-located services** – The user moves, the provider does not move. Some examples are tourism, medical services, and education services (to extents).

The goal of many service companies is to provide all of the three in the best possible and cost-effective mix. For example: An outsourcing service is a highly separated service with its datacenter and helpdesk and remote infrastructure monitoring service, however the on-site support and the service management component is demander-located.

The internationalization of firms is affected to the extent by different locations. The financial strategy writer Suzanne Segal-Horn (Segal-Horn, 1993, p. 40) for example notes that historically, service firms were seen as "local" in character. Thus, service firms have chosen to internationalize because of networking motives and this strategy leads to greater degrees of risks for the firms. They were considered as poor candidates for globalization.

However, Segal-Horn (Segal-Horn, 1993, p. 43) notes that the sources of competitive advantage in services are changing, especially scale and scope economies can also be achieved by service firms, and services can become "industrialized". This can also be seen in Outsourcing Services, as von Gamm has noted at various examples (von Gamm, 2009, p. 60f).

2.1.4 Porter's Diamond

M. E. Porter (Porter, 2008, p. 45) did shape the concept of the International "diamond", a set of conditions that generate a certain shape of the industry in an international context, as depicted in Figure 2-2: Porter's Diamond – (Porter, 1990). For Porter, internationalization is composed of:

- **Organizational Strategy, structure and Rivalry** – definitely, how the starting conditions of the industry will prevail will generate further prerequisites of success. An example is the Pharma industry around Basle. It has been founded in the late 19th century along with scientific breakthroughs of several pharmacists and three founding families – Roche, Hoffmann, Sandoz who did compete fiercely for a developed domestic market and thus out of superiority of their research have been able to export globally.
- **Demand conditions** – typically, what end-users want and whether this need is encompassed by an industry shapes that industry, too. If this need can be satisfied, users typically buy it. If the demand is high, such as for special steel in the railroad industry, steel producers also will try to excel on this demand.
- **Factor conditions** – these conditions, according to Porter are the infrastructure of success: education facilities that provide a new feed of graduates and a base for research, infrastructure per se, like communications highways or simply speaking transport. For raw material transports, rivers have been a

preferred way of transport for ages. As a result, many cities have been built along rivers, either as there are bridges across rivers that generated a toll focal point to cross – Munich is an example. There are also harbors on rivers for related industries.

- **Relating and supporting industries** – Most industries rely on a further industry or are a spin-off of other industries. An example is the chip manufacturing industry in Silicon Valley which was a spin-off of the defense industry of the 60ies. Later this chip manufacturing industry did generate a full supporting industry, the software industry, also residing in that area. It is similar to the automotive industry, which has cross-nurtured the fine mechanics industry, i.e. the watch manufacturing industry in Switzerland.
- Imputations such as the **Government** and just "**Chance**" – Porter here refers to the fact that sometimes a creative place just happens by itself, he calls this "chance". Florida (Florida, 2002, p. 78) did investigate this "chance" concept a bit further and has found parallels between an open-minded environment with a multi-structural industry, a culture that supports entrepreneurs and inventors and an explicit gay lifestyle. Florida then concluded that this would increase the chances of success of an industrial or service cluster. However, besides this, Government structural imputations can also support (or destroy) industrial development chances. A good example might be cited with the biotech industry around the Munich fat belt, which has received high government subsidies from privatizations of the Free State of Bavaria (Biotech Cluster Development GmbH, 2010).

Together, all these factors generate a Diamond nucleus for a certain set of industries in an international context and thus would generate a prerequisite for success.

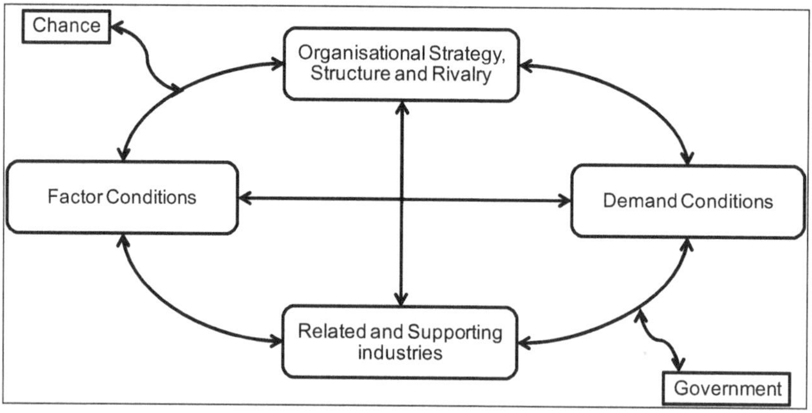

Figure 2-2: Porter's Diamond – (Porter, 1990)

2.2 Strategy, Resources and Competitive Advantages

Strategy in itself has been defined as "the match an organisation makes between its internal resources and skills [...] and the opportunities and risks created by its external environment" (Drucker, 1995, p. 89). Strategy itself is then necessary to carry out the goal from coming where a company is currently positioned to where it wants to be and what it wants to be. Strategy is therefore the way to achieve a certain goal and not the goal itself, as people often confound.

Many books have been concerned with strategy implementation and the analysis of the organisational environment around it, and less with the selection of a strategy based upon the current and future resources a company does have. This resource-based view to the firm is now being widely used in management literature. In particular, Grant (Grant, 1999, p. 138) has performed a single-integrating framework and has also done research about the practical implications of this theory. He especially put out an organising framework for the strategy formulation using a five-stage approach.

The five stages according to Grant are as follows, as depicted in Figure 2-3:

- Identification and classification of the firm's **resources** and the appraisal of strengths and weaknesses relative to competition. Identify opportunities for better utilisation of the resources.
- **Identification of the capabilities**. Capabilities are defined by Grant about what a firm *can do* with its resources, and merely spoken, more effectively than its competitors. In this part of the process, it should be noted that the resources inputs to the capabilities are required and then the complexity of each capability. At the same time, finding new capabilities based on rearranging or re-utilising resources is the key in this process.
- **Appraisal of the rent generating model for competitive advantage:** Here, the resources capabilities a company does have should be looked at in order to provide sustainable competitive advantage and the appropriability of their returns.
- **Strategy selection:** Here, Grant recommends selecting a strategy that best exploits the firm's resources and capabilities, relative to external opportunities.
- **To close the loop, Grant then recommends investigating resource gaps.** These resource gaps need to be filled in order to achieve supreme competitive advantage. The firm needs to invest into replenishing, augmenting and upgrading the resource gaps.

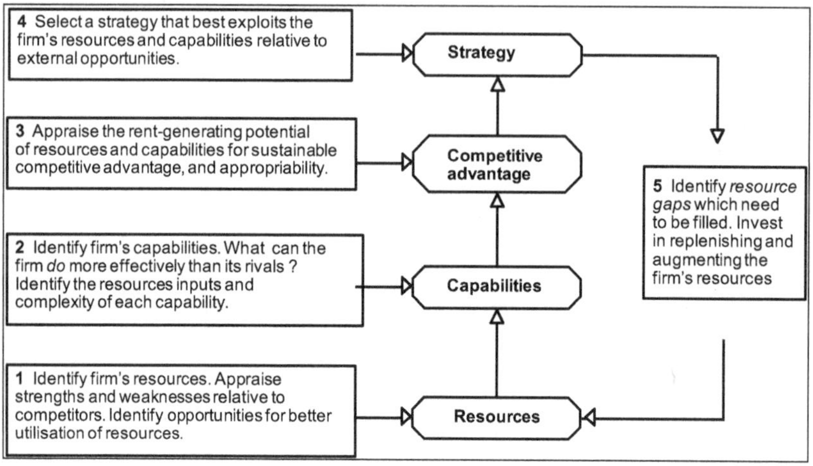

Figure 2-3: Resource-based model for strategy formulation (Grant, 1991, p. 113)

2.2.1 What are resources and capabilities?

As Grant points out, it is merely not that much about what a company is now but rather what it wants to be, it is about a “firm’s identity and propose… what is our business?”, which then leads further to the question: “Who are our customers?” and lastly: “Which are the needs we are seeking to serve”. However, the needs of customers are changing; the customers themselves tend to change frequently and the technologies are changing as well. Thus, it makes some sense to look into what a company can provide and lastly what is it capable of doing.

Bowman (Bowman, 1990, p. 120) for example suggested that companies should better define themselves rather broadly in what they “can bring to the table” and less into what they actually do. An example might be, as Grant noted, railroad companies. Of course themselves being in the business of transporting people or goods using railroads from A to B, they also can define themselves in being good in managing tangible assets and real estate and being less competent in the transport themselves, leaving this to third parties to whom they rent out their facilities. Similarly, automotive companies in Germany, such as Daimler in the 90s did revisit their strategic stance not considering themselves as a car manufacturer but rather in being an “integrated technology company”, managing technologic progress resources. This unfortunately lead to a series of costly false decisions, such as the acquisition of DASA, later EADS, Dornier, the foundation and dissolution of debis Systemhaus and later the merger with Chrysler, and so on. The Daimler case is widely reported as a series of over-stated resource and capability ambitions.

2.2.2 Inventoring resources

In order to take stock of resources, it makes sense to classify them along side two aspects: Barriers to entry into an industry and providing competitive advantage.

Kay (Kay J. , 2004, p. 15) did classify resources with a source of advantage as follows, also shown in Figure 2-4: Classifying resources and capabilities, (Grant, 1995, p. 113).

Distinctive resources:

- Natural monopolies because of existing market share
- Exclusivity as a barrier to entry i.e. through patents, brands and a retaliatory capability
- Sunk Costs because a firm had a first mover advantage, and the existing clients already paid off the investment.

Competitively advantageous resources:

- Cost-advantaging resources, such as process technology, size of plants, access to low-cost inputs.
- Differentiation advantage, such as brands, product technology, marketing, distribution and service resources.

In addition, Grant classifies commodity classifications as:

- Human resources – skills & knowledge, communication and interaction, motivation
- Intangible resources – technology, reputation and culture
- Tangible resources – physical and financial resources

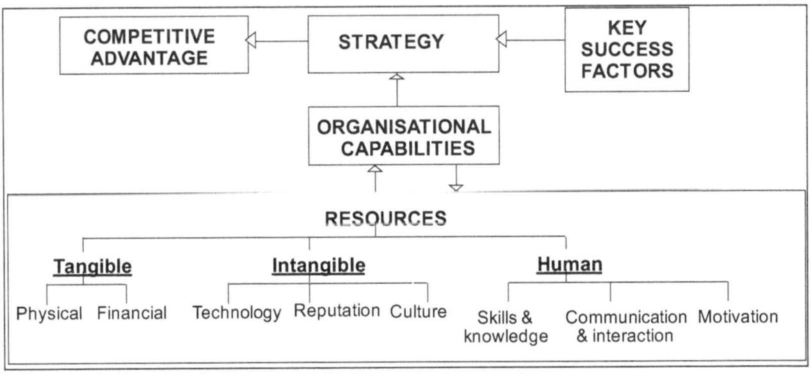

Figure 2-4: Classifying resources and capabilities, (Grant, 1995, p. 113)

Culture in itself therefore can be seen as an important resource that generates a capability and same the capability to interculturally manage these cultural domains across different entities, countries or clients. However, being an intangible resource, it is worth noting that often it cannot be quantified and typical financial ratios have a hard time doing so. Often, it is correlated with brand values, and companies. Interbrand (Interbrand, 2010) try to calculate the brand values thus roughly speaking subtracting the book value of physical and financial tangible assets from the total enterprise value of a company – often calculated in numbers of shares outstanding times the share market value. Looking at Figure 2-4: Resources and capabilities, classifying resources, (Grant, 1995, p. 113)", theoretically the subtraction of the enterprise value by the total value of resources and capabilities then might be intangible and human resources[1]. However, this then leads to the valuation of the capabilities, the strategy derived out of it and the competitive advantage.

The key mandate as Grant argues taking the resource-based approach is to

a) Take care of what opportunities do exist for economizing the use of resources and to maximize the utilization of the resources. The key is to see whether there are economies in re-using the same resources again and all over. An example might be to take the same management holding for a series of subsidiaries or the success of IBM Corp. in acquiring software companies and thus using its sales arm in order to take the software companies' assets and re-sell them through their existing sales and distribution group's channel at virtually no extra cost.
b) Make sure that there are possibilities for using existing assets more intensely and in more profitable employment, before buying new assets, in other words: to "milk out" the resources as much as possible. The returns can be substantial. An example is the re-utilization of the Disney Company's resources such as its film library for second use for cable TV; videos and syndication.

2.2.3 What are capabilities?

As noted previously, capabilities is the capacity of a company to "do something" with its resources, as the resources themselves only "exist" but not necessarily will be put to productive use. Those capabilities can be appraised and extracted by listing up the firm's activities.

Hamel and Pralahad (Hamel & Pralahad, 1994, p. 139) use the term "core competencies" to describe central and strategic capabilities and call strategy as a "stretch" to achieve a distinct goal.

Central capabilities might be in general:

- To sell a product or service
- To produce a product or service

[1] It needs to be noted that there are a series of companies whose Share value is lower than its book value; there might be numerous reasons for it, such as a market downturn, a value-destroying management and so on.

- To integrate partners and various suppliers into an amalgamated product/services bundle.
- To be able to hire and fire human resources on demand of the clients
- To be able to deploy resources across the world

For companies, in example this might be:

- McDonald's capability to setup branches that look similar across the world and to market a common experience, globally.
- Microsoft's capability to bring out a new release of software that pushes the whole industry once every three years.
- BMWs capability to re-leverage its resources for development and production across a whole range of series of cars, starting from the 1 series to the 3, 5 and 7 series and now even Rolls-Royce, yet having the same development and design elements.
- IBM's capability to sell similarly with IT technology and services across the globe.
- Migros' capability to connect local brand experience of "Swissness" with a highly industrialized outreach at an affordable price.
- Capgemini's capability to organise human resources in a cost-effective way across the globe, called Rightshore®.

Capabilities therefore are not only about collecting a set of resources, but they involve - as Grant states - a "complex pattern of co-ordination between people and between people and other resources" (Grant, 1999, p. 125). Here, the concept of *organizational routine* can be applied: somehow this routine is codified within the company as an intangible fabric that is hard to formulate and codify. As a result this then draws a linkage into the following, as Grant further elaborates:

- **The relationship between resources and capabilities**. The potential ways of performing an assembly between those individual resources and the capabilities are unlimited, vast and numerous. The organization's style, tradition, values and leadership are hard to copy for competitors even if they have exactly the same or similar resources and capabilities.
- **There is always a trade-off between efficiency and flexibility.** Kay (Kay J. A., 1993, p. 224) calls this "strategic choices". Scale efficiencies do not necessarily generate flexibility, as there are then base costs attached to it, a too flexible organization might not scale.
- **Economies of experience do exist**, also known as sunk costs. As soon as experience is made – i.e. in designing and crafting a larger deal or services experience, it can be re-leverage for the next deal, easily. Therefore there always exists a certain sunk-cost experience of an experienced firm over a newcomer, who needs to make this "experience curve" with all its drawbacks and failures in-between.

- **Complexity:** Capabilities can be more or less complex and sometimes can be derived from more or less one resource. Sometimes even the most scaling firm might just have a simplistic capability. An example might be 3M to re-utilize the form of paper and sticky material for all kinds of applications that come into the mind of the inventor, the key capability is to look at applications of a very simple concept, like at Post-It. Similarly simple might be the capability of Goldman Sachs to generate advantage in currency trading by high-performance computing – they just trade faster than everybody else.

2.2.4 Gaining a competitive advantage

As Grant (Grant, 1999, p. 129) states, in order to gain a competitive advantage, the capabilities need to have a certain set of features:

1. They need to be durable; thus, they do not need to be re-invented all the time.
2. The need to be transparent, thus not easy to be replicated by competition.
3. They need to be transferable from one division and one geography to the next; however, they need to stay within the firm. As it is often said, this is only possible in an imperfect way, as capital equipment tends to become immobile similar to gifted employees.
4. They need to be replicable. They should be able to be copied within the firm at low incremental cost; however, they should not be replicable outside. An example is employee loyalty towards a firm or the commitment to work overtime if the business situation demands it.

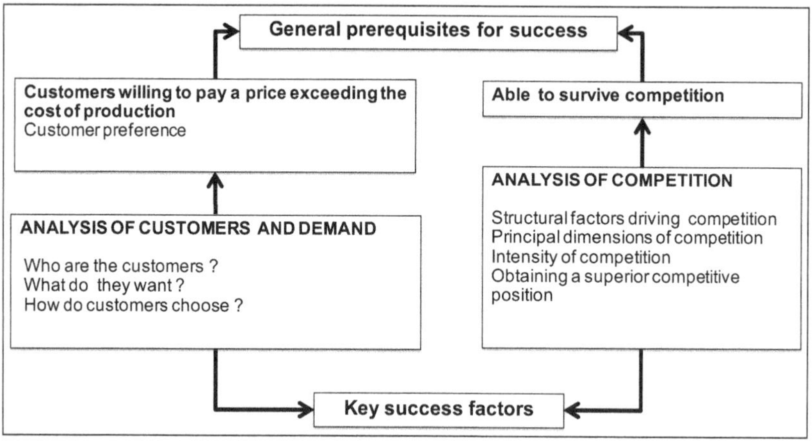

Figure 2-5: Key success factors, after Grant (1995, p.91)

These set of features are then key success factors. These key success factors then can be grouped into two sides.

1. To let the clients pay a price higher than production costs
2. To be better than competition still.

A diagram can be seen in Figure 2-5.

2.2.5 Formulating a strategy

Strategy formulation therefore needs to be in line with the resources and capabilities a company has. The analysis of a rent-generating potential of resources and capabilities are those essentially no one else has but somehow want to utilize and therefore willing to pay a price premium. Therefore, it is essential for strategy formulation to encompass exactly this: What do other people want to have from the firm but cannot get without paying a premium price? It might even make sense to test everything else as a "me-too-strategy" and think of redeploying the resources and capabilities only to those parts that are really not only valuable but valued. Those resources are those that are durable, non-transferable and irreplaceable to other companies.

Grant states: "The ability of a firm's resources and capabilities to support a competitive advantage is essential to the time frame of a strategic planning process" (Grant, 1999, p. 118). In contrast, failure to recognize the right resources might result to failure to formulate the right strategy. It is therefore also a certain risk to employ pure outsiders – like consultants - for strategy formulation; yet they can provide a "second opinion" at things.

However, strategies might be tested and discarded, as Mintzberg and Waters (Mintzberg, 1999, p. 238) depicted. A new strategy emerges as a learning effect of the old, non-working strategy, as shown in Figure 2-6. At the same time, resource gaps will be discovered.

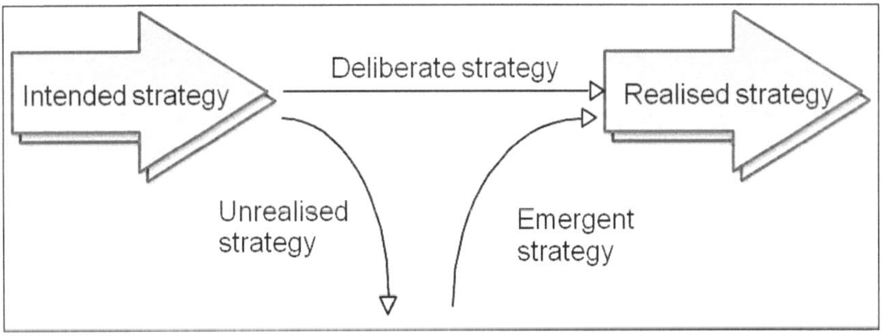

Figure 2-6: Intended and Realised Strategy, after Mintzberg & Waters, (1995, p.221)

2.2.6 Defining resource gaps

Resource gaps become apparent when the rent-generation of the existing resource and capability stock is insufficient in satisfying a company's ambition to grow, in other words, when a current strategy has failed. Thus, it should be looked at which resources need to be replenished in order to make the puzzle "look sound". As Kay noted that corporate success is based on an effective match between the external relationships of a firm and its own distinctive capabilities, the same applies for the replenishment of resources. They need to be addition to new capabilities, and generate better key success factors.

2.3 Intercultural dimensions

Culture as depicted in the previous chapter can be a key success factor in generating a rent of a company. However, what is culture exactly? It is a fact that things are done differently in different cultures. One might ask any manager with experience outside their home culture and there is always a favourite "war story" about the difficulties or peculiarities of the ways things get achieved in the one country or other region.

Whole books point out the blunders made by managers who have not fully appreciated just how profound those differences are.

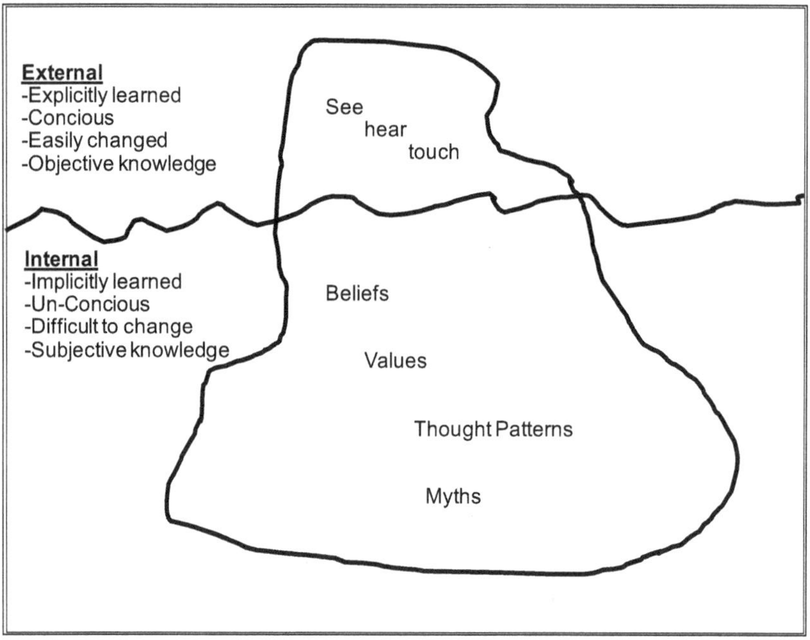

Figure 2-7: The iceberg model, after Bolten (Bolten, 2007, p. 95)

In a multinational services environment, those cultural differences need to be bridged and utilized for the firm in a way that it generates a competitive advantage. In essence, for a well-working company, it needs to become a key capability which then helps other firms who are less capable of performing those matters in benefiting from those experiences. Nevertheless, it needs to be emphasised how important cultural differences really are. Moreover, should cultural difference be taken as a "lame excuse" for low-performers not to perform in a given function regardless of culture?

Culture is something that often stands between people. It is a sum of habits, beliefs, processes and even mechanistic systems (i.e. taxation, financial incentives) that shapes people's behaviours and responses. As in working with international companies, it is important to understand culture as part of an international dimension.

Many business outsiders think that this is only about hard facts. Sure, facts matter, but culture and working together even much more. Culture is about the bottom of the iceberg. However, there are risks in intercultural study:

- Risks of creating a generic profile of an entire group of people (stereotyping, generalization)
- Greater risk of failing to understand cultural context and its influence
- Probability of certain patterns of behavior
- Each person: Universal/Human + Culture + Individual

For example, do the differences in organizational functioning between Germany, France and Poland really matter? Is managing an organization in the developing world that is fundamentally different – or is it at the end merely about providing a good and service at a cost lower than the price it can generate with its clients – regardless of culture? Can it be rather so that the understanding of culture has its cost and price tag attached to embed into an operation and a cost-effective, cultural-agnostic company can live without it, but then can operate at a lower cost?

2.3.1 The communicative act and the concept of "understanding"

Culture and understanding go hand in hand. If people do not understand each other, it is argued the reason behind is culture and vice versa. Els Oksaar (Oksaar, 1993, p. 15) has performed some good research about the topic of "understanding". He defined the process of "understanding" or "Verstehen" as the way in which relationships are established by which new topics, new things and new matters are identified through known matters. Oksaar hereby follows the concept of Coombs & Hull (Coombs & Hull, 1997, p. 43) who have elaborated that knowledge happens in a path-dependent way. In the process of learning, Oksaar hereby differentiates between two sets of competencies, one being the *Produktionskompetenz* (production competency), the other being the *Interaktionskompetenz* (interaction competency). In the process of understanding language as the process in which what is heard and read is recognized through already current lingual, which means formal and semantic structural patterns and building blocks. Oksaar emphasizes on the knowledge of the semantics, the meaning of words etc, plus of course of the context such as mimics, gesture, body language etc. As the latter might cause irony and turn the spoken or written word into the opposite, he emphasized that this communicative act needs to be considered and reduced to a minimum in intercultural workings. Therefore this intangible knowledge needs to be codified and made abstract in a terminus technicus. This then becomes of foremost importance when transporting knowledge from one part of the organization to the next, means letting other parts of the organization "understand". In summary, total base of texts, habits forms and methods can be called a "knowledge base". As a result of this process of understanding, the knowledge base can be variously interpreted, being quite closely connected to the technologies and clients currently familiar to the firm or one department closely working with the next. It therefore consists of a "shared mental framework of fundamental design concepts" (de Liso & Metcalfe, 1997, p. 87) as mentioned above. Besides this, there are more aggregate levels of knowledge bases in firms which can generate action and behavior. In essence, it is argued that in order to "understand", the firm has a capacity to merge individual views, habits, abilities and execution preferences of its employees. This capability is driven to some extent party through the ability of the firm to generate trust and loyalty, but also through the perpetration of a "corporate culture". As a result, Coombs & Hull then argue that this path-dependency my therefore be seen not only in the knowledge base of a firm but also more broadly defined with the culture of the organization.

Coombs & Hull then elaborate this further into the knowledge management process (KMP) within organizations. They consider this knowledge management process as a set of routines that deploy an existing knowledge base not only by sheer repetition but also through codifying tacit knowledge into explicit knowledge.

Oksaar then goes back and caprices into the "communicative act" as the main feature of the knowledge process:

He sets seven elements of this communicative act:

1. The interaction partner: listener and speaker, and the auditorium
2. The topic and the subject of the discussion
3. The verbal elements
4. The para-lingual elements
5. The nonverbal, kinetic elements
6. The extra-verbal elements
7. The totality of the affective behavioral features.

Oksaar (Oksaar, 1993, p. 20) then emphasizes that the learner or the one who receives information within this knowledge gathering process needs to understand the situation in order to know *what* she then says *whom what when* and *where.* This situational perception is then never identical, as everyone is imputing his subjective expectation and previous knowledge into that situation.

In a multicultural environment, this then is elaborated to a further level. Learning and knowledge gathering is then biased by each other person's originating culture, which then might generate the necessity to differentiate and identify each other group's specific behaviorisms.

Oksaar has made some good research about German language. However, it needs to be noted that in a global environment, English is now *the* international language. Many international companies, both UK and US-originating or neither of both use English as their common language in order to communicate, such as IBM, Siemens or Royal-Dutch Shell and the French-originating Capgemini Group. It is estimated that three-quarters of the world's post mail and 95% of the world's e-mail is now in English, and certainly more than 80 Percent of the world's data stored in computers is stored in English language. It needs to be noted that this International English that has evolved over time is an "artificial" language with a lingual subset and has been developed for convenience and related to the mother tongue of those who speak it. There are many dialects of Business English such as German-English ("Genglisch"), French-English ("Franglais"), Indian-English ("Hinglish") or Chinese-English ("Chinglish"). Native English can be described by being far more idiomatic, flexible, rich in metaphor and as a result more difficult to understand than the reduced set of "International English". However, it serves its purpose as a lingua franca of understanding within companies quite well.

2.3.2 Management-Related elements of cultures

Global convergence will take a long time, if it happens at all. As Robert Louis Stevenson pointed out "There are foreign lands; only the traveler is foreign", or as the sponti proverb says: "Wir sind alle Ausländer, fast überall", this underlines the need for international firms and its managers to approach other cultures with consideration and respect.

There are some features of culture that occur frequently in cross-cultural situations to suggest that they are of key importance in relation to managing. These are several attitudinal aspects, as Fons Trompenaars (Trompenaars & Hampden-Turner, 1995) has elaborated:

- **Attitudes to Authority**: Authority of superiors depends in all societies upon a mix of function, status, money, personal or acquired competence and power. However, this mix is different by culture. In some countries, competence matters more than status or money and leads to promotion, in other countries promotion only happens by origin. Even within Europe, this can be observed, for example the author when travelling in a multi-country environment, he observed clearly the difference between the relationship of the manager and his employees in the same division of a multinational company in Spain, France and Sweden. In Spain, people were heavily oriented towards the boss both in terms of listening and body language and let the boss talk first. They only answered when the boss allowed them. In France, everyone was talking, however the boss at the end made the summary in his own view, often even contradicting the whole team. In Sweden, it was hard to recognize who the boss was. Everyone was talking and listening, it was almost a discussion within peers. It only turned out over time who the chief executive was.

- **Attitudes to others:** As most people are born and educated within families, some countries tend to take a focus on working with the "extended" family, means taking care of cousins, uncles, nephews etc. more closely and with higher priority than of others. This especially then touches the relation within companies when dealing with new and scarce resources, such as jobs or supplier contracts where one person might have a good say on decision making. In some countries, it is absolutely a common practice to prioritize family members; other countries would call this bluntly "nepotism" or "Göttiwirtschaft" (in Swiss). Nepotism in some countries is far from being a sin or even a crime, it is a virtue and strongly upheld. Even in highly developed western countries, such as Switzerland, it is seen as common practice as Matthies (Matthies, 2001) points out. In other ways, some special careers cannot be explained otherwise, such as the rise of Martin Blessing to the CEO of Commerzbank being the son of a former head of the Bundesbank Karl Blessing, or Ursula von der Leyen, born Albrecht, being the daughter of the former prime minister of Lower Saxonia.
- **Attitudes to self-management**: How people see themselves in relation to what they want to achieve – in other words – what is the gap between a person's present and future state is affected by the culture in which they have been brought up. Questions for example arise whether "The goal is the Goal" (western culture) or "the way is the goal" (eastern culture). In an achievement-oriented western world, it is sometimes difficult to believe that other people take a different way. Even in the West, there is a classic distinction between German and British managers in attitudes on how they place humor in management (Moore, 2006, p. 399). More emphasized is that for Germans, business is a serious matter and joking about it is inappropriate, whereas British are more relaxed and consider humor as acceptable in any management situation to "make the wheels go round."
- **Attitudes to time**: Trompenaars further elaborates that there are different attitudes to time. Most western countries are "monochromic" and the clock is ticking away minute by minute in an unforgiving way. Others have a polychromic perception of time; many things can be done at once. This then especially draws the attention when timing in a western sense is crucial, which means people are to be "on time" or have an appreciation for delays or not. However, there is nothing frivolous or trivial about that situation. Especially within negotiations in working with multi-chronic teams it is important to adjust to each other. This implies that often those who have the lower bargaining should adjust to the other person's behavior, i.e. giving more time to informal talks during the first days of a negotiation session, it might pay off later.
- **Attitudes toward nature**: The ways in which cultures relate to the external and natural world vary significantly. For example natural tribes of southern Asia not consider themselves to be part of the fabric of a living whole world. They do not set themselves apart from the world; they "are the world". Part

of what they do is part of the nature, as Trompenaars states (Trompenaars & Hampden-Turner, 2001, p. 140). Technological cultures of the west rather consider the "world as their oyster", they command and control it. As a result, there exists a clear hierarchy of living with rocks and stones on the bottom, plants above, animals below humans, the latter being worth more than all of the rest. Trompenaars asked people from different cultures to choose between the following two statements:

"**A**: It is worth while trying to control important natural forces, like the weather

B: Nature should take its course and we just have to accept the way it comes and do the best we can."

It is interesting to note that the Czech Republic ranges on the edge of continuum towards A, whereas Brazil, Portugal and Hungary lean on the edge of continuum B, Germany more B than France, and Switzerland, Austria and Sweden even more leaning towards A.

The relationship between humans and nature, themselves, their peer, position and powers is therefore highly dependent upon the culture they are living in.

2.3.3 The Lewis Model

As Lewis (Lewis, 2007) writes in the magazine "HR Director": "Cultural behaviour is not something willy-nilly, accidental or whimsical. On the contrary, it is the end product of millennia of collected wisdom, filtered and passed down through hundreds of generations and translated into hardened, undiscussable core beliefs, values, notions and persistent action patterns." Schröder calls the "undiscussable core beliefs" as "taboos" and focuses on the breakage of those taboos (Schröder & Rothe, 2008). Lewis continues: "As such, a culture cannot be depicted satisfactorily at random or evaluated according to impressions or recent observations. It is a largely finite, predictable and enduring phenomenon – the essential key to survival for a nation or cultural group."

He then further elaborates that the purpose of a model for cultural behaviour is to formalise the study, starting by analysing the genetic and environmental background and writing a blueprint for the subsequent historical development.

Lewis then formalised a model of Linear-Active, Multi-Active and Reactive cultures that help understand the different cultures of different countries, shown in Figure 2-8. However, it should be noted that even though the case in India is on the other extreme of Germanic cultures, a corporate culture might supersede in parts a country-wide primary culture.

As it can be shown especially in India, large corporations try to import their own culture as much as possible (Kumar, 2008, p. 126), key success factors, however, as Carmel (Carmel, 2003) notes include human capital and to include national orientation and traditions further.

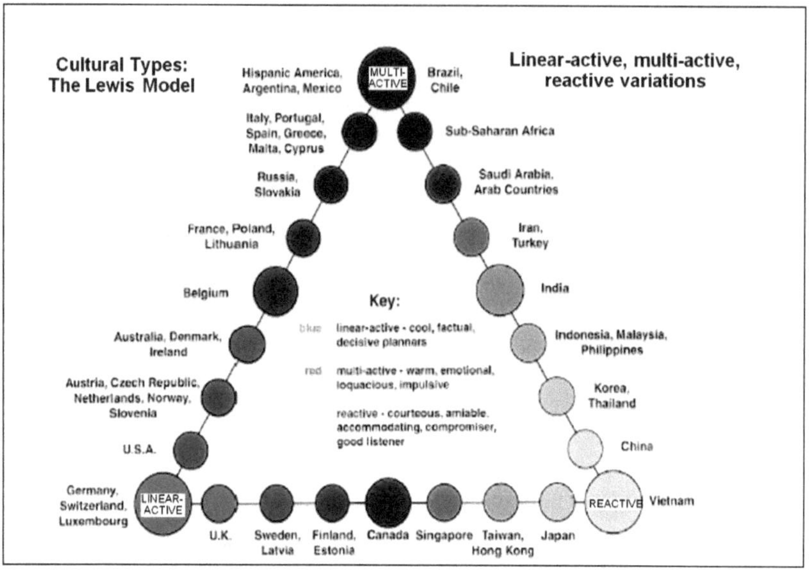

Figure 2-8: Lewis model of cultural dimensions (Lewis, 2007)

2.3.4 The Hofstede Model

Gert Hofstede's Framework for Assessing Culture has brought many advances to intercultural work and can be considered as one of the cornerstones of intercultural business science: Hofstede (Hofstede, 2001, p. 79f) has found five dimensions of culture by researching work related values of different nationality groups. Other researches have shown to some extent some similar results.

Hofstede collected those samples in two waves, first in the larger 39 countries have been conducted, later in some 30 plus countries of smaller size. Hofstede did most survey in the sales and services departments of IBM but not exclusively. Typically people from the upper middle class have been surveyed – sales assistants, top manager, sales executives, some professional scientists – using the language of each country, in total 20 language versions have been produced, under the assistance of IBM Corporation.

The key work of Hofstede did entail that typical other biases such as the ones of different profession, company belonging or job role could mainly be evened out as most respondents had similar professional background, servicing and selling IBM products. Hofstede therefore argued that the main difference was the national difference. Moreover, he also concluded that because of a similar social class of people the survey respondents were coming, the cultural differences found within IBM were much lower than in the total countries' population.

Hofstede then applied those studies in different countries using his research into the IT Company IBM; however, the concept can also be applied in divisions of a multicultural enterprise.

The dimensions researched by Hofstede in the 1970s inside IBM Corporation using more than 116'000 questionnaires from 70 countries are:

- Power Distance
- Individualism vs. Collectivism
- Masculinity vs. Femininity
- Level of Uncertainty Avoidance
- Longterminsm.

Small vs. large power distance: Hofstede invented the concept of power distance after looking into the way people act towards power and how superiors exert power. In a large power distance culture such as Philippines or India, the boss is the boss and his opinions are valued much more than individuals' expertise. Less powerful members of companies and institutions presume and acknowledge that power is not distribute equally but rather autocratic and based on their hierarchical positions. In cultures with small power distance - Australia, Austria, Denmark, Ireland, Sweden, Switzerland – people do consider themselves more as colleagues and believe that inequality in society should be minimized. At the same time, they expect and accept power relationships are to be more equally distributed, even democratic and equal, much more than just formal. People working as subordinates do ask more for the "why" and argue and discuss and also dare to criticize their bosses openly. Thus, Small vs. Large Power Distance does measure how people do view their inequality versus the others from a personal perception perspective (Foucault, 2005).

Individualism vs. collectivism: The individualism-collectivism dimension is the degree to which a culture is willing to support individual versus collectivist or group concerns. The emphasis is on individual achievement, and people are supposed to mainly take care of themselves plus their people near to them, like their family. In collectivist cultures (for example Iran, Hong Kong), the population views itself more by being a member of a life-time group. At the same time, they have a more dense social framework, such as the family, their professional belonging, their respective age peers or their co-members of the same religion. The goal is to be a good member of the group and to be part of it, whereas – in the individualist culture the aim appears to be a good leader, there is less emphasis on good job training since – as Hofstede argues – it increases commitment to the company. For example, it appears that in collectivist countries, it matters more who people are and not just what they actually "do".

Before Hofstede, Hall (Hall, 1976) had already investigated the differences between high-context and low-context speech across different cultural countries. In a low-context culture, the aim is for the message to be explicit as possible, and how the message is put depends relatively little upon the context in where it stands. English and German are low-context languages by this definition. In High-context languages, the opposite is the case, and the spoken words indicate the message implicitly and only a part of it. Japanese, Arabic and Latin American Spanish are language of this high-context and implicit speech languages. It appears that there is a high correlation between Hall's (Hall, 1976) dimensions and Hofstede's Individualism-Collectivism continuum.

Masculinity vs. femininity: Hofstede calls one dimension of differentiation between countries "masculinity" at the one end to antagonize it with "femininity", attributing values as such to it. In so-called 'masculine' cultures, people regardless of male or female – put a high value on competition, are more ambitious, strive for a higher material goal and tend to go for money. Hofstede points out that in a "masculine" culture people tend to focus onto an opportunity for high earnings and less importance to work within a co-operative group, whereas in a "feminine" culture people value to live in a pleasant area and put less recognition from others for a good job done (Latour, 2005).

Weak vs. strong uncertainty avoidance: Avoiding uncertainty means that cultures can either cope with new things and encourage risk taking or not. As change is inevitable, it is more a question how to deal with change and to adopt for it. Hofstede found a considerable range across cultures in people's attitudes. In cultures with strong uncertainty avoidance such as Greece, Portugal or Japan, people prefer explicit rules and formally structured activities and employees tend to stay longer in the same employment role, or at least with the same work place. In a weak uncertainty avoidance culture – such as Denmark or Hong Kong – the uncertainly in life is more readily acknowledged and each day is taken as it comes and people cope with it. Hence, they appear to experience less stress.

Long vs. short term orientation: Hofstede, similar to Lewis and Trompenaars, has found a difference to time aspects. Theories about culture itself will be affected by time. A society's "time horizon" or the how the past is connected to the future and weighted. In short term oriented societies, the immediate rewards are preferred over long-term sustainability, shortly speaking. In long-term oriented societies, the more distant future rewards are being less discounted compared to a reward in the immediate rewards. It might be worthwhile investigating whether short-term orientated have higher interest rates for financial than long-term-oriented societies. In the cases of Switzerland or Japan, both highly long-term oriented societies, at least the interest rates are comparably low, since years.

Hofstede especially made a comparison between different countries, based upon his original study with IBM. However, it shows that groups within companies based on their systemic and beliefs also show different behavioral patterns.

Hofstede then performed a clustering of those dimensions and countries, grouping them together as shown in Figure 2-9: For example, more developed Latin countries are those with "high power distance, high uncertainty avoidance, high individualism and medium masculinity", comprising Belgium, France, Argentina, Brazil, Spain. Near Eastern countries have been grouped together with Greece, Iran and Turkey.

Hofstede's model of culture being essential and static has attracted some criticism. Criticisms about Hofstede's work come from a multitude of origins, as it is inevitable in all management research. The six main criticisms are presented below.

1. All original respondents came from one multinational company: IBM. It is not known how much this effect fell into place and biased the survey in one or other way. However, it can be noted that IBMers to a large extent have a higher degree of education, often have an origin of science or business or mathematics due to the nature of the IT business which might bias their frame of horizon. At the same time, IBM has its very specific shape and configuration with not all the subsidiaries having the same tasks – thus the Israeli sample group might have been distorted with its larger research lab there. Moreover, the Latin American sample group with some considerable amount of manufacturing facilities might also distort the picture, same as pure sales and distribution group outlets, such as in the Nordics (IBM Corp., 2010).
2. Definitely this also comes along with the next criticism, that it mostly represents the attitudes and values of IBM employees. Values indeed affect people's behavior but certainly not everything. Especially when filling out company questionnaires, people might adjust their responding in a way where they think they ought to respond, what their bosses want to hear and not what they really think. Additionally, it might be argued that that Hofstede's survey is about what people say what they intend to do and not what they actually do (Jones, 2007).
3. Thirdly, Hofstede's analysis does compress and simplify, this is something what all analysis is for. Lastly, it characterizes national work cultures by using the average for the respondents of each nation. One has to acknowledge that this is an oversimplification, as the differences of attitudes in all cultures can be vast – there might be German risk takers and Brazilian uncertainty avoiders that definitely can distort this average. Hofstede then has developed a cluster of countries' work attitudes and cultures, such as Germanic, Nordic, Anglo on the basis of those dimensions, generating even a further simplification. Regarding Austria, Switzerland, Israel or even Italy as a Germanic culture because of having both a low power distance, high uncertainty avoidance, a high masculinity and a medium individualism is a sheer gross oversimplification. Swiss, in particular, do not regard themselves as Germanic, and same Germans consider themselves to be vastly different to the Italians. The same is with stereotyping Denmark, Finland, the Netherlands, Norway and Sweden as Nordic because of their low power distance, their low to medium uncertainty avoidance and a set of low masculinity and a medium individualism. People from Finland are very likely to see significant differences

from the Dutch, as well as Danish and Swedish people note their differences very obviously when they compare each other.

I: More developed Latin High power distance High uncertainty avoidance High individualsm Medium masculinity **Countries**: Belgium; France, Argentina, Brazil, Spain	**II: Less developed Latin** High power distance High uncertainty avoidance Low individualsm Whole range on masculinity **Countries**: Columbia, Mexico, Venezuela, Chile, Peru, Portugal, Yugoslavia (former)	
III: More developed Asian Medium power distance High uncertainty avoidance Medium individualsm High masculinity **Countries**: Japan	**IV: Less developed Asian** Low power distance Low uncertainty avoidance Low individualsm Medium masculinity **Countries**: Pakistan, Taiwan, Thailand, Hong Kong, India, Philippines, Singapore	**V: Near Eastern** High power distance High uncertainty avoidance Low individualsm Medium masculinity **Countries**: Greece, Iran, Turkey
VI: Germanic Low power distance High uncertainty avoidance Medium individualsm High masculinity **Countries**: Austria, Israel, Germany, Switzerland, South Africa, Italy	**VII: Anglo** Low power distance Low to medium uncertainty avoidance High individualsm High masculinity **Countries**: Australia, Canada, Britain, Ireland, New Zealand, USA	**VIII: Nordic** High power distance Low to Medium uncertainty avoidance Medium individualsm Low masculinity **Countries**: Denmark, Finland, Netherlands, Norway, Sweden

Figure 2-9: Hofstede country characteristics, adapted by Henry (Henry, 2001, p. 137)

4. Fourthly, and at the same time it can be argued that Hofstede then has over-complicated his cultural maps, as the dimensions depicted have a considerable amount of overlap. Power distance and Individualism do correlate significantly in Hofstede's cultures with cultures having a high power distance at the same time depicting a low individualism and being rather collectivist in their nature. Only Costa Rica has a small power distance and is collectivist at the same time, which might be originating from the small sample of questionnaires put out in that country given the fact that IBM at that point in time only had very little employee population there (IBM Corp, IBV, 2010). Same;). Similarly, it appears that high- and low-context speech relates closely to the individualism and collectivism dimension.
5. Fifth, the assertion of masculinity vs. femininity is also quite biased by one trend. In the early 1990s, more than 70 Percent of the population inside IBM – a truly IT and engineering company were male, with a higher propensity of males within the upper and managerial ranks. Only since the end of the 1990s, IBM made great strides in putting more "diversity" into its workforce (IBM Corp, 2010). This then implies rather how much "femininity" a more or

less male workforce did have and / or whether in some countries more women had already been employed for various reasons. As this "masculinity" is also a tendency for people to earn more money, it might also be queried that people in those countries observed have just a need to "earn more", as there might be less of original wealth resources available, i.e. from inheritances or other family members, whereas "feminine" countries such as Sweden might just have all the stuff they need, especially in the Upper Middle class where IBMers typically tend themselves to exist.
6. Lastly, Hofstede's country clustering was a snapshot of the 70s (Jones, 2007). One might wonder how Iran would fare after the Iranian revolution or Argentina after the 2001 crisis. Are they both still in the "developed" cluster, or did the external environments generate more pressure?

To conclude, it might be worth to look at a simplification by putting the financial dimension as the main dimension of Hofstede's work. The more money cultures and societies have in average and overall, it appears that the more cold, rich, individualist and small power distance they have, the less money societies have in average but only a few a lot of money. The more hot, poor and collectivist and with a large power distance they appear to be. In the middle, there are many cultures in-between.

Using the rich-poor continuum it can be argued that the Lewis model and the Hofstede model do concur. However, given the fact that Hofstede is widely used not only within academia but also within the professional environment, it is worth more than a couple of sentences. In essence, it shows that the Hofstede model can be used to depict differences between enterprise cultures – either between different enterprises, different enterprise parts or different countries within the same enterprise.

2.3.5 Implemented intercultural work in international management

Intercultural work has a main field of application in the improvement of business flows, as Bolten (Bolten, 2007, p. 157) expands. Unlike the common intercultural communication science, he writes, "the Intercultural Business Communications is designed to work with concrete economic and business practice by linking questions of organization theory, marketing and human resource development." As Bolten expands, there is still little research on intercultural business communications in the fields of finance, accounting, controlling and production. However, there is more with sales, as here selling often is a boundary-spanning role (Rogers B. , 2007, p. xxi). In business, there are two approaches of managing culture:

- One is by ignoring it – the economistic, "culture-free" approach.
- The other one is the culturalistic, "culture-bound" approach.

Classic theories often assume little influence of culture towards business and enterprises are purposefully oriented and technocratically plannable and controllable. Bolten, in particular, refers to this approach as too short-minded and expands in his critique that a "culture-free" approach neglects the individual aspects of different cultures which might be an inhibitor for business flow. As a result, it is worthwhile investigating and working a way through culture because cultures might impede a free, globalist business flow.

The "culture-bound" approach, as discussed through with Hofstede, Ouchi and other writers connects culture with business. The culture-bound approach especially also sees a strong influence of culture as an economic and competitive motivator. Samuel Huntington (Huntington, 1996) in his oeuvre: "The fight of cultures" considers religious and cultural differences even as a source of future conflict.

When working together company to company across different cultures, the culture-bound approach however should be observed. Bolten (Bolten, 2007, p. 161) further expands that cultural differences and cultural diversity "are not to overcome but rather to be conceived as a chance for the construction of synergetic scenarios of action, which would not be achieved when suppressing it or synthesizing it in a "best-of-both" synthesis."

Using the three schools of understanding of international management,

- The classic/neoliberal international management
- Cultural-comparing international management
- Intercultural international management

Bolten concludes that despite the higher efforts, the intercultural international management approach might yield the highest results.

2.3.6 The individual and its context using Dülfer's layered model

To explain the entrepreneurial action and its connectedness to the environment, the layer model of Dülfer (Dülfer, 1999) is often referred to. Being closely connected to the iceberg model and resembling highly to the Maslow pyramid of needs (Maslow, 1943), it depicts a model that states that the actions of managers are closely connected to six layers that are interlinked to each other. A picture of this model is shown in Figure 2-10.

Starting from the natural environment and climate, supported by the reality of recognition and technology, together with culture techniques, sense constructions and religions, Dülfer then sees a connection to social relationships and values. These generate public order policymaking and norms of which acting individuals can draw from.

Dülfer has made some ground-breaking research; wherein those matters do generate managerial action and form this action altogether. It is also highly interlinked to the eclectic OLI theory mentioned before, and can be shown upon some examples:

- In Switzerland of the 19th century, trade happened from north to south via the alps by passing several lakes, amongst other the lake of the four cantons (Vierwaldstättersee), the Zugersee and the Zürichsee. As a result, shipbuilding has been a major industry, same as then the emergence of steam engines. This then in result also generated the spread of railroad companies as a viable substitute for ships (Reimann, 2009). However, at the same time as every ship operator and trader was responsible on his own, it generated a highly participative culture with a high-degree of self-responsibility.
- In North Germany of the 19th century and as a result of the industrialisation, trade happened in a different way. Steel barons who have been able to accumulate huge resources and capital assembled large companies who have been able to scale up. The individual though had to be taken care of within the overall construct of the company itself (Pamp, 2004).

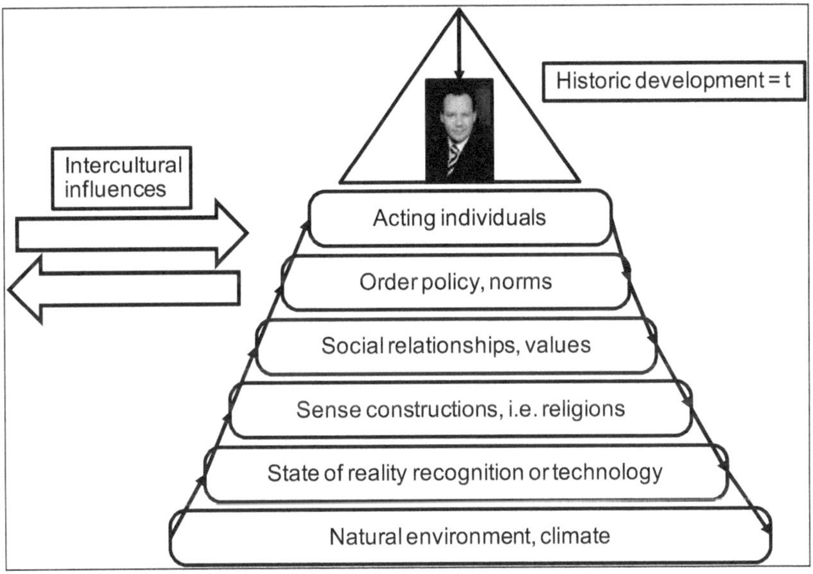

Figure 2-10: Dülfer's layer model adopted (Schichtenmodell) (Dülfer, 1999, p.221)

2.3.7 Relationship orientation vs. matter-orientation

In the intercultural research, there is a differentiation between relationship-oriented cultures and more matter-orientated cultures (Homburg & Pflessner, 2000) or (Bolten, 2007, p. 201). To give an example: While the accent on business relationship in Germany appears to be rather on business, in China the aspect of relationship is more in the foreground first; business appears to come later.

To state it righteously, this means that the contract itself is the base for the business relationship and it determines highly what both sides have to perform and do receive. At the same time, it is a hedge in case a contracting party is not keeping up to the services or payments committed; it can be taken as a base for a lawsuit and penalties.

In more relationship-orientated cultures, where the codification of contracts in itself does not that long exist, i.e. in India or China, the investigation into the reliability of the business partner is much more perennial. A due diligence is therefore needed in a higher degree prior entering a contract. Part of this due diligence is small talk, same as joint events, dinners, receptions or any other type of social program that enable relationships.

The predicate of being a good business partner is therefore not only by being competent in the expert domain, being timely and reliable but also by being a good host and caretaker, i.e by bringing people to the airport, making sightseeing or having a special spouse program within the business development phase. This can be seen as a fallback instrument against odd situations (Ihlau, 2006, p. 62), as then people know each other much better and have established a good knot of relationships.

Members or more matter-orientated cultures might appear to be irritated by this behavior, especially when they are supposed to answer to private questions or when they feel a pompous wine and dine program might be a waste of time. As a result of this relationship-oriented culture, nepotism can be considered as usual and near relatives are preferred in good jobs.

Nevertheless, a business relationship should not be confounded with friendship within these cultures, as often those relationships have to be taken care of purely egoistic rationales.

2.3.8 Merging enterprise cultures using "Theory Z"

Ouchi (Ouchi, 1981) has developed a "best-of-both" synthesis. For enterprises that have the characteristic features A and B, he argued the each best feature might be developed and integrated, for example in the area of leadership, social welfare, process organization etc. and to assemble this into a new enterprise culture.

As Bolten (Bolten, 2007, p. 169) argues, Theory Z as shown in Figure 2-11, is the starting model for the still used model of "lean management" or "lean production". It has yet never been realized in this synthetic form. Even though Ouchi has developed this model as culture-neutral or culture-agnostic and globally deployable, some further adoptions have been necessary to employ this model into Western Europe.

However, it can be said that this model can be looked at the integration of a value chain (Porter, 2008, p. 45), which has been adopted widely within the IT industry, i.e. for the Component Business Modeling of IBM. (IBM Corp, IBV, 2010).

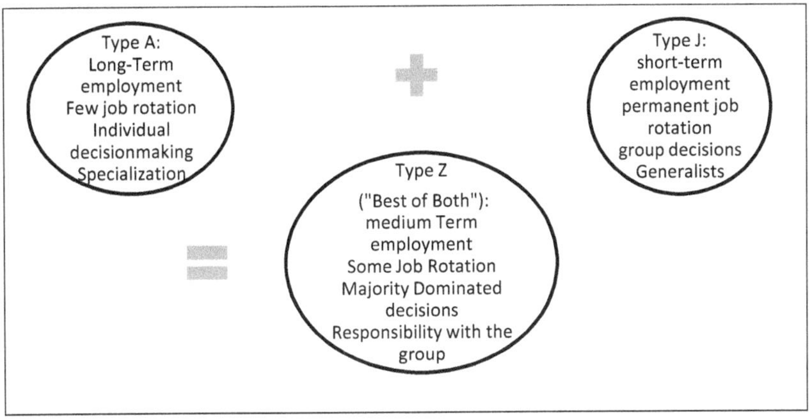

Figure 2-11: Theory Z (after Ouchi, 1981)

In the component business model concept, IBM argues that during the last decade, "businesses across the globe struggled to comprehend and adapt to the changes brought on by the ubiquitous growth of information technology and the Internet. Today, those uncertainties are no longer so uncertain; the tech-driven upheavals of the 1990s and early 2000s have coalesced into a new, era defining set of imperatives". It needs to be proven that this is really a "new era".

IBM in this paper further elaborates, that by "using widespread adoption of standard communication technologies such as e-mail and the internet and open data standards like XML", companies were able to further automate business transactions. This then has resulted in a dramatic increase in flexibility and a "race to the bottom" in transaction costs..

By this automation and standardization, many traditional barriers to entry have been removed, to categorize this with Porter's Five Forces (Porter, 2008). IBM then further lines out, that whilst new entrants flood the marketplace, customers "find it easier than ever to switch providers", which increases competition again.

IBM concludes that only specialization – and a focus on the few activities that confer real advantage and profit – will enable firms to deliver full value to their key stakeholder groups of customers, employees and shareholders. This specialization would then be set on two parallel tracks: external and internal.

However, it needs to be said that most enterprise architectures have some deficiencies. As Grant argued that companies cannot be good at everything they do, however they need to have "a distinctive competence" (Grant, 1999, p. 118) and make strategic choices and trade-offs and focus their resources and capabilities towards the right place.

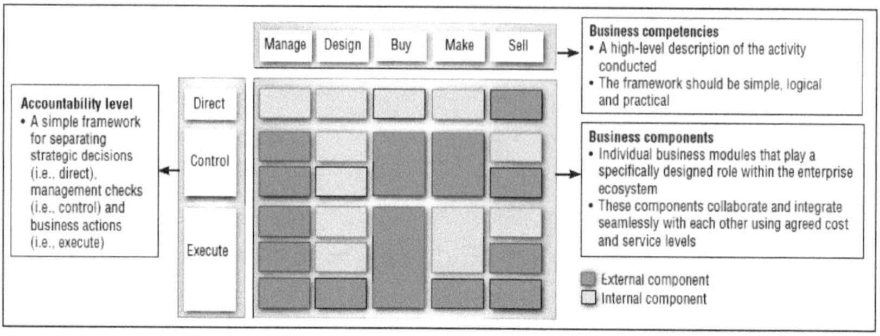

Figure 2-12: IBM Component Business Model, Source IBM Corp (IBM Corp, IBV, 2010, p. 7)

Using the IBM component business model (IBM Corp, IBV, 2010, p. 7), the traditional value chain can be dissected into three parts, the "Execute" part (or day-to-day operations part), the "Control" part that supervises the execution on a tactical and adjustment level and the "Direct" part, a kind of strategy level.

However, it needs to be said that the model of defining capabilities do not come together, thus Grant's (Grant, 1999) model goes here way beyond.

2.3.9 Enterprise and Individual, Language typologies

The enterprise itself is composed out of individuals who then perform tasks within a certain frame of reference and expectation. For example: A chief finance officer is mostly asked to be on the "Direct" side of the Finance process, whereas a shop floor engineer might be more on the "Execute" side of the operations stream. Bolten (Bolten, 2007, p. 71) in his work about Business German ("Wirtschaftsdeutsch") here argues that a "business language" might generate artificial boundaries that divide a company into sub-cultures and therefore the typical language division within science will here result into a language division within enterprise divisions. Bolten roughly divides the enterprise language within the following main sections as depicted in Table 2-2. Bolten argues that there is little empirical work that sustains this assertion, especially within the German language. He sees this as a need to further elaborate this and also to look into the different language barriers within companies in order to hopefully overcome it.

Bolten further argues that in order to improve communications amongst companies, that the following three key characteristics should be developed by science:

- Development of a base dictionary of German Business language.
- Analysis of morphological and syntactic particularities of the business German
- Research of verbal communication

By the author's personal experience, it needs to be noted that similar language barriers also do exist within US-based companies where the chasm between the senior executive language and the operational execution language often becomes an unbridgeable gap. The same experience can be realized within French-Originating companies. With his personal experience, Swiss-Originating companies have a more common denominator using a business sub-set of Schwyzerdütsch (Swiss German) in order to communicate across hierarchies.

	Text material	Communication partners
A	Theory Language Monographies, Research reports, educational literature etc.	Scientists, Students (Economy, MBA, Politics, Law), Executives, Senior Staff managers, area leaders, economic policy makers
B	Professional Language Business reports, Balance Sheets, Contracts, Protocols, Newspaper and Journal articles, inter-company memorandums etc.	Mostly the people amongst A plus representatives of the operative management, trade journalists, trade interpreters and translators
C	Division-specific company Language Business mail, Advertisements, Prospects, Sales negotiations etc.	Mostly those amongst A and B plus the representatives of the "execute" section within enterprises, consumers.

Table 2-2: Language typologies (Bolten, 1991, p. 71)

What needs to be noted further is that the rise into a hierarchy often is conjured together with an up-leveling of the language accustomisation, which means people coming from lower levels need to learn the speak of the higher-ups in order to be acknowledged within their ranks; the other way round often appears to be fraternizing and populistic.

2.3.10 Conflict handling – Indirect vs. Direct communications

Avoiding a conflict is a common trait for most animals and humans. A conflict usually costs resources and the outcome might be unpredictable. Smiling and the act of "showing face" to each other are means that enable a flawless course of life. Even when most humans – especially in the Western hemisphere - are being used to discuss most conflicts openly and discuss things through, this is not necessarily the case in all culture, even in the Western hemisphere.

Swiss for example consider Germans as too direct in discussing touchy points, as Küng points out – this even has been grown "over centuries" (Küng, 2007, p. 34). In Asian cultures, this is even more paramount (Lewis, 2007). In those cultures, the "western battle culture ("Streitkultur")" is not that paramount. An issue is not being brought up that openly, in most cases. Conflicts are often not uncovered but rather avoided by an "unnoticeable intervention" (Chen, 2001, p. 51). The goal is a flawless course of every day's life. In contrast, especially in academia in European higher education, the giving and receiving of "constructive criticism" is exercised quite often as a virtue by discussing in a professional and specific way around a topic.

Categories	West	East
Understanding	Direct, clear and short Free use of praise and criticism Confrontation of the counterpart with own matters and opinions Discussing and questioning at every price, mostly verbal communication	Indirect, often via third parties Consideration of the context (right moment, right mood, etc). "sitting-out" and delaying of conflicts, no discussions Increased sensitivity for body language and "reading between the lines", communications without words Passive listening, little eye contact
Language	Often complex, abstract patterns of thinking and language Objective exchange of opinions, constructive feedback -> aide for development Emotionality, honesty and trust (but also irony) are values in society	Replay of learned matters and proverbial Highly differentiated addresses, even within the family Different levels of language for different events (i.e. family, religion, upper class or government) Little negative or emotional uttering (consent orientation)
Center of discussion	Own free exchange of opinion Same right for everyone in the course of discussion without considering the social rank of the people Counterpart as equally righted and free discussion partner. Explaining if necessary – speaker centrism	"Keeping the face" of both the own and the counterpart has highest priority Orientation towards the counterpart – language, addresses, behavior by position, profession and age. Orientation towards context and collective -> centrism towards the meta levels
Society	Individualism, egalitarianism and libertism as part of a self- understanding of a democratic state Emphasizing of creativity and self-initiative, emancipation and autonomy. High age = senility – a taboo. Fast and short-term orientation and problem solving (capitalistic orientation)	Collectivism (individual is part of a group) Hierarchy and authority as structural features of the Asian society (patriarchate, clear distribution of roles) Education as a prerequisite for a secured life and societal reputation Age = wisdom "Perseverance" for more overview, long term decisions ("long breath")
Family	Equal righted, libertarian living together Joint decision making Early self-responsibility and maturity of the child.	Family is the most important reference group Authority of and duty to take care for the parents towards the young Kids have mostly no decision power and – duty

Table 2-3: East and West communication differences (Schulz von Thun, 2001)

Similar aspects have been found in handling criticisms out by Schröder et al. (Schröder, Reuter, & Tiittula, 1989) in comparing German and Finnish cultures. As it shows, fair criticism and friendship do not necessarily stand in contrast.

In Asia, this is to be handled with more care. Open criticism in best case is considered a sign of bad manners as Günther (Günther, 1991, p. 302) writes, "in the worst case it is being seen as an intended insult." Criticisms in front of third parties can be particularly considered as highly humiliating and does not correspond with the concept of friendship.

Therefore, criticism happens more in an indirect way, as Chen elaborates. For European business leaders, this especially means talking about the positive aspects and commonalities with the Asian counterpart and then late coming to "suggestions of improvement" the Asian counterpart might envisage, often transported by an ambassador.

Schulz von Thun (Schulz von Thun, 2001) has developed a framework that contrasts the direct and indirect communication and has also been elaborated by Schröder (Schröder, 1993, p. 517ff) in investigating through academic and professional texts. Schulz von Thun differentiates the categories of Understanding, Language, Center of Discussion, Society and Family, as shown in table Table 2-3.

There are many ways to handle conflicts and to resolve them. One method in order to overcome conflicts can be humor and laughter. Schröder (Schröder, Das Lachen der Kulturen., 2008) has researched this component of culture across different nationalities and has found out that humor is a means of conflict resolution. He especially has shown by examples that laughter is a "system of signs" that has its semantics, syntax and pragmatic, however it is language and culture dependent. Schröder describes the laughter of Vietnamese women having experienced extreme stress in an American bomb terror as a means of conflict resolution, same as the black humor that differs by culture. Laughter and its little brother, the smile, therefore can be seen as an acknowledgement of conflict and a way of resolving it.

2.3.11 Intercultural work: Working with Rightshore, Poland and India

As soon as trying to take advantage of factor conditions (Porter, 2008), the trade-off that needs to be made is to work with extra transaction costs that come from overcoming those factor conditions. Many of those extra transaction costs come from the differences in culture and of course location distance. The more successful organisations try to overcome those factor conditions with a set of concepts on how to bridge those gaps.

Typically, organisations also have to work with stereotypes, lacunas and ethnocentrisms that need to be analysed and overcome in order to stay effective. Definitely, as Schröder (Schröder, 1998, p. 41)writes, they need to be acknowledged, and the "pre-supposed base truths" need to be spoken out as they often do not correspond to each other." In order then to overcome this and to become effective, they essentially need to be translated into a correct meaning, often using a common process framework or a lingua franca technical, such as ITIL (ITIL Organisation, 2010), a framework for describing meanings within a technical services community.

To research intercultural communications processes questions besides research around argumentation and hermeneutics, the cognitive psychology and procedural-dynamic models and text linguistics and ethno-semantics and ethnomethodology do play a role, just to name a few important points of references. As Schröder et al write (Reuter, Schröder, & Tiittula, 1993), language and communications should not be seen in an isolated way, and it always should be seen in its context and contents. They especially emphasise that theoretical and methodical knowledge about business administration and economics is more than helpful.

To research on intercultural communications, they do recommend the following aspects to consider:

1. The degree of verbosity in the communications
2. The degree of formality in communication
3. The rhythm of the discourse
4. The degree of linearity of the discourse

As a result, it shows that communications happens in a different way besides the language and the discourse. In technology and services, it is therefore important to find a lingua franca to describe similar terms across the world, globally, especially when working with front-offices on-shore and back-offices off-shore.

This then helps in finding a common denominator across the organization to talk about.

2.3.12 How do communicate with a process model – The ITIL model

Braun (Braun, 1991, p. 193) argues that representatives of multinational enterprises do increasingly recognize the importance of language and culture skills. She especially reflected this in the area of tourism, where often a multinational crew caused by labor supply shortage in the own country is meeting a multinational set of clients, either because of the fact that they are working in an international environment or vice versa.

As a result, she realizes that besides typical domain-specific languages, a reduced English comes into play which increasingly is highly normed in an "impersonal way" and functions merely as language containers. This language is also caused by a clearly described role distribution between guest / client and personnel which prevent people from the individual language use.

What Braun expresses is that in a services industry the service process itself is becoming standardized and industrialized in an increasing way, in order to enable scale efficiencies and the replicability of personnel (von Gamm, 2009, p. 57). As von Gamm further elaborates, this is a key feature of industrialization inside the IT industry, which is further instrumentalised using common process such as ITIL. ITIL being the abbreviation for IT Infrastructure Library, developed by CCTA, now the OGC (Office of Governance Commerce) in Norwich (England) developed on behalf of the British government. "Today, ITIL is the worldwide de-facto-standard for service management and contains broad and publicly available professional documentation on how to plan, deliver and support IT service features", as the ITIL organization boldly states.

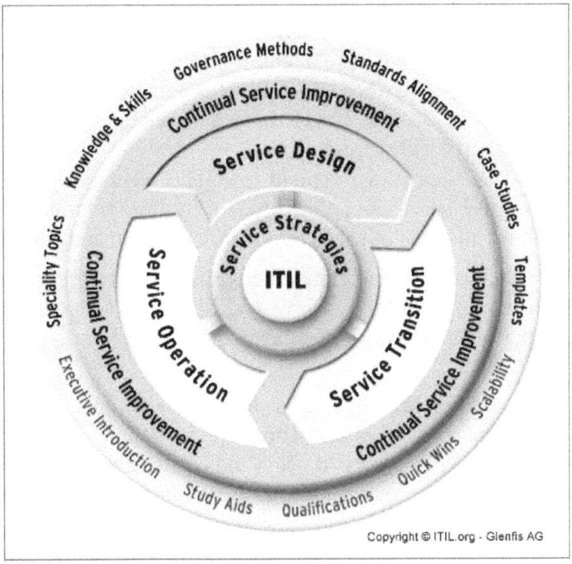

Figure 2-13: ITIL Overview (ITIL.ORG 2010), taken from website

ITIL (ITIL Organisation, 2010) mostly contains a process description methodology and tool language – a set of reduced English that helps in the following areas, also shown on Figure 2-13:

- Service Strategy
- Service Design (models for productive operation)
- Service Transition (service implementation/launch)
- Service Operation (productive operation of services)
- Continual Service Improvement

The following sub-types of ITIL as a common denominator are described below, as described in a longer text on the ITIL web site. The distil of ITIL can be seen as follows:

- The **Service Strategy Manual** delivers guidelines how services are being defined and positioned.
- The **Service Design manual** provides guidelines for the design and the development of services and service management processes. The scope of ser-

vice design comprises both on how to perform improvements and changes on existing services as well on how to design new services.

- The **Service Transition Manual** writes about how to improve and develop skills for bringing new services into operation, also called transitioning services.
- The **Service operation Manual** provides a guideline how to manage services on a day-to-day operational base. Here, both the delivery side as well as the support side is being described. By following this manual it is believed that both the client as well as the service provide have an efficient and effective operation and receive a clear added value.
- The **Continual Service Improvement** manual (CSI) provides instructions in on how to improve services continually and by this introduce cost-effective and efficient amendments of services in both operation and design.

As ITIL has become the lingua franca between IT services providers and its clients and also within IT Services providers, the ITIL concept it has found a wide-range adoption and has now become an often-found pre-requisite of operations for public tenders.

As a result, ITIL has been developed as a simplifying language to overcome culture-barriers between companies and company parts and in order to ensure a continuous process flow. However, it needs to be said that as a result of the richness of ITIL the language around ITIL has become dialectal. Thus, there is for example an IT Infrastructure Dialect of ITIL and an Application Management dialect of ITIL, too.

Nevertheless, ITIL serves as a good tool to overcome language and culture-depending barriers within enterprises and thus can enable the codification of language, which then helps to transform businesses into front-office and backoffice organizations and to further outsource parts of it.

Lacity et al, in particular, realized that the outsourcing of back-office operations (Lacity, Willcocks, & Rottman, 2008, p. 13) do correlate widely with the use of common language. Common language has been developed in order to capitalize upon the maturing Information Technology Outsourcing (ITO) and Business Process Outsourcing (BPO) markets by firms. Again here, the concept of Understanding (Oksaar, 1993) different cultures is paramount and if this cannot be achieved, a common framework such as ITIL serves to provide a trans-cultural bridge. The main lessons are that executives need this lingua franca in order to build significant and effective internal IT capabilities in-house – those capabilities to develop are hard to do, and in consequence, service providers who have developed that capability, have a further competitive advantage. Same is with the processes to manage global outsourcing. One of the main issues results in finding a common language of communication and control especially in regards to alignment of the back office, to incent suppliers and clients the right way, how to transfer and manage the knowledge and to retain key parts of it and to work on the sustainability of outsourcing relationships.

2.3.13 Offshore and Rightshore Concepts

Outsourcing companies increasingly employ a concept called "Offshoring" in order to achieve economies of factor conditions from labor arbitrage into the countries they serve. Capgemini employs a concept called Rightshore® that has the following triple aim (Capgemini S.A. , 2008):

- Provide an effective service on-site where clients want the service to have.
- Supplement the service with cost-effective resources from places where cost-effectiveness can be generated.
- Have high-quality center locations that accumulate skills and knowledge.

One of the biggest locations for Rightshore is India with currently 22'000 employees. Compared with other IT providers, Capgemini has a similar number of employees now in India than their competitors (IBM: 400'000 employees, 100'000 people in India; Accenture: 200'000 employees, 40'000 people working from India).

It therefore is notable to mention the Indian culture and working practices in a separate chapter.

2.4 Sales - Managing the bridge between cultures and firms

The initial contact between one company – a buyer – and the other – a prospective supplier – happens through a sale. The sale therefore is the "Build of the bridge" that establishes the ground between a long-term relationship between company A and Company B.

Sales itself has become "a boundary-spanning role" (Rogers B. , 2007, p. xxi) and a key role of interpreting the relationship between supplier and customer towards both sides. As Roger further elaborates, it is essential to understand the customer's point of view and to reconcile it with the needs of the company for profitable growth. At the same time, sales people, besides the work as relationship builders, forecasters, planners, people managers and business leaders, they are the standard-bearers of a company's reputation. Sales people are expected to ensure high standards of behaviour; despite the contradictions represented by some of the targets they are given.

Rogers then further differentiates between strategic relationships, prospective relationships, tactical relationships and cooperative relationships. Additionally, Rogers noted that the exit-relationship is important; and indeed, in outsourcing services, the termination services are often heftily debated already during contract negotiations.

- **Strategic Relationships -** these are relationships where it is believed on the basis of rational customer attractiveness analysis that the client has a strategic value to the supplier and where the client's buying decision-makers believe on the basis of rational supplier performance evaluation believe the supplier can add value to the company and its customers. The relationship itself is then of high quality, with integrated processes and day-to-day interactions. The relationship itself might be value creating, but besides the value creation needs to be tangible from both sides, thus fostering the relationship. Piercy & Lane (Piercy & Lane, 2005, p. 572) argue that account management should take place; however, it is too big. The client can also destroy value to the supplier and vice versa.
- **Prospective Relationships** – relationships that emerge and might become strategic. Roger argues that it is imperative for every supplying company to develop prospective relationships as clients often change their buying behaviors, or get merged and bought over time and thus would disappear from the clients' list of the company. The key imperative is to be economic in selecting and working the right prospects. Key tasks involve segmentation, targeting and positioning of each other's companies in order to redirect the efforts to the right place.
- **Tactical relationships** are those that have a low-priority purchase from the client's side, adding marginal value to either side. Typical tactical relationships are where the situation is given, the requirements are evident and thus "one-dimensional", as Drucker (Drucker, 1995, p. 147) describes it. The key feature of relationship is about the most economical option (i.e. price or price over time) and that the transaction costs are minimized on both sides. Nevertheless, they can be a source of opportunity for the supplier and might provide mutual value with a group of customers that might otherwise lose to competition. In addition, tactical relationships might be a good driver to bring down production costs, and sales here might provide a good contribution to develop lower-cost processes using IT tools and the right set of marketing. It has been proven that those tactical measures then might contribute to strategic relationships as those tactical measures – i.e. catalogue ordering, automated tools – add comfort to a strategic relationship and thus even increase the strategic value there.
- **Cooperative relationships** might just be the opposite of the tactical relationship. The buying company has a real strategic interest to keep the supplier; however, the supplier sees the buyer's value as low or medium. A typical cooperative relationship is where a supplier provides services or parts for an old or obsolete but often-used piece of equipment that cannot be easily substituted. An example in the services industry might be application maintenance for legacy software which is in operation since 30 or more years.

It is essential to look into a good definition of the sales management discipline. The Marketing and Sales Standards Setting Board MSSSB (MSSSCB, 2004, p. 12) describes the following key processes of sales management:"

- Establishing sales force objectives
- Developing sales force strategy, plans and associated structure
- Recruiting and selecting sales people
- Training and developing sales people
- Supervising the sales team
- Evaluating the overall performance of the sales people"

This chapter will focus on the individual sales management aspects, such as market planning and territory planning then leading opportunities, leading the sales people towards the right deals and then closing the transactions and managing and measuring the performance of the teams.

2.4.1 Establishing Sales force Objectives

Marketing and sales are in an "endless war" as written by Kotler, Rackham and Krisnavany (Kotler, Rackham, & Krisnavany, 2006, p. 23) write and builds a key cornerstone for the organisational layout of the company according to Claycomb et al (Claycomb, C. Germain, & Dröge, 2000, p. 219), and this lack of alignment might end up hurt corporate performance. Hence, it is of key to understand from the sales side how to develop the market and for marketing how to develop a sale. As Kotler writes, "all too often, organizations find that they have a marketing function inside sales and a sales function inside marketing", it is of clear importance to:

- Integrate the activities by jointly involving sales and marketing in product planning and in setting sales targets
- Integrate processes and systems by implementing systems to track and manage sales and marketing joint activities
- Enable the culture by emphasizing shared responsibility for results between different divisions of the organisation, to emphasize the metrics and to tie rewards to results
- Integrate organisational structures by splitting marketing into upstream and downstream terms and to hire a chief revenue officer

This then should help a company to grow in the market. Looking at the market and market size for Capgemini in Switzerland and Germany, here a market share of 5% might be a reachable goal.

2.4.2 Growing the business

Business growth is important. In order to be able to repay dividends, repay debts, and pay salaries that are competitive and to stay ahead of an inflation curve, growth of a business is a condition sine qua non. In essence, profits per owner can grow either by cutting costs or by increasing revenues or by paying out an owner and giving more to the rest, i.e. in the form of share buybacks. Given the fact that both the GDPs of the countries in the West covered (Central Intelligence Agency, 2009) as well as the IT market itself is slightly shrinking (BITKOM, 2009), (SwissICT, 2010), growth does not necessarily come from an ever-expanding market but needs to be fought away from other competitors.

2.4.3 Options of growth

As discussed, with revenues of 8.4 billion Euros, Capgemini is not a market leader in any of the domains. The market leader in IT Services is currently HP or IBM, depending on how numbers are being counted (Niklowitz, 2009). As the IT market grows globally according to IDC (2009) by 4%, there is an imperative for growth in order not to lose market share. In Germany, the IT market is sized at 66 bln Euros, with Capgemini only having a less than 5% market share overall. Given the fact that both the GDPs of the countries are currently covered (Central Intelligence Agency, 2009) as well as the IT market itself is slightly shrinking (BITKOM, 2009), (SwissICT, 2010), growth comes from gaining market share.

In general, there are two selected strategic options for growth:

- One is the inorganic growth through acquisitions of local IT Services providers and then integrating those services providers into Capgemini. This topic has been left out in this consideration.
- Organically, by setting up pursuit teams and work deal by deal in order to grow the business, also called organic growth, best by organising sales in a well-concerted manner.

2.4.4 An-organic growth through acquisitions

An-organic growth through acquisitions is always a viable option to grow. However, in consulting services and in outsourcing, this option is determined by the following factors:

- The amount and nature of players available. Unfortunately, it is found out that the players available are either not up for purchase due to the specific strategic impetus of their owners, or they would not fit into an integrated Capgemini picture by being either too small, too niche or not culturally fitting to the Capgemini brand promise of a brand that enables transformation and enables freedom (Capgemini, 2010) brand.
- The fluctuation or non-fluctuation of human capital with an acquisition as services business mainly consists out of people and some residual assets, as written by (Alaganandan, Bhowmick, & Mohanty, 2010). Most services leaders and senior managers are very likely to be hired in a burgeoning market such as outsourcing – and even in a decline - by the next available company. Once they would see their independence to be touched or once they see that a painful and time-consuming integration, it might affect their ability to

gain new clients on the market. Therefore, with every acquisition, key human capital – like senior consulting principals, chief architects and other people - need to be given incentives for long-term stay with the company. However, most of those incentives have failed, such as shown with the integration of several players, like IBM and PWCC, as described in IT World (Bennett, 2002).

- Price. The price can be determined by the portfolio of contracts, its profitability and its duration, plus a certain forward-looking synergistic value or brand place expansion value (goodwill (Wardlow, 1988, p. 27)). Figure 2-14 provides a pricing model for a company value in the services area, derived thereof.

$$P = \sum_{i=1}^{n} npvk(i) + Valres + pbrand + Pgoodwill - restructuring$$

Figure 2-14: Pricing a company value consisting out of a series of single services

The following elements are being used:

- npvk(i) being the net present values of the individual services contracts
- *Valres* being the residual value of synergies
- *pbrand* the brand price to be bought
- *Pgoodwill* any other goodwill
- *restructuring* – any restructuring obviously needed.

Given these factors, many acquisitions in the services area do not pay off its purchasing price over time - unlike the economic conditions that favor this. Below are some examples:

- A future economic climate where key employees rather stay instead of going away (motivators do not count, as they are part of the deal!)
- Other competitors disappear suddenly and therefore contracts do migrate away less easily than forecasted.

2.4.5 Organic Growth through Target Account Selling

Organically, growth comes from building up a pipeline of new deals by the company itself by carefully selecting the right targets and then work from there an expansion of the business. Barash & Mitchell (Barash & Mitchell, 1998, p. 3) even go further and depict business forecasting using an accounts-based model. Woodburn (Woodburn, 2001) especially suggests considering qualitative aspects when looking into Pipelining and CRM implementations.

If deals are being won through a good pipeline management system together with solid relationship planning, the following effects apply:

- Every deal won is then carefully understood and selected by both the client and the supplier. This therefore should add solidity towards a client-supplier relationship in services (McDonald, Millman, & Rogers, 1996).

- The business development costs of the deals can be understood well and with every new deal, there is a learning effect, if configured in a stable, hit team approach (Clutterbuck, 1998, p. 153). This is not always the case; hence, it will be subject to further research.
- As the deal is understood and well implemented, outsourcing cases, in particular, can go faster through the "implementation dip" or known as "valley of tears" (Lewin K. , 1947, p. 34).

However, being unappealing for the propagators of big M&As, many companies have found this business to be more profitable and a lower risk for the following three reasons:

- Every deal won is then carefully understood and selected by both the client and supplier. This is at least the case in outsourcing, in other areas, such as Consulting and Technology Services, Time and Material type services do dominate thus imposing lower risk of liability.
- The business development costs of the deals can be understood well and with every new deal, the business development team has a learning effect, if configured in a stable, hit team approach (Clutterbuck, 1998, p. 153). This is not always the case, and will be subject to further research.
- In outsourcing, especially, instead of integrating a large delivery team and then trying to leverage a team which has performed only half ways well in a market whilst going through the usual "pain of consolidation" – means: displacing half of the employees whilst moving the workload to India and Poland, aka Rightshore® - Capgemini then can handpick the right people though executive search agencies from the market.

In order to understand the market, it then needs to be made through a market sizing analysis of companies that would be interested to leverage. Notably, market share depends upon the right market definition and especially in services can be captured either as broad including all potential in-house services i.e. Finance, Admin, HR that can potentially be outsourced or only the distinct set of services that is already "out on the market". In conclusion, the potential "market reserve" is larger than the numbers depicted.

2.4.6 Growth and Organizational setup

Organisational setup is of importance for sales forces and in order to determine growth. The MSSSB (MSSSCB, 2004) sees three different ways of structuring sales forces:

- **A geography-based sales force** – sales staff are responsible for all sales activities necessary to sell their organisation's product and services. District sales people are responsible here.
- **A product-based sales force** – organisations with a diverse range of products and services, especially where these include technically complex products

- **A market based sales force**, where sales staff is organised by the different markets or customer types.

Deriving from the organizational setup, Capgemini in Germany/Switzerland has a mixed type of sales force: It is mainly driven around service categories (product type sales force), entailing the divisions of Technology Services, Consulting Services and Outsourcing Services – all of those sales forces selling their product distinctively. At the same time, within those product groups, some regional or market based types of sales forces do exist, such as "Geschäftsbereiche" inside Technology Services or "Market Units" inside Consulting Services (3M, 1997). However, there is no consistent type of approach to develop a joint framework under both consulting services and technology services, which might be one root cause for the dilemma researched.

2.4.7 Performance management and measurement

As firms are groups of people, the total performance of a firm is composed not only of the sum of the performance of individuals; it shows otherwise, every individual could be also performing independently maybe even better. As the "3M experience" (3M, 1997) depicts, the key in managing and measuring performance is a commitment to up-front planning and the support and buy-in of senior management. Besides investment in training, the empowerment of the team should be enabled and the team itself should manage the risk and control the budget.

2.4.8 Winning and losing

Winning is better than losing, financially speaking. Unfortunately in business, being Number 2 in a sales competition is not a "silver medal", it is the highest price to pay, as business development efforts usually do not get repaid, unlike in other branches such as architecture or construction services (Hamel & Pralahad, 1994, p. 34). So the question is how losses can be avoided in order to improve the win-rate.

2.4.8.1 Winning

Lastly, businesses are being conducted by winning deals. And most business environments are being dominated by a "the winner takes it all" situation, thus the rewards of winning are high and the pain of losing might be high aswell. For example, a deal won in outsourcing might then last for five to ten years of committed business for a provider, whereas the losers continue with zero again.

The lesson learned depicted in Figure 2-15 has been drawn by practitioners and professionals in order to distil in one page the recipe to win in engagements (von Gamm, How to win, 2009).

WIN
- Know the customer inside out
- Demonstrate to the customer that they are important to Capgemini - value proposition
- Understand the customer business plan and competitive environment
- Build a value proposition around the customer's key business objectives, without access you will fail

EXECUTE
- Your first proposition should knock them off of their seats – value proposition
- Raising the bar, be paranoid, never stop selling – value proposition
- Embrace change, innovate, innovate and innovate – value proposition
- Understand risk transference – i.e. Unit pricing is about risk taking away from the client
- Be pragmatic, winning something creates a platform but be obstinate about the Capgemini uniqueness.
- Winning is everything but the journey is the real experience for you

TEAM
- Winning is a team game, use Capgemini global, TS, CC have many highly skilled resources that you can exploit
- Work harder than the customer and the competition all of the time.
- Perseverance, don't lose confidence, it is a roller coaster, enjoy the ride
- Small, highly skilled and motivated teams are better than average armies, know the process, know the journey
- Include the support teams and Delivery from the outset, bring everyone along the journey with you
- Sell internally all of the time
- Be humble, however, know when to walk away

You are part of the best IT and consulting companies worldwide, believe in it

Figure 2-15: How to win (von Gamm, How to win, 2009)

It reminds that winning is a multi-dimensional, often non-repeatable process that despite all uniqueness of a win might be dissected in three main phases:

- The **Win** phase itself – having a clear **goal** in front of the mind on where to win and what to win and why the client wants to strike a deal
- The **Execution** phase – during the deal **what to do** best, how to craft a deal and understand the core of what clients buy and
- The **Teaming** phase – **how** to behave and compose within a winning team.

In essence, this Figure 2-15 suggests that there are no real recipes of winning besides those ground rules and its specific application to a deal.

2.4.8.2 Losing

The downside of winning is losing. And in competitive environments, usually only one player can win, and all the others do lose. This implies that dealing with losses as an individual and as an organisation is wise to do and it should be learned from losses. Clearly, losing can be painful. Especially in larger pursuits, where people have worked for months on a deal then lose, a thorough analysis is required then. Hence, a post-bid review analysis can make sense. In that respect, Capgemini has developed in its sales guidelines a post-bid review analysis (Capgemini S.A., 2007), that captures the expectations of winning – prior to the loss compared to the actual state of situation, after

- Interviewing the power sponsor to win
- Interviewing any consultants and intermediaries
- And making the own conclusions.

There are obvious reasons for loss, such as overpricing, wrong solution or not enough client access or wrong depiction of real client pain (McDonald M. H., 1998). However, there are other little trigger events that might cause a loss, e.g. a cultural wrongful adoption of client teams. Simply, reasons of losses often come out of the unexpected and are the unknown unknowns, as Taleb (Taleb, 2008) describes it in his book for Investment analysis. In services particularly, people focus on minimizing risk, be as professional as possible as Piercy & Lane state (Piercy & Lane, 2005, p. 563) and to have the sales process well under control.

2.4.9 Planning to win: Territory-, Account- and Opportunity Planning

To plan ahead the territory served and then work on the target accounts selected by identifying the right opportunities that fit to the organisation helps improve the win rate (Piercy N. F., 2001). The accounts should be served where a supplier can add value with specific cases and opportunities.

As most account planning bases upon existing structures, such as existing sales personnel, business relationships and opportunities, it is perennial to integrate the desired goal of a new to-be account and territory structure with the current situation. Hence, either an evolutionary approach might be needed or a hard-cut by setting up a new sales organisation for a new opportunity landscape.

2.4.9.1 Account and territory planning

Typically, account and territory planning is a key element after designing a marketing plan has been performed. Smith (Smith B. , 2003) et al (Smith, E., & Blair, 2000) emphasises that territory alignment might motivate a sales force to rethink its planning around different clients. Definitely, territory planning is to be performed best in a group of experienced sales people, across different disciplines in order to have a full picture of the planning. It is indeed necessary to look at a territory alongside a methodology as Rogers (Rogers B. , 1999) depicts or using a very similar metric like Capgemini is using, dubbed KARMA (Key Account Relationship Metric Analysis) (Capgemini S.A., 2007). In both – highly similar cases - a territory will be divided into four quadrants of clients – strategic, anchor, and target and tactical. Fiocca (Fiocca, 1982) points out that concepts and techniques which have been developed for analysing might strategies also be utilized to assess strategic position of companies in industrial markets. The emphasis on supplier/customer relationships by Fiocca is analogous from the interaction approach to marketing and purchasing strategy.

As companies develop a symbiotic relationship, strategy evolves as proposals made by either side are either accepted or rejected. KARMA is more simple but in many ways useful for a first usage of a territory definition. Using the KARMA Analysis of Capgemini, it can then be determined which clients are currently strategic, anchor, target or tactical clients. Rogers (Rogers B. , 2007, p. 71ff) uses a slightly different taxonomy to KARMA – in brackets are Rogers' words. KARMA is a very Capgemini specific taxonomy, which in essence is compatible to the framework of Rogers (Rogers B. , 2007, p. 139).

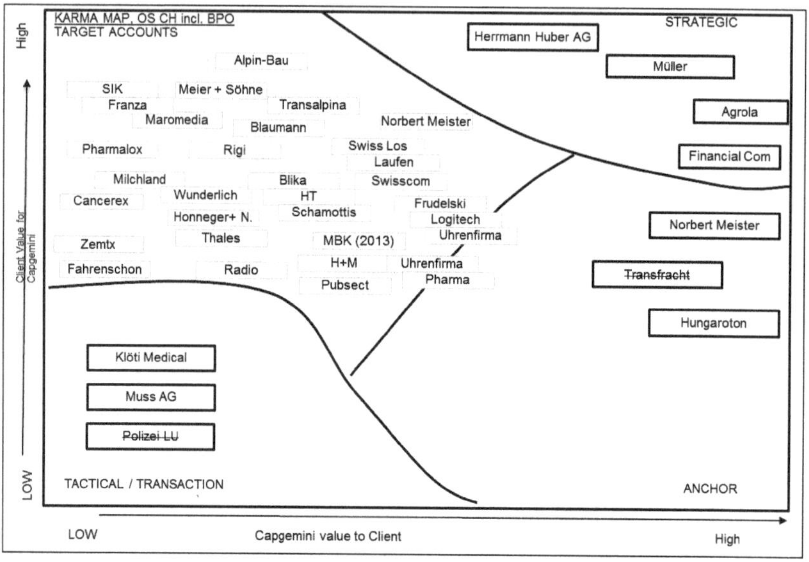

Figure 2-16: KARMA example map

- **Strategic**: high value to Capgemini and High Value to the client. A strategic client should be served by a key account manager in order to develop the client for further growth and share.
- **Anchor (Cooperative** (Rogers B. , 2007)**)**: High value to the Client, but of only medium to higher value to Capgemini. This client type might best be compared to a "cash cow" client as it is being used often in the BCG matrix (Grant, 1999, p. 257). Thus, the current value for Capgemini might be very high but the incremental value might be limited, for example because the market share within the client has peaked.
- **Target (Prospective** (Rogers B. , 2007)**)**: Potential high value to Capgemini and therefore worth investing. These clients have been identified as target accounts and would represent with a certain investment a future revenue and profit source for Capgemini. Therefore, these clients are both worthy and require a certain amount of investment in order to **become** strategic accounts in the future.
- **Tactical**: Some value to both parties, but highly opportunistic. These types of accounts might be interesting to get if the price of investment is not high.

A KARMA target map with phantasy names can be seen at Figure 2-16. As it is key to work out a client classification system that both fits the client and the company, MacDonald and Rogers (McDonald M. H., 2000) argue that developing account plans is of paramount importance.

2.4.9.2 Target Account selection

Selecting target accounts is in that respect a matter of empirical trial and error. The following checklist has been developed by using a checklist similar to the UVOP concept of Knox and Maklan (Knox & Maklan, 1998).

- Future value for the client
- Future value for the supplier
- Pain that can be resolved by the supplier
- A need to act now
- A client access that can be leveraged and target
- A "Strategic fit" in terms of other existing client bases, such as references
- Size of opportunity
- Existing client of a competitor whom then might be easy to switch because of dissatisfaction and expiration of contract, especially in outsourcing.

2.4.9.3 Target account list

In order to rate and prioritize the target accounts, a prioritization should be applied. It is key to prioritize accounts on in a target field, as the targeting process itself is already expensive enough. their A methodology as this is being applied at several firms, here the example of IBM, as Pop (Pop, 2009) highlights it, will be presented. Pop makes a good argument by raising those three most important points.

- **Client access**: Does the provider – by any means – have client access to a decision making level? Client access might exist through existing relationships or through a likely accessibility – means openness. The openness here might exist if the executives recently have changed and are therefore still in a "learning mode", being open for new ideas. This client access also sometimes can be found through influencers, who then need to be incentivized, somehow.
- **Pain**: some current pain known from the client? Pain might be coming from two sides: one is personal pain of a decision maker – like the ambition to move forward or at least survive without having any real good idea on how to impress the bosses - or some business flaws, likely impeding the profitability of the client in the mid- or longer term whilst at the same time impeding the personal growth of a decision maker, who then might be a power sponsor for a good idea, such as outsourcing. Typical areas of pain might be exploding costs, sluggish sales, inflexibility to setup new subsidiaries or new business caused by a too balkanized IT and business process environment, and therefore as main pain the risk of losing a year-end bonus. Those pains are dependent upon the level where people are and which function they have in the company – ground rule: The higher the level, the more important the pain.

- **Story** – Does the provider actually have a story that would solve and heal the pain of both the target client company and at the same time the decision maker? An example: Outsourcing is not a panacea for many decision makers, so it only can be applied to those who are open to it. Other clients might rather prefer a consulting engagement just to impress with good ideas, but not the actual delivery and taking over of people. It also needs to be made clear, whether the offer really solve the pain and the story is concrete by numbers and actions. In order to be effective the story should center around increased sales, reduced IT cost, demonstrably reduced process cost or cycle time, improved flexibility, and less risk. How exactly the story then is intonated, depends upon the level and situation of the target client.

Another very important factor can be introduced by sales managers themselves. It is called the "gut feeling", an amalgamate of professional experience, personal view of the world, integrated into the subconscious feeling. It is said that the best sales people and executives are paid for their gut feeling, first and foremost.

- **Gut Feeling Stars**: Quite a deciding factor, this then is really what it is – gut feeling – of the sales director whether something pays or not. This "gut feeling stars" system is simply based upon the year's long experience of the sales director and therefore differentiates a good choice of a sales director versus simply a bad choice.

The target rating *tR* is then determined by the following formula Figure 2-17:

$$\boxed{tR = GutFeeling \cdot (Story + Pain + ClientAccess)}$$

Figure 2-17: Target rating formula

The following elements are used:

- *GutFeeling* – a qualitative indicator of the sales management function to prioritize or de-prioritize sales events - ranging from 1 to 4 stars
- *Story*- qualifying whether Capgemini can provide a reasonable value proposition to the client ranging from 1 to 10
- *Pain*, qualifying the "need to act" of a client, ranging from 1 to 10 and
- *ClientAccess*, the level of access to the client ranging from 1 to 10

The formula has been developed further from a sales qualification rule of thumb, i.e. found at IBM, called the magic triangle as documented amongst other by P. Pop. (Pop, 2009, pg. 24), shown in Figure 2-18.

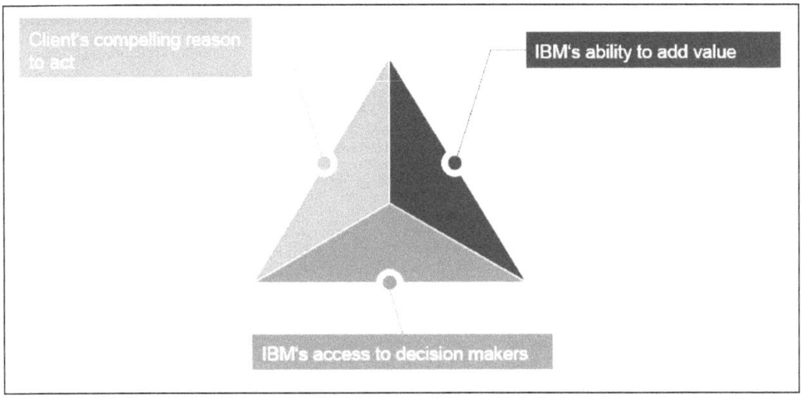

Figure 2-18: Qualification Metric, here used by IBM, Source Pop (2009, p. 24)

Therefore, the maximum t_R points number can be 120, the minimum is 3. With this rather simple mechanism, it then can be determined further the first wave of target clients, as shown in Figure 2-19. What then comes to importance is a "sudden change of behaviour" of the client, also known as "trigger event". Pop (Pop, 2009, p. 17) qualifies the following events as trigger events:

Internal trigger events such as New CxO (CIO, CEO, CFO), Strategic misalignment, Financial performance, Overall restructuring required, Non performing business unit, Non performing business process, Non performing IT, Merger / Acquisition, Expand into new markets, Expand into new products, Strong growth

External trigger events like Changing customer behaviour, Share price underperformance, Missed earnings / market surprises, Changing market demands, Changing market structure, Competitive dynamics, Technological changes, Regulatory / Economic changes, Major event (e.g. catastrophes)

Pop, like many people in sales, however, forgets one point – the external trigger event typically causes an internal effect within the company. This internal trigger event then results into a change in strategy which forces the company to rethink its position for example towards outsourcing or towards the introduction of a new system, like a better customer relationship management system.

An example might be constructed as follows: Because of the higher exchange rate between the Swiss Franc and the Euro, an exporting company in the middle of Switzerland earns less Swiss Francs in Euro. As a result of the reduced revenues in Swiss Francs, the profit declines. This forces the board of directors to the strategic decision to import more goods and services from the Euro room to hedge its position. At the same time, the cost effectiveness of the imported service is better than the service performed in-house. This might lead the board to decide to outsource the IT department. In consequence, services might be supplied from outside of Switzerland.

Target Rating *	Gut Feeling Stars	Bemerkung	Firma	Market Cap Mia CHF	# employees	Revenues	DDS Potential MCHF	DCS excl. DDS Potential MCHF	AM Potenzial MCHF	Total Potential MCHF	Client	Acc Pain	"Story"
96	4	bidding, currently Nr. 2		4.78	2'541	1065.6	6.40	12.36	6.18	24.94	8	7	9
76	4	kein Outsourcing, haben aber AGBs geändert.		48.68	80'000	31980	158.40	1'918.80	959.40	3'036.60	4	8	7
72	4	Not interested in pursuing further		18.29	19'795	11000	39.19	330.00	165.00	534.19	8	3	7
72	4	Outsource IMAC (DDS) bei Swisscom, Netz bei BT		54.45	48'200	45000	95.44	900.00	450.00	1'445.44	5	7	6
51	3	Christoph Locher hat Outsourcingüberlegungen, und beschäftigt Bearingpoint damit, so		19.49	11'702	31600	23.17	632.00	316.00	971.17	5	6	6
51	3	voll outgesourced: BPO bei Capgemini, IT z.T. bei		39.37	60'000	38900	118.80	427.90	213.95	760.65	8	4	5
51	3	konsolidieren gerade ihre IT Truppe, neuer CIO			6'000	512.5	11.88	10.25	5.13	27.26	7	5	5
51	3	wollen "das beste vom besten"		private	2'000	142300	2.52	284.60	142.30	429.42	4	6	7
48	3	hat kein Outsourcing, Pain?		5.64	8'457	13300	16.74	266.00	133.00	415.74	5	6	5
48	3	haben 18% IT Expense, grössere Restrukturierung		government	4'446	2126	8.80	255.12	127.56	391.48	3	7	6
48	3	gehört zum Renova Konzern (Thomas Borer),		private	9'497	3900	11.97	78.00	39.00	128.97	6	5	5
42	3	Outsource mit T-Systems, läuft 2010 aus.		2.46	20'000	8500	25.20	170.00	85.00	280.20	1	7	6
42	3	Syngenta hatte BPO bis Ende 2007 mit Capgemini.		24.30	21'000	10000	26.46	200.00	100.00	326.46	5	5	4
36	2	RfI verschickt, RfP qualified out			1'500	1000	2.97	20.00	10.00	32.97	4	7	7
36	3	SAP 1. Generation Globe Projekt fertig seit 2006.		184.38	200'000	107600	180.00	645.60	322.80	1'148.40	3	5	4
36	3	Outsourcing mit Swisscom und T-Sytems läuft 2010		keine - Staat	27'438	7600	54.33	152.00	76.00	282.33	3	4	5
33	3	BT und IBM im Outsourcing, letztes Renewal 2007		155.05	54'613	41420	68.81	828.40	414.20	1'311.41	4	3	4
28	2	Outsource mit IBM seit 2003, 10-Jahresvertrag		51.09	157'000	31809.5	197.82	636.19	318.10	1'152.11	4	5	5
27	3	sehr hoch bewertet. Bei starkem Börsenabfall mag		17.96	9'000	3000	11.34	60.00	30.00	101.34	3	3	3
26	2	haben in der IT keine bekannte Strategie. Haben		128.64	80'000	46000	100.80	920.00	460.00	1'480.80	3	5	5
22	2	Baloise Versicherung kein Outsource, SoBa (Bank)		3.88	3'100	82.3	6.14	1.65	0.82	8.61	3	4	4
20	2	kein Outsourcing bekannt.		6.64	23'577	5900	29.71	118.00	59.00	206.71	2	4	4
16	2	kein Outsourcing		23.22	89'364	27000	112.60	540.00	270.00	922.60	1	3	4
14	1	Management Pain, only			130	40	0.26	0.80	0.40	1.46	1	6	7
12	4	mit exec changes möglich			51'075	20975	64.35	419.50	209.75	693.60	1	1	1
12	4	keine Pain			2'615	2810	5.18	56.20	28.10	89.48	1	1	1
12	4	Pain wg. China evtl.			9'400	2559	18.61	51.18	25.59	95.38	1	1	1
10	1	Outsourcing-Bemühungen mit IBM im Jahr 2003,		12.92	3'869	2800	7.66	56.00	28.00	91.66	3	4	3
10	2	Planung für 2012 outzusourcen, ähnlich Modell		keine - Staat			-	-	-	-	1	3	1
10	1	Pain wg. Gescheiterter Fusion			300	96	0.59	1.92	0.96	3.47	2	2	6

Figure 2-19: Sample Target account list, using target rating formula, names omitted

This example shows that if this change in external environment is recognised, a selling company can address that change in external environment early enough to construct a well-fitting value proposition that then leads the decision makers within the company towards a purchase.

2.4.9.4 Target account selection through cross-selling

A further way of expanding the business is to take current consulting engagements and technology services engagements of Capgemini and check whether they are able to leverage those engagements into an outsource, in essence to "clothe" deals with components of a different division. In order to leverage outsourcing within existing technical or consulting services engagement, a high degree of trust between the internal parties is necessary.

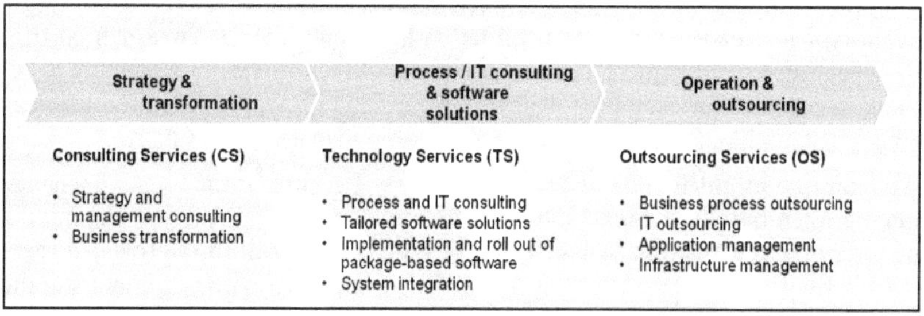

Figure 2-20: Capgemini Value Chain – simplified view , Source: Capgemini collateral

The internal trust needs to be achieved through changing the behaviour of the people. This correlates with the view that Capgemini does encompass the full value chain of projects from Design, to build and Run, as depicted in Figure 2-20. It is believed that strategy and transformation consultants can determine the technology solution depicted and implemented "downstream" and thus Capgemini Technology Services can have a lead advantage in implementing it. Outsourcing services then would be able – due to tighter integration with Technology Services to operate and run the whole IT installation at lower price. The whole process would be self-funding from a client perspective with increased business benefits.

2.4.10 Sales and Managing Key accounts

2.4.10.1 Key account management models

Key account management gains importance in large scale organizations. A big reason besides efficiency gains on the supply side, is buyer pressure, as Ryals and Rogers (Ryals & Rogers, 2006) do argue. Procurement organisations have grown up and have become a strategic business function that helps buying organizations reduce risk and increase efficiencies in buyer relationships. Ryals and Rogers (Ryals & Rogers, 2006) expand that this then also is a direct mirror back and forth towards an increase in buying organizations. Especially with the tighter integration of the value chain, Ryals and Rogers as well as Millman (Millman, 1994) envision a stronger role of purchasing not only in supplier selection but even into strategic decision making.

In sales, Piercy and Lane (Piercy & Lane, 2005) elaborate that a transformation from conventional transactional sales activities towards a more strategic customer management would impose a major challenge for executives. In parallel, key account management becomes a career step for sales managers from individual divisions. Companies like IBM (IBM, 2009) focus on key account managers as managing directors and formulate a strategy for career progression with beaconing executive visibility inside.

2.5 Selling into global Accounts

A specific work needs to be conducted with Global or International Accounts. Special points come to play:

- Not only the service provider – in the respected case – is working globally, but also the client company is a global player.
- The demand for services provided is to be implemented by the global account in different places; then the demand for services is executed.

There are in essence seven different configurations that might come into play, as shown on Table 2-4. These are the types of configuration sets that need to be respected when dealing between international clients and international service providers. Services can be exported, imported, determined by a local headquarter towards a foreign subsidiary or a foreign headquarter might purchase local services. With the on-going centralisation of procurement power (Rogers B. , 2007, p. 27) towards headquarters for economies of scale, scope and professionalization, sales managers must increasingly think of this international dimension and scope, simply, as on both sides there are international entities to work through.

Type	Service Provider	Client Headquarter	Client Service provision
1. Local to Local	Domestic	Domestic	Domestic
2. Local to Foreigners	Domestic	Abroad	Domestic
3. Imported Service	Abroad	Domestic	Domestic
4. Local Subsidiary provision	Abroad	Abroad	Domestic
5. Headquarter-controlled Service	Domestic	Abroad	Abroad
6. Local for Headquarter Provision	Domestic	Domestic	Abroad
7. Specialist Service Provider	Abroad	Domestic	Abroad
n/a	Abroad	Abroad	Abroad

Table 2-4: International Client Service configurations

Moreover, this means, that both sides might have teams that need to be integrated in a global way for this specific client configuration.

Example 1: An Indian Service provider sells to a Swiss-based multinational a service contract that essentially then will be executed for its U.S.-based entity. In order to be successful, all of the following entities need to play together:

From the provider's side:

- The sales manager of the Indian Service provider in Switzerland
- The Service delivery team in India
- The Service implementation team in the U.S.

From the client's side:

- The original service requester, i.e. a specialist department in the U.S.
- The global headquarter in Switzerland
- Potentially, a global centre of procurement excellence, which might be located elsewhere, for example in Singapore.

It needs to be noted that this example is not constructed but is existing in reality. This would be a "Type 7" configuration from the table above.

Example 2: A Swiss subsidiary of a French Multinational Service Provider receives the request to host data of a Russian global client in its Swiss Datacentres.

Similarly, the following parties ideally need to work together, a "Type 5" configuration.

From the provider's side:

- The Swiss Service Provider, together with its French Headquarter
- The Russian Subsidiary of the service provider

From the client's side:

- Mainly the Russian headquarters plus its service requester. If it is a centralised service and the Russian company does not have a Swiss subsidiary, the business here can be quite direct.

Each of these situations has implications in building the right sales and delivery team, executing the service the way clients want it, coordinating with the right resources from the client side and then executing the invoicing and billing in a way that is both taxation conform (i.e. the avoiding of value added tax "round-tripping") and cost efficient.

2.5.1 Planning accounts and opportunities

After assessing the potential territory prospects, the selected "strategic" or "target" accounts require planning. Ryals and Rogers (Ryals & Rogers, 2007) emphasise that strategic planning has been part of the management function for "as long as anyone can remember", there was not much focus on key account plans as a critical part of the marketing and business plan. As a best practice, they describe to first determine what a key account is – this should be done using territory planning as emphasized in chapter 2.4.10.1. Then, a "hierarchy of key relationships" might be instrumental in determining how much planning an account justifies. The following step marks the need to be easy to remember and as simply possible to use, as Dueck (Dueck, 2007, p. 15) postulates are suggested, to quote: "

- Identify the KAM team
- Train on analysis, objective and strategy setting, and then writing plans
- Brief on the planning process
- Brief on the analytical process
- Identify the responsibility for production of plan document – this is usually done by the key account manager
- Agree client involvement
- Communicating on the planning process
- Communicating on the output (plan and the results)"

Content-wise, Ryals and Rogers (Ryals & Rogers, 2007) suggest a combination of several aspects of the plan. It should start with a PEST (Political, Economic, Social, Technological or STEEP when the ecological component is added) (McDonald M. H., 2001) analysis and then using Porter's five forces of competition for the client. An example will be shown in Chapter IV for the country selection. At the same time, they suggest to in-depth discuss with the client's decision makers and maybe shareholders what is really demanded and required, especially when it goes to business-critical selling. It is also suggested that an actionable SWOT (Rogers B. , 2007) analysis should be produced and a determination what the client should perform as strategies for the next 3-5 years. As a resolute thereof, priority opportunities should then be identified.

A further often observed challenge is the non-existing alignment between the account plans, often developed by individual teams and the management or executive decisions, plus the out-datedness of account plans after a while. Thus, the account plan then often does not become reflected at the selling organization's top executive level and therefore the planning of business and opportunities is done without this key critical element.

Jackson et al (Jackson D. Jr, 2006) formulate though their conceptual model, which can serve as a checklist for sales managers to evaluate and alter their programs. The conceptual model provides a framework for tying together disparate areas of career development. Piercy and Lane (Piercy & Lane, 2005, p. 570) provide a template that improves the client focus of senior management. In particular, they focus on the following aspects:

- **Infrastructure**: Change in sales force structure and process
- **Involvement**: In strategic decision making
- **Intelligence**: Market sensing and interpretation
- **Internal Marketing:** Selling the customer inside the company and
- **Integration**: Working around cross-functional interfaces.

Piercy and Lane particularly recommend focusing on clients with larger potential sales outcomes and with higher customer relationship and service requirements, while in parallel building up a simple "mass channel" for small and low volume sales in order to provide a base for expansion. Both see a bigger focus onto who really at the end of the day would be the end-user of the services purchased, often referred to as well as "business user" instead of "purchasing"; at the same time, the seller organization needs to be bought in by the buyer organization into providing this service. Piercy and Lane (Piercy & Lane, 2005) then put a stronger focus on long-term client relationships, including assessing customer value and prioritizing the most attractive prospects.

2.5.2 Opportunity development and Pipeline management

From developing the market towards pursuing opportunities and ending up closing a sale, there is a so-called "buying funnel", described by Kotler, Rackham and Krisnavany (Kotler, Rackham, & Krisnavany, 2006). They identified the following steps in closing a sale:"

1. Customer awareness
2. Brand awareness
3. Brand Consideration

4. Brand Preference
5. Purchase intention
6. Purchase
7. Customer loyalty
8. Customer advocacy".

These steps are elaborated in the following sections. As Kotler et al (Kotler P. , 2003) write, "there is the view that marketing should take care of the early steps of the typical buying funnel, and sales is in charge of the last four steps. Often, those steps are not integrated with each other."

2.5.3 The sales process Selling stages

Sales Stage	Kotler's stage	Description	Ownership	Key activities	Typical Check-mark
1	Customer awareness	Sales Planning	Business Development	Territory Planning Account Planning	Territory and Account Plan
2	Brand awareness	Demand Creation	Busienss Development	Opportunity Planning	Opportunity becomes clearer
3		Identified deal	Business Development	A distinct transaction is on the horizon	Qualification Review
4	Brand consideration	Qualified Deal	Business Development	A deal is on the table worth engaging	Qualification Review
5	Brand consideration	Solution reviewed	Delivery	Crafting the solution and designing the deal	Solution approved by delivery management
6	Brand preference	Offer submitted	Business Development	Pricing, Define Terms & Conditions	Price review
7	Purchase intention	BAFO	Best and Final Offer	Final Offer is submitted to client, final Terms and conditions are being used	Verbal Client acceptance of offer
S	Purchase	Sold	Delivery	Deal is being handed over to delivery, signed	Signature
L	n/a	Lost	All	Deal has been Lost	Loss review
D	n/a	Dropped	Client	Client has dropped deal after initially writing out RfP	Drop reason
Q	n/a	Qualified out	Business Development	A trade-off between investing and winning has shown that this deal would not win positive results	Qualification after Stage 3-6

Table 2-4: Sales Stages Holden in relation to Kotler

Many companies, including Capgemini - employ a more filigree approach compared to Kotler. Holden's sales method is amongst the more widely used within outsourcing. It employs a pipelining model, supported by a Customer Relationship Management (CRM) implementation.

Holden (Holden International, 2009) and other sales step methodologies – i.e. SSM (IBM, 2002) used by IBM Corp. (IBM, 2002) – usually go hand with those CRM tools like Siebel Sales, now being maintained by Oracle. Capgemini has adopted a so-called "collaborative selling principle" with several sales stages into its sales process very much like its competitors, probably also because of the way the Siebel Software is being designed. From stage 2, an opportunity for a client might exist; Stage 1 does only size the territory.

Practically speaking, in most of the steps, sales stage concepts look very similar and try to associate check marks and toll gates towards the completion of the each steps of the sales funnel or pipeline in order to minimize business risks and optimizing business developments funds spent, as Table 2-4 highlights.

The logic behind the sales stages and check marks is like an iterative strategic approach: To progress a deal only makes sense if the win chances do increase by the deal progression whilst at the same time the expected business value is still positive, which means it delivers a profit or a strategic advantage (McDonald M. H., 2001). At the same time, the costs of progressing a deal further in terms of deploying resources along it are being measured and controlled. Capgemini globally dissects those sales stages from purchase intention to customer loyalty into seven distinct stages that are being discussed here.

2.6 Leading deals

In leading a pursuit, new aspects come to life. Sales people and deal leaders are often amongst the same group of people. However, experience shows that sales people are good in initially identifying an opportunity or help close the deal at the end with their existing relationship map, however in complex services business to business discussions, deal leadership becomes a profession on its own. During the leadership of a deal situation, several phases do come to bear which are being captured well along the sales stages of 2.5.2, implying different dynamics and client focus activities. When managing the a pipeline of deals in various sales stages, a sales manager needs to keep in mind that deals in early stages albeit with large amounts might be weighted with a lower entry probability than deals in later stages. Typically, most known pipeline management systems do reflect this thought. An example: A large deal, 10-times as large in early stages with a low entry probability (10%) might overshadow a forecast of a small but "sure deal" in a later stage, which might be weighted already much higher, say: 70%.

2.6.1 Deal phases and buyer concerns

According to Lemke (Lemke, 2009), different buyer concerns during a deal phase will occur alongside the phases of the deal, as shown in Figure 2-21.

They need to be encompassed towards the client in order to be successful at selling:

- **Need determination** – In this phase, clients will have an in-depth discussion with advisors and with several select constituents - board members, suppliers - on their needs.
- **Solution Finding** – The buying organization looks at how to fulfill the needs by the right solution tailored for the client. This solution finding is especially looked after by evaluating alternatives – both in solutions but also by revisiting needs.
- **Price/Cost** – Initially, playing a certain role is not of key eminence during the selection of alternatives. Often, clients at that point in time will revisit their price point completely by realizing that their needs have been overshadowed by a new solution.
- **Risk** – Risk is to be associated with a discount if it has to be taken or a premium if a certain risk – like lacking quality, follow-on costs, and brand awareness – is being taken on by the supplier. Interestingly enough, the risk comes to play at the last phase of the buying cycle and can kill a deal, if not managed well by the seller.

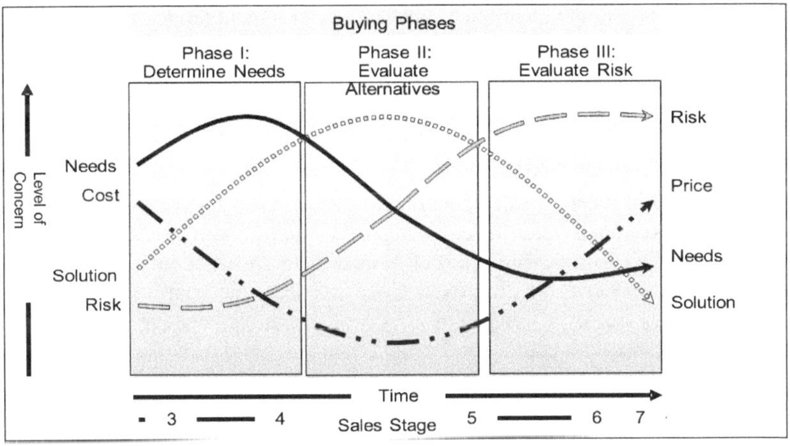

Figure 2-21: Buyer Concerns during deal phase (Lemke, 2009)

2.6.2 Planning to win the deal: Opportunity Analysis and Client pursuits

All business ventures are being undertaken under the working hypothesis that there is a certain chance of winning. Consequently, planning to win does help. Holden's (Holden International, 2009) Winning Sales plan methodology – adapted to Capgemini utilizes a full analysis of the opportunity as shown in 1. It is worth noting that the opportunity analysis will be reviewed after a post-bid pursuit.

2.6.3 Meeting the client

Client meetings itself are of importance to move a sale further and to drive it to close. Without client meetings – be it personal or virtual, there are rarely any transactions possible. Some companies – such as IBM - have a high focus on planning client visits highly in advance and provide series of books to their sales force.

IBM postulates (IBM Corp., 2004, p. 15) in its client briefing materials is emphasising onto setting a key objective for meeting the client and to have a "thorough planning process that begins with what will happen after the meeting: the desired outcome". Thus, it is viewed not only as "crafting a well-prepared agenda", but also map the topics discussed to objectives and thus steer the client into the direction IBM wants it to have. In order to be effective, for larger client meetings, "effective speakers" should be recruited inside the company and put a high focus onto presentation.

2.6.4 Client facing activities and client face time

Client facing activities and client face time make a difference. According the MSSSB Occupational sales map (MSSSCB, 2004) many people involved with selling especially in the business to business environment are too much preoccupied with non-client facing activities, therefore reducing the number of client touch points. At the same time, McGovern et al (McGovern, 2004) highlight on focusing on senior executive visibility towards the clients – as they point out – to "bring customers into the boardroom", thus having a direct influence of the clients towards the supplying organization.

Unfortunately in meeting sales people, executives from clients often do not appear to receive much value in engaging from them. Santucci (Santucci, 2010) presupposes that salespeople are well-prepared to speak about their company, products and services, but few executives feel that salespeople can empathise with what they do for a living. Only 34% of executives believe that the salespeople they speak with usually understand their roles and responsibilities.

Later on Santucci elaborates that executives, in general, do not feel that salespeople do understand their businesses. In particular, business leaders (24%) are slightly less than IT executives (29%) to believe that salespeople are knowledgeable about their specific business. In addition, the references and examples salespeople shown are felt as not relevant. As a result, most executive-level sales calls fail to add value.

Consequently, executives avoid talking to sales people by shortening meetings, deferring to subordinates or just neglecting the meeting follow-up at all. Frustration therefore occurs at both sides. However, Santucci recommends in order to overcome this feeling to be specific about the key messages about what and whom they are selling to; to define clear objectives for sales people; and to be obstinate about specific training and to have the right but not too much supporting material at hand. At the same time, people need to acknowledge the comfort zone of the current sales force in order to make them an effective bridge builder. This research especially implies not only to be both specific as a sales person and well prepared towards a client in his specific, but also to have the right supporting organisation that understands the sales support that a salesperson needs to have at hand.

2.6.5 Capitalizing upon existing success - Reference usages

The capitalization of existing successes – especially in the services business helps winning. References do count and often help more than advertisements or a good "we are great" presentation, empiric studies show, as Salminen (Salminen, 2001, p. 487) underlines. Besides good personal relationships, a freedom of selection and a good preparation, Salminen sees an important element in following up onto the reference given.

2.6.6 Border-crossing activities - working together with other entities

According to Grant (Grant, 1999, p. 113), a key importance on how to generate new competitive advantage is to combine a company's resources into new capabilities. Inside Capgemini, service delivery resources such as Consulting Services, Technology Services and Outsourcing Services are distinct resources that might be – client case based into new capabilities, such as for example a consultative outsourcing transformation approach which might generate a new business unit at no cost for the existing business unit.

2.6.7 Winning and losing - Reasons of loss of opportunity

Reasons of loss of a deal often do include the following aspects, as found in Capgemini loss reviews:

- Lack of fitting product or service to the client need
- Price expectation is differing
- Lack of client intimacy
- of knowledge of the political agenda
- Lack of empathy with the sales person – no build-up of rapport
- Lack of trust to deliver, especially in services sales situations

The key point is now how to eliminate the weaknesses of a sales situation and to emphasize on the strengths. The good news hereby is that winning is always relative. If there is little or competition in a sales situation by whatever reason, then winning might be easier than if competition is hefty. However, it is important to qualify the losses and to perform a thorough loss review. Capgemini uses pre-made templates in order to post-analyse the bid and to compare it with the OARI pre-analysis as shown in "Planning to win, Chapter 2.6.2" and in "1 ".

2.7 Measuring and rewarding performance

Sales performance measurement is at least as difficult as selling itself. MacKenzie, Podsakoff & Rich (MacKenzie, Podsakoff, & Rich, 2007) rightly state that there is a huge impact of transformational and transactional leader behaviours that affect the performance of sales personnel. Smith and Blair (Smith, E., & Blair, 2000) emphasise the importance of an environment in which employees feel trusted and empowered to make decisions and focuses on learning. Kellen (Kellen, 2002) argues that the purpose of measuring performance in customer relationship environments is to measure "leading" indicators and refers to Kaplan and Norton's (Kaplan & Norton, 2009) balanced scorecard. Lastly, the performance measurement is important to influence and validate decision making. The five categories to be noted are given below:

- **A hard ROI approach** – that shows return on investment models which seeks to deliver actual cash benefits to the company. It is important to consider cost savings, revenue generation opportunities, or expense to revenue models. Capgemini uses this model for overall business unit considerations.
- **Intangible benefits and assets** – Software benefits or intangible assets are identified and quantified. Examples might be brand equity or knowledge capital. Despite a largely outspoken knowledge culture, this model is not used at Capgemini.
- **Competitive assessments**. - This approach measures how competitors do work with clients and whether the company's approach is at or above par to completion. This model is only being utilized in a spotty way.
- **Value driven** – The economic value delivered or derived from a client is measured. This also involves building a model of customer value exchange. This model is used heavily to calculate deals over the duration of the deal.
- **Instinct and experience** – This approach uses manager's individual experience and intuitions. Capgemini is uses this model for an overall business steering approach it seems, especially in Consulting and Technology Services. However, this instinct and experience based model is then becoming often very hermeneutic (Apel, 1973), means that it is experience biased and therefore often precludes experiences coming from different sources of consideration.

2.7.1 Sales Compensation

Sales Compensation and bonus plans are a heavy debate of today's discussion, as people nowadays often refer to it as a way to generate moral hazard. However, sales people are often entrepreneurial type of people and want to see a distinct financial reward for the revenue they generate and broker. They support the idea that motivation is the critical item affecting sales performance and that resistance to change and an organization's structure and strategy can directly affect motivation.

Cooke (Cooke, 1999, p. 80) describes sales performance as how salespeople are motivated to increase profitable sales of products to clients. Cooke especially believes that money is the key motivator. According to Deci and Ryan (Deci & Ryan, 1980, p. 43), money can either motivate or de-motivate. However, as people increasingly see their full on-target earnings (OTE) as the real financial target, a sales plan has a certain de-motivating element.

Lastly, profit- and loss bearing organizations want to pay only what they get for, and this implies a debate on how to motivate sales people, especially when they are key account managers in charge of selling not only one single service but rather a multitude of services which all have different delivery elements and characteristics. Locke (Locke, 2004, p. 130) emphasizes on a consistent sales and incentive plan and realized in his studies that most sales and incentive plans only work "somewhat well" and especially recommends the combination of actions and outcomes and a design that avoids moral hazard. The key is that most incentive plans only work somewhat well but at least – as Locke writes this is better than no incentive plan at all.

2.7.2 Measuring business success using a balanced scorecard

Measuring sales success only upon a pipeline perspective might be a good start, however it will not show the underlining efforts and progresses made in order to move the organisation forward. Therefore, in order to track the hidden changes in behaviour and culture, reporting and steering based upon the following parameters, leaned upon from Kaplan and Norton's Balanced Scorecard model (Grant, 1999, p. 43). Grant points out that balance Scorecards should be top-down in order to be really effective. However, it is believed that at least measuring success of such an emerging business unit might make sense to be scored separately, anyway, as long as it fits into a larger framework. The balanced scorecard suggests that the organization is viewed from four perspectives (Kaplan & Norton, 2009). Along those perspectives, measurement metrics should be developed, data should be collected and analyse it then furtheron:

- **The Learning & Growth Perspective:** This perspective suggests to metrics around cultural attitudes in the company – especially how to improve the culture and climate, as well as individual and group training measures for employees. In the current climate of rapid technological change such as with Capgemini, it is becoming necessary for knowledge workers to be in a continuous learning mode. This metric should also be in place not only for major business units, but also for "sales clusters", enabling the sales leader to guide towards training funds where it helps the most. Kaplan and Norton highlight that 'learning' is more than 'training'; it also should include maven-type of personalities like mentors and tutors within the organization. At the same time there should be a climate that rewards sharing of communication and collaboration amongst employees in order to allow them to help each other. Moreover, technological tools also need to be taken into account like self-aid portals, internet tools etc.; what the Baldrige criteria (NIST, 2010) call "high performance work systems.". Key is especially on the learning and growth perspective to find the measurement metrics that are both accurate and leading indicators into the future.

- **The Customer Perspective:** Rogers (Rogers B. , 2007), (Salminen, 2001) and many other management writers have focused on listening to the clients and especially satisfied clients in every transaction. It shows that if clients are not satisfied, they are likely to find other suppliers that match their needs. As consequence, unsatisfactory performance that should be measured in customer perspective metrics can be regarded as a leading indicator of future decline, despite the current fiscal year still may look encouraging. Besides customer satisfaction, companies therefore should develop metrics about client density, means: are they just buying a single product line or multiple product lines and beyond that they also should measure the frequency of interaction. For existing clients, client satisfaction might be measured through surveys. Some companies do then include the result of the client satisfaction survey into account for allotting bonuses for senior management. With this, client satisfaction has then a direct impact to pay.

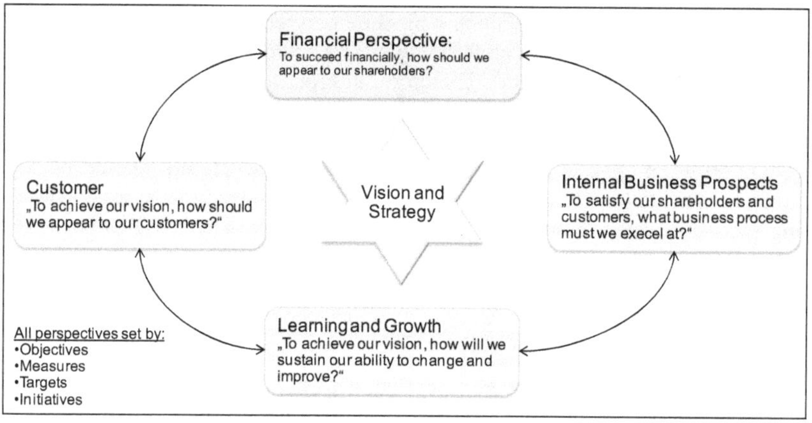

Figure 2-22: Balanced Scorecard Sample, (Kaplan & Norton, 1996)

- **The Business Process Perspective:** This perspective refers to internal business processes. This perspective is designed with metrics that should enable the executive management – and especially and the sales leader to know how the business is running according to client requirements and according to the business process requirements. Good measurement indicators might be around turnaround cycles per service provided and not only by department, as typically a service is provided throughout multiple company departments, and as a result the flow of information and product around multiple departments can be measured alongside. Here, a good example for the automotive industry might be the turnaround cycle of how fast a car might go through the assembly line as a top-line internal process indicator. Also, other metrics can be used, such as "on-off" metrics like a passed quality certification, like ISO 9001 or numbers of deviations within internal audits.

- **The Financial Perspective:** Despite the current focus onto financial data, Kaplan and Norton do not disregard this and emphasize on selecting an implementation of this perspective, such as timely and accurate revenue, cost and overhead financial data as key. Mostly, financial perspective data do entail trailing indicators, thus they are less forward looking, except order entry or signings data, as signings metrics can forecast revenues for the future, simply because they are contractually committed revenues over time. Besides the financial data, also business risk data should be put into this category here, as well as pipeline information from CRM systems, such as Siebel. Thus, it important that the data entered is accurate and the system is used, as Dueck repeatedly states (Dueck, 2007). Often, financial data has a very direct impact to management's pay, typically sales people are measured upon revenues or order entry numbers they make, thus the financial focus of management is of course high.

All of those four perspectives are to be designed by the following parameters:

- **Objectives**: What should be achieved?
- **Targets**: In what quantitative way can the objective be achieved?
- **Measurements**: How can the target be measured in-between?
- **Initiatives**: What are the initiatives that move the status-quo towards the targeted objective?

Balanced scorecards can become highly industry-specific and company specific. The key challenge for implementing balanced scorecards is less the development of the metrics on a top line, but the un-bureaucratic and yet constant and timely collection of the data needed throughout the organisation in order to keep the metrics up-to-date. The implementations of a balanced scorecard – despite being debated in corporates since years is still spotty. By own experience, the mandate for implementing a balanced scorecard is being given the controlling department, part of the CFO function. As a result, balanced scorecards still are heavily financial-perspective-weighted, whereas the other perspectives, such as the customer perspective and especially the innovation and learning perspective are more being seen as a "nice-to-have" view, which in result is a good recipe for failure of such a project. A very thorough overview on the theory of Balanced Scorecards, applied for example to insurers can be found at Wimmer (Wimmer, 2008, p. 31).

2.8 Chapter Summary

As a strategic stretch, companies go international because they want to grow and often cannot grow otherwise. This does not happen often as a clear strategy aspiration but rather in a emergent way, trial-and-error like. Eventually, some companies succeed and go international. When dealing with international environments, intercultural encounters do materialise that need to be dealt with. In international environments, intercultural work becomes increasingly important - especially not only when dealing with the same company, but also when dealing with clients. This needs to be encompassed into the sales research, increasingly.

Sales management consists out of a severe and cycled planning process, while the typical sales execution – meeting the client – is rather a thinner part of the overall sales process.

The planning part in sales is too often neglected towards a more cowboy-like mentality. It needs to be added that Strategy formulation is important; however, the hard part is the execution of the strategy once it is defined.

Execution comes from working together with different people, across cultures and making an enterprise work. Execution in front of a client is often a sale, and the close of a sale is the signature of a successful execution plan.

3 Outsourcing into non-western countries

As elaborated in the previous chapter, due to cost reasons, IT services providers tend to find lower cost services sites that can be combined with their client establishments as easily as possible. Those providers that have the best and most flawless model of combination between on-and offshore might therefore have a competitive advantage.

Outsourcing countries need to have a special factor condition, to follow with Porter's Diamond model (Porter, 2008, p. 140), that consists of the following:

- Initially low labour costs
- A high scalable degree of education allowing for higher productivity over time
- Stable and economy-friendly political influence
- Flexible labour legislation in order to be able to scale up and down the company population
- A sufficient infrastructure

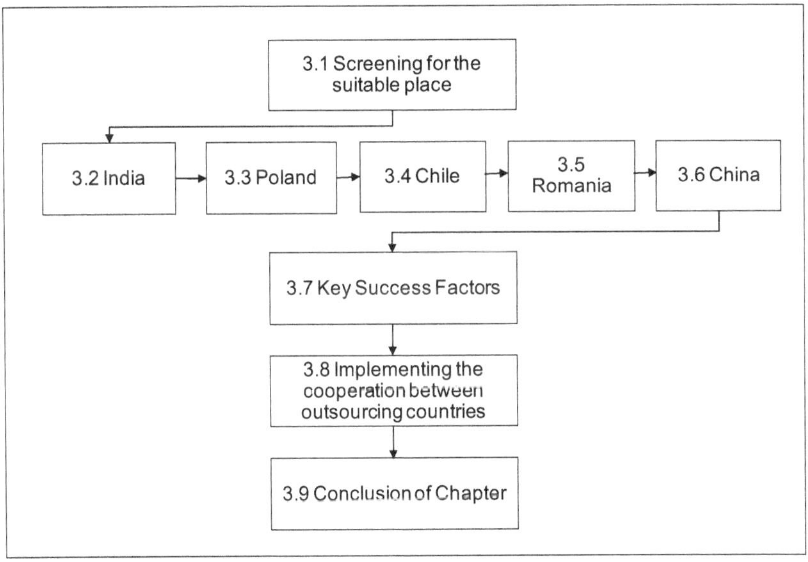

Figure 3-1: Chapter III Overview

This chapter deals with choosing the right country for outsourcing for a European provider with mostly European clients, compares five countries given a certain set of characteristics and then further on considers aspects on how to choose and implement a setup of global cooperation. Figure 3-1 provides a flow diagram of the chapter.

3.1 Global operations – comparing countries

As noted already by von Gamm (von Gamm, 2000), companies increasingly seek to optimise its development and service capabilities globally. As a result, they are in a constant screening process for new facilities in order to grow and adjust their business.

Especially in Information Technology, service providers try to mitigate risks – such as inflation risk, location risk, political risk and skill shortage risks by balancing their operations globally. As Kumar (Kumar, 2008, p. 214) notes, Indian providers go a different route and export where they are good in domestically. They start their venture from being strong in India and establish there; Erhan Carmel (Carmel, 2003) also supports this. Capgemini employs a set of centers globally to mitigate this risk while capturing a location based opportunity, such as labor cost shown in Figure 3-2.

In the following chapter, several advantages and disadvantages of global offshoring countries will be enumerated and depicted. Amongst others are Poland, India, Romania and Chile. First, the financial rationale for an off-shored outsourcing is evaluated.

3.1.1 The financial rationale for an off-shored outsourcing

Outsourcing and Offshoring often come together as a pair of synonyms. However, the terms are very well coined: According to Turnbull (Turnbull, 2010), Offshoring comprises the motion of moving parts of an enterprise off the own shore, means to foreign countries; however, according to Gabler (Gabler Verlag, 2010) outsourcing is about transferring parts of an enterprise value chain towards suppliers, also known as the outsourcer. With this, outsourcing results in a shorting of the value chain for the client. By taking advantage of specialized firms, for production, services or development activities, cost advantages might be realized and the own strategic market position might be improved. Gabler believes that one's own key technologies and competences should not be abandoned in order not to enter into a strategic dependency.

Other reasons for outsourcing besides cost reduction resulting into a strategic advantage often quoted, for example by von Gamm (von Gamm, 2009) are:

- **Improved flexibility**: The outsourcer might have economies of scale the client does not have, thus enabling a fast scale-up or scale down of the operations depending upon the business needs, which might improve time to market and cost-dependencies.
- **Access to talent:** As the outsourcer operates within her own core competencies, the access to talent might be easier to manage in this specialized domain skill.
- **Risk transference**: with the operation transferred to the outsourcer, the outsourcer then has the risk of performing and can contractually be forced to take over the financial and business risk of a service delivered.

- **Capital allocation**: An operation outside of the core business might still bind financial capital designated otherwise to core operations. The capital designated to core operations might provide a higher return.

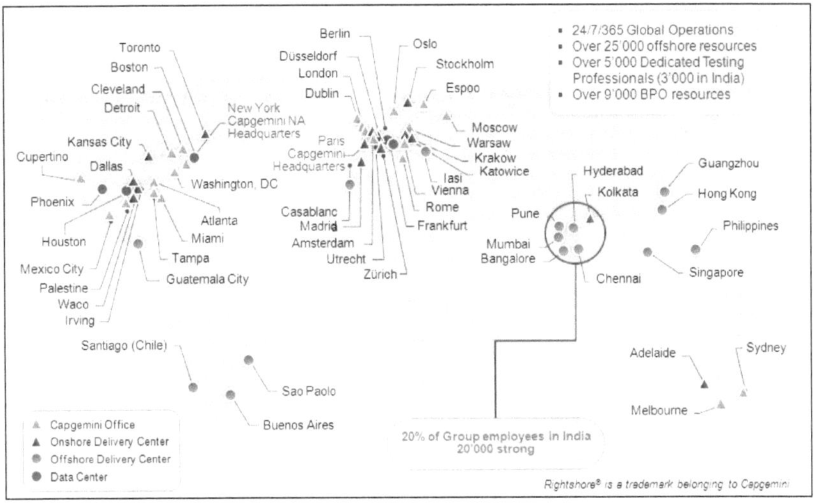

Figure 3-2: Offshore Delivery Centre locations, source Capgemini (2010)

Additionally, several benefits might occur during this process, such as further instant savings, less risk in delivery and as part of the acquisition, an initial payment for cash-strapped organizations, and literally speaking, a hidden loan for the takeover of assets at a good-will price.

In total, as Figure 3-3 depicts, the savings contribution and quality improvement of an outsourcing solution might be more predictable than a do-it-yourself operation, at least it can be contractually guaranteed[2].

However, an outsourcing company does not perform an outsourcing solution for "free"; it has associated some extra cost:

- **Margin for the provider**: In order to perform the service, the provider wants to see a certain margin, usually between 5 and 20% of the total service delivered. This margin is typically used for business development activities, administration of the overall outsourcing operation and profit.
- **Transition and Transformation cost**: In order to move the outsourcing operation from one company to another, several activities are incurred that generate effort, such as knowledge transfer, operations setup etc. This transition and transformation cost might be up to 10 to 15% of the total outsource.

[2] Still, surprises do exist and the life is not black and white, as several large and prominent examples of an outsource show, such as the famous failed outsource of the UK NHS (Beckett, 2009)

- If **people transfer** or take-over is part of the outsource, then redundancy fees and termination fees need to be accounted as well, including the minimum stay of people transferred from one country to another, as described in German law under BGB § 613a or Swiss Law OR Art. 333[3].
- **Value added Tax (VAT):** If a client is a VAT-except organization, such as a bank or a public sector company, then the outsourcer – usually under VAT duty - is handicapped by the VAT rate, as then previously internally performed people services from own employees then need to be burdened with VAT. In situations with high VAT, i.e. Germany, Austria with currently 19 and respectively 20%, this artificially inflates the price.

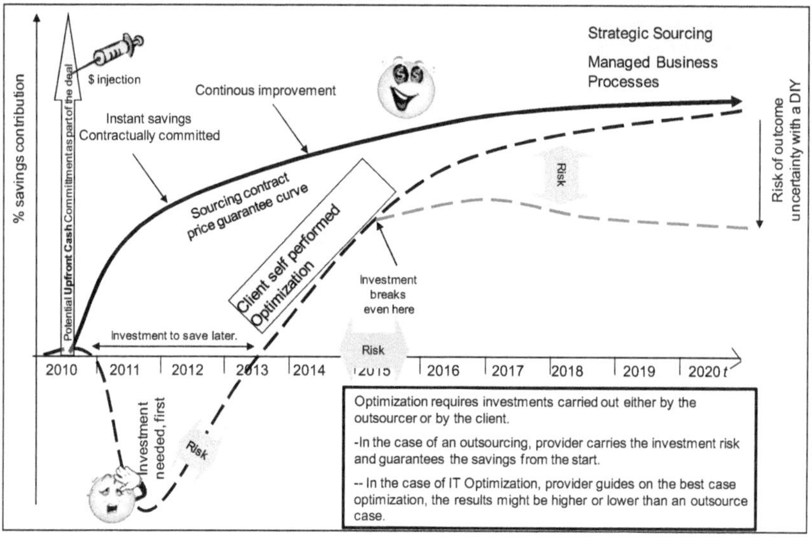

Figure 3-3: Savings contribution of an outsource compared to a do-it-yourself IT optimisation, (von Gamm, 2008)

At the same time, the client has to setup some parts of the organization to manage the outsourcer. Depending upon the quality of the contract, the client has to put on a "retained organization", managing the supplier.

Combining outsourcing and off-shoring, two factors come together: the outsourcing of parts of the enterprise towards a supplier who then chooses to perform the service from abroad. Additional costs and risks come to bear what need to be encompassed:

[3] Other European and Non-European countries have similar laws, typically people transferred from the client to the outsourcer need to stay at least twelve months, in some countries such as Germany they literally keep their employment rights notwithstanding any company transfer. (§613a, BGB) This impedes the financial attractiveness of some outsourcing engagements dramatically.

- **Cultural risk**: As described in Chapter 2, different countries have different cultures. There is a risk and a price associated with dealing with the different culture.
- **Currency risk**: If the outsourcer operates within a different currency environment, these currencies might fluctuate to each other.

In total, the business case for outsourcing only works if the effective service performed including all burdens can be done at a much lower cost than previously. The total schematics is described in Figure 3-4, in that case for an IT outsourcing operation, which typically both integrates a capital equipment component and a people cost component.

In consequence, this business case then only works if the following premises do apply:

1. The infrastructure cost can be drastically lowered i.e. by better purchase conditions, sharing of resources or better utilization of capital equipment employed.
2. The people cost can be significantly lowered either by
    a. A much better utilization of the people and condensing people's work, i.e. by sharing the same skill over several clients or a higher degree of automation.
    b. Lower labor costs by using labor arbitrage and putting people offshore.
3. The risks approportioned are manageable and therefore can be lowered, i.e. by a culturally capable team and by standardization and specialization.
4. The service management costs from both sides – provider and client (Retained organizations) are contained and can be as friction-less as possible. Here, common standards such as ITIL as a lingua franca do play a significant role in order to reduce the service management costs, see Chapter 2.3.12 on ITIL.

To conclude: A sustainable low-cost place is the main driver for off-shoring, and a high VAT rate in developed countries as a result will even aggravate this driver, especially within financial services. It might therefore be argued that Switzerland with its low VAT rate might not that be under pressure for Financial Services offshoring than other places. However, especially the larger financial institutions such as Credit Suisse, Deutsche Bank and notably Zurich Financial Services[4] have an outspoken outsourcing strategy.

[4] Zurich Financial Services is a Capgemini Outsourcing reference client, Deutsche Bank is working with IBM for a global datacentre outsourcing, however due to the asset intensity, the VAT issue is not that preminent at the latter.

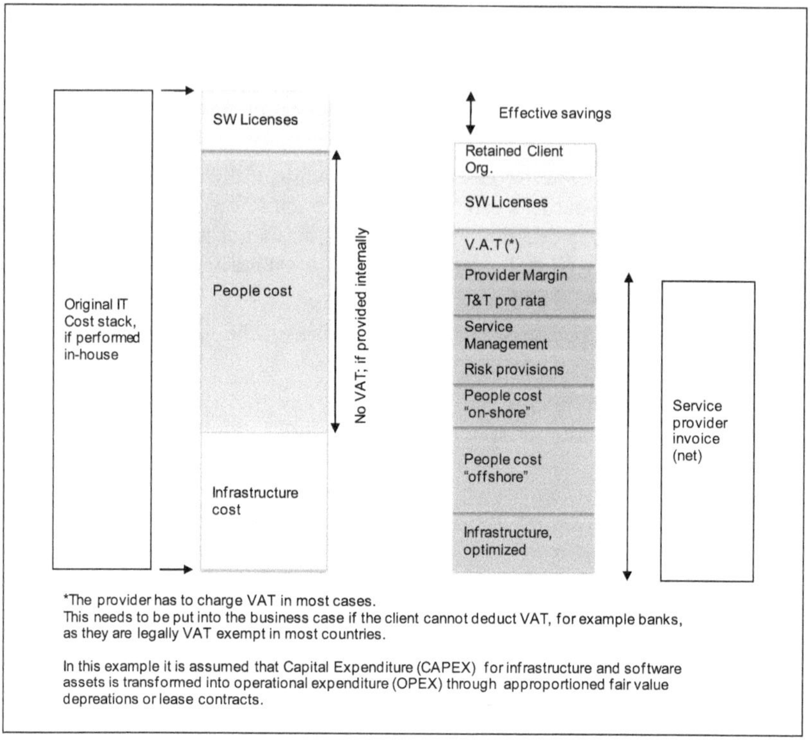

Figure 3-4: The business case scheme of an off-shored outsourcing, (von Gamm, 2010)

3.1.2 Screening for a suitable place

Many IT companies already have setup a significant proportion of its service center activity in Europe, the possibility to yield additional gains out of a relocation of development activity in an amount greater than 1000 developers is quite limited and complicated to undertake, especially also due to an already heating labor market on scare IT skills (Germany is already more than 100.000 people short on IT skills, similar situations do exist in the UK and in France), it is more suitable and feasible. Saying that, two options do essentially exist: either importing that additional resource back into the main country, for many IT providers, the U.S.A (i.e. IBM, CSC, HP) or France (Capgemini), Germany (Siemens, T-Systems), or by exporting the service centers close to where on a long term IT skills can be drawn out of the population.

Using the strategic tests of Rumelt (Rumelt, 1995) to look into other parts of the world for additional resource, the country selection can be structured. Rumelt focused on

- **Internal consistency**, bringing a coherent framework of organizational action
- **Consonance**: The sustainability, of societies valuation of a product or services
- **Advantage**: The ability to capture economic value through superior skills, resource or position and
- **Feasibility**: The ability to resource strategies, meet performance targets and cope with competitive actions.

As a result, the following key factors need to apply:

- The service provider organization can scale internally in a consistent way.
- The skills available on the market can easily be drawn from.
- The advantage exists through lower costs
- It is doable from a legal and operational perspective.

Furthermore, we need to assumed that once there are IT skills in the population at a significant amount, those IT skills due to the global IT skill shortage will be demanded not only by one company. Thus, it also will be assumed, that there is a need for a sustainable strategy to attract and retain the best of the best IT skills of that chosen location plus setting up a management system that matches with the cultural attitudes and governmental / geographical situation of that chosen country. This section focuses on choosing the right sites outside the United States and Europe and will give an overview onto the advantages and disadvantages on the right country based on empirical and statistical information gathered from public and nonpublic sources. As a follow-on, an installment and implementation strategy that shortly covers HRM, marketing, structure and culture will be discussed. Now, after looking at some generalist views of different areas of the world, some screening will be undertaken that is trifled: Exclusive, comparative and specialized. A first essay on this topic has been published by the author 10 years ago (von Gamm, 2001).

3.1.3 Exclusion of inappropriate regions

First, in order to investigate into several countries, it is best practice to exclude countries that prevent global companies from installing a sustainable rent generation throughout its service activities and provide too high barriers of entry (Kay J. , 2004). These are for example unacceptable standards and socio-cultural factors, economic barriers - here especially lack of sufficient IT skills or other activities. Supply barriers are especially those where shortage of factors of production do exist - even though both hardware and software development are quite disconnected from typical manufacturing supply problems, it has an indirect effect the standards of life of the employees and thus as a consequence an effect onto human resource attrition, because that prevents high-class people from staying long-term at the same place.

Unacceptable standards, safety, socio-cultural factors, etc. will start the first exclusion: political barriers boycotts, sanctions, mandatory local participation, state monopolies, etc.

Political barriers do exist in countries like North Korea, Yemen, as well as the "jerk-states" like Iraq, Iran, Syria, Pakistan, Afghanistan, Nicaragua. Also, crisis-countries like Israel, Lebanon (no IT skills) etc. fall into that area.

Economic barriers: non-transferability of funds, barter trading, price control, etc. - Also, other non-developed countries like Bangladesh, Thailand, Vietnam, the Oceanic, etc. fall under that cluster.

Legal barriers: anti-trust legislation, labor laws, patents, environmental control, etc. - do exist in countries of the former Soviet Union, especially Belorussia, Azerbaijan, Ukraine (to some extents) . **Supply barriers**: shortage of factors of production, skill or infrastructure, etc. Are Here, to exclude countries from the list are all countries with a low level on IT education. Here, all countries of Africa except South Africa and Egypt fall into that cluster, Skill shortages in a significant amount in the IT space also do exist in Chile, Paraguay, Peru, Middle America (except Mexico), Argentina, Australia (IT skills available but same situation as in Europe).

As a next criterion, a minimum population needs to be there that guarantees a certain critical mass of middle-class labor to guarantee a growth/renewal of IT knowledge.

Thus it remains on the short list a set of countries like Saudi Arabia and The Emirates, Brazil, India and China, which then will be compared further.

Of course, this selection is biased upon the current business knowledge.

Five countries in overview: Table 3-1 shows a STEEP analysis with a view on global trends and additionally a view of divers different countries which fall into that area. This screen does only give an overview but still does not rate the factors that are important.

Except China which has been excluded for services outsourcing due to a still higher lack of English language and financial export barriers, the countries India, Poland, Chile and Romania will be presented in the following chapters in regards of its suitability for services outsourcing.

STEEP	Global	India	China	Chile	Poland	Romania
Social / Culture	Americanization	Caste system with stronger middle class due to economic upturn.	social conflicts between regions and groups	Lower criminality Population Social differences	Becoming highly westernised EU Member	Becoming westernized New EU Member
Technology	Fast moving, Internet networking Commoditisation	Increasingly High skills in middle class - good education system Labour resource People	Low wages, thus cheap labour Different languages but unified writing system, local market	Low wages Mining technology available	High affinity to Germany Steel and mining technology	Rather developing market.
Politics	Global convergence Governmental Control Internet Tax Internet Content Control Intra-company trade	Political Stability Some "brain drain" into USA and Europe due to better opportunities vast labour pool	Internet regulations law tax political system US export regulations	Education Privatization Stability Removal of competitive impediments	EU regulations now in place Increasing liberalisation	EU regulations now in place Highly liberalised, Ongoing corruption
Economics	Trading blocks Country embargos 24x7x365	High economic growth, liberalization of trade markets and intellectual property laws	High growth due to wealth generation and special economic zones.	unequal income distribution	Growing economy, increased middle class	Growing economy despite global downturn
Environment	Globally Increased sensitivity, buildup of UN offices on environment Regulations in developed countries	High pollution and waste in cities, unwooding of tropic rain forest	Lack of water in larger cities Higher energy consumption than the USA now overall	High pollution and waste in cities	Lower sensitivity to environment, however not relevant to services industry	Low pollution, some toxic waste from oil exploration.

Table 3-1: STEEP analysis of China, India, Chile, Poland and Romania

3.2 India as a country for Outsourcing and Offshoring

According to the CIA World Fact Book (Central Intelligence Agency, 2009), India is the second largest country by population with about 1.15 bln human inhabitants. Furthermore, the CIA states: "The Indus Valley civilization, one of the world's oldest, flourished during the 3rd and 2nd millennia B.C. and extended into north-western India. Aryan tribes from the northwest infiltrated onto the Indian subcontinent about 1500 B.C.; their merger with the earlier Dravidian inhabitants created the classical Indian culture. The Maurya Empire of the 4th and 3rd centuries B.C. - which reached its zenith under Ashoka - united much of South Asia."

3.2.1 India as a country

Economically, with a GDP at PPP of $3.56 trillion (2009 est., [5].), now-being the fifth-richest country world-wide, and on official exchange rate of $1.095 trillion, and a growth rate of 6-7% over the last five years, India has become a real superpower. Twenty percent of Indians work in the industrial sector, 17.5% in agriculture, and 34% in services, which includes local services but more economically important, global services. Still, despite the economic growth, 25% of population are below poverty line which implies some political instability.

Figure 3-5: India Overview, Source: CIA

Infrastructure-wise, the CIA continues and "supported by recent deregulation and liberalization of telecommunications laws and policies, India has emerged as one of the fastest growing telecom markets in the world"; total telephone subscribership base is approaching 600 million, an overall tele-density of 50%, and subscribership is currently growing nearly 20 million per month; urban tele-density has reached 100% and rural tele-density is about 20% and steadily growing. According to several sources, 7% of Indians are now Internet users and growing; however, mobile phone users are now more than half – reflecting those 600 million stated above, even though there are many rented mobile phone users.

[5] Data 2009 US-Dollars

3.2.2 Four different Indias

Economically, there are now four different Indias, a traditionally structured India, a modern structured India, a traditionally unstructured India and a modern unstructured India which co-exist and co-fertilize each other to some extent.

India is the size of Europe with a large variety of cultures, languages, religions and values; there is a traditional India and a modern India.

- Individual communication styles depend to a large extent to exposure to western cultures and professional experience
- Technology and software industries are leading modern India in evolving business attitudes and communication style. A "high-tech" sub-culture has emerged = Indian values + Silicon valley

3.2.2.1 Traditional Structured India

In the traditionally structured India, traditional agriculture and services dominate; the caste system is still dominating and – as apologetics of the cast system are propagating – is providing a connex within society. Ihlau (Ihlau, 2006, p. 42f) estimates that even though in 1949 the caste system has been abolished officially, it still dominates the rhythm of life.

Figure 3-6: Traditional structured India, a Hindu festival - Source: Kiran (Kiran, 2009)

Thus, members of the same caste are marrying each other in most of the cases, and work in professions that are predetermined. Origin and social class can be derived from the skin colour, the most family names and the appearance. The top-most class called the Brahmans once the priests and preachers of the holy writings should take care of spiritual and intellectual matters.

However, as observers note that a real sense of social solidarity within Hindus does not exist, they rather appear to be machiavellistic or cold-blooded, determine bad destiny as a punishment for bad behaviour in former lives, and refuse therefore to help each other. The caste-less, also called "paria" have the hardest destiny and appear to be rightless within society.

The castes in the middle as shown in Figure 3-7 are the Kshatriyas or Warriors; then the Vaisyas, means herders, farmers, merchants and crafts people; and then lower caste the sudras – often to be found within farm workers, servants and labourers, as the Guide to the Essentials of World History elaborates (Prentice Hall, 1999, p. #IN). However it needs to be noted that the caste system increasingly becomes less of importance in modern India.

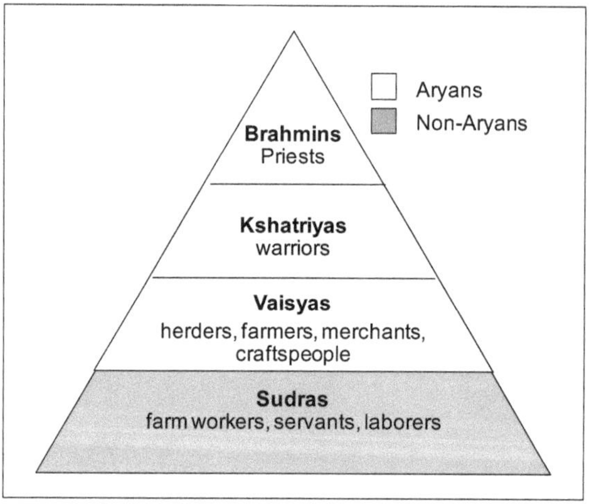

Figure 3-7: Indian Caste system, Source: Prentice-Hall, 1999

3.2.2.2 Modern structured India

India has experienced a significant growth and is now one of the economic superpowers of the world. With the advent of IT industry, an increasingly large middle class has emerged which has a similar habit, spending and living profile than an U.S.-American middle class, a Chinese Middle class or a Western European middle class. More often, the rate of academics is higher than in Western Europe within this middle class (Ihlau, 2006, p. 48ff). Alongside with this, the typical middleclass features, now amounting to more than 300 million people are increasing:

- 350 shopping malls in India in 2007, in 2001 only three
- Increase of 30% per annum of mortgage volumes

- More than 670 million mobile phone users.
- Increasing density of populations in the mega-centres such as Mumbai, Bangalore et al.
- Increasing domestic flight capacities
- Increasing car loans, individual car transports.

Caused by and thanks to this westernization, the middle class contains a rich potential for western-originated services firms to provide skilled labour with a minimum of knowledge of western habits.

Figure 3-8: Modern structured India, Mumbai Shopping Centre, Webcam

3.2.2.3 Traditional unstructured India

The traditional unstructured India is the India of the Parias, amounting about 250 million people. People try to survive – less than life as Ihlau writes (Ihlau, 2006, p. 108) as street dealers, pedlars, day-to-day workers and other. This traditional unstructured India can be found in the agglomerations and slums of the larger megalopolis such as Mumbay, Madras and others.

3.2.2.4 Modern Unstructured India

The modern unstructured India can be found as an emergence of the Traditional unstructured India and increasingly works in support services such as, restoration, street dealers and others. It has a high tendency to be found in-between the modern structured India.

The "Dabbawallas" in Mumbai are a good example of a mixture between a traditional unstructured India and the modern structured India. The Dabbawallas provide the lunch provisioning from the individual's homes to the office boxes, using "tiffins" - special tin boxes for lunch - to transport more than 175,000 meals from home to office on time. Apparently the accuracy – despite 5,000 individual entrepreneurs working together and organizing the billing and payment to each other first appears highly chaotic – the efficiency is at more than 99.9999% according to observers, which is better than the often-mentioned "Six-Sigma" and better than any other delivery and courier company.

Figure 3-9: Traditional Unstructured India, Source Capgemini (Capgemini , 2007)

3.2.2.5 Work habits

Historically individual identity came primarily from family and the belongingness to a caste or a village. Since liberalization of India, (1991) work has become more important/more profitable and is increasingly a source of identity but family is still very important (Ihlau, 2006, p. 28ff).

Hierarchy and the influence of castes: influence of caste system on acceptance that power differences exist have a rightful place and should therefore be acknowledged, accepted, and respected. However, it needs to be noted that the caste system is not a main criteria for decision making and professional development of an Individual in modern structured India of the IT industry. Vice versa, not all the superiors are Brahmins, as now increasingly a meritocracy allows for lower castes to rise up the hierarchy ladder or high casts to be excluded out of the hierarchy.

Nevertheless, the hierarchy concept still appears to be paramount and the pyramid system of traditional enterprises (Kumar, 2008) has a good fit within this caste system. As now increasingly hierarchy-less forms of enterprise set-ups or senior leaders without people reporting power (empire) come into play, this new form of enterprise setup is a challenge for Indians to observe.

Figure 3-10: Modern Unstructured India, Source I.Z.Reloaded blog (izreloaded.com, 2007)

3.2.2.6 Approaches and beliefs

The following section will guide through Indian -specifics of communication and leadership styles, problem solving domains and negotiations.

The communication style is mainly based upon hierarchy, thus the vertical flow happens from superior to superior upwards and downwards. Working horizontally – in a team – often appears to be a challenge, as the power-distance between people prevents often an open flow of communication. It is said and observed that Indians try to be respectful and harmonious, at the same time the communication style appears to be ideological and details and trivialities tend to be avoided.

From a leadership style, personality and charisma of people plays a big role. A good leader is a "Guru", a "raja" or a "father" who has responsibility for his subordinates. His success determines the success of the overall group. Dharma and Karma do play a big role, a guided destiny where results will yield in the long term do overshadow the short-term problem-solving attitude of Indians often. At the same time, high ideals, a higher tolerance for risk-acceptance does exist, risks often are not avoided.

Figure 3-11: Dabbawallas from Topnews.IN (Dabbawallas, Topnews.IN, 2009)

From a problem solving domain, problems are often tried to be fixed with inventiveness, means a quick solution is better than a long-term rethinking of a problem. Heroics often come above processes; a good way how to circumvent a process appears often to be better than following the process step by step. Alongside this comes improvisation.

Nevertheless, Indians appear to be very analytic and highly active than reflective in their analytics. This feature has been used by many firms in taking advantage for outsourcing tasks such as data collection, data mining and data cleansing into India (Alaganandan, Bhowmick, & Mohanty, 2010).

The negotiation style of Indians needs to overcome power distances and show rapport. Professional guides often mention that the establishment of relationship and familiarity between people takes a great deal of time (Bölscher, 2009, p. 15ff). Respect needs to be shown, at the same time the avoidance of losing face is a paramount feature for Indian counterparts. People should start with high aspirations in order to gather the attention of senior executives; to gather as much information as possible and not to be concerned with time.

3.2.2.7 Indian Culture values – A blend of east and west?

Culture in India has been influenced by a wide variety of sources that comprise the philosophy of Hindus, the colonial style and habits of the British, Islamic neighbours, and recent independence politics since 1948. Amongst other, Arabs were seen the first ambassadors of globalisation. They transferred Indian science, literature, medicine and mathematics to Western Europe from where it has been developed further. At the same time, the influence from Western Europe back into India has also been transferred by Arabs (Bölscher, 2009). Islamic influences have certainly affected the social texture in large parts of the country. Moreover, the Hindu philosophy does have profound impact onto the basic belief structure of the Indians, given the fact that 80 Percent of Indians consider themselves to be Hindu (Kumar, 2008), same as later the adoption of British style during colonisation. A unique mindset of Indians is the combination of individualism and collectivism in an amalgamated way (Hofstede, 2001, p. 150f). Indians appear to be goal-oriented and aggressive, at the same time they appear to be family-orientated with a higher tendency for loyalty. Maybe because of this, the caste system and the culture itself, larger services organisations in outsourcing can flourish.

3.2.3 India's outsourcing landscape

Outsourcing in India has become possible with the information technologies itself. They are the backbone of the knowledge society. Technology and teleworking has provided a new dimension into this economy with knowledge and the management of knowledge increasingly becoming a factor of production. The key success factor is, as many writers note, low labor plus an abundance of skill (Nollen, 2008, p. 72), even when compared to the world's largest country, China. For India, a key limiting factor of for example also China does not exist: managers who speak the English language for contracting.

With about 380 universities in India and about 11 million of students (Auswärtiges Amt, 2010), India has a huge potential of graduates coming out of university every year. It is estimated that half of them are trained to work in the IT industry or related businesses, therefore generating a potential of students similar as the total amount of IT graduates within the EU (BITKOM, 2009).

Big outsourcing providers from the West have become present such as:

- IBM with more than 50'000 employees in India of their total population of 400'000 (IBM Corp, 2010), making a Q4 2010 services revenue of 9.9 billion Euros[6].
- Accenture with more than 30'000 employees (Accenture , 2010) in India.
- HP Services with estimated around 20'000 employees in India.
- Capgemini with reportedly more than 20'000 employees in India and a total revenue of 2009 of 8.4 billion Euros and a total population of 90'000 employees.
- Other IT and services companies include Logica CMG, Genpact, Siemens, T-

[6] IBM does not disclose individual numbers of revenues per country, sub-division and head-count.

Systems etc., however with smaller reported Indian populations.

Indian originating players according to Gartner Group's study (Gartner Group, 2007) such as:

- Tata consulting Services (TCS) with 150'000 employees, most of them in India and ca. 4 billion Euros of revenues
- Infosys with 109'000 employees and ca. 3.2 billion Euros of revenues (2009)
- Wipro with 102'000[7] employees and ca. 3 billion Euros of revenues (2009)
- Cognizant with 78'400 employees and 611 million Euros of revenues (2009)
- HCL and further other companies

Additionally, there are captive outsources of several Western Non-IT Services companies, such as UBS with 2'000 employees[8], American Express, Siemens, Philip Morris, Dow Chemical, Lufthansa, EDF etc.

According to (Businessweek, Top Outsourcing places, 2009)), the largest places for Outsourcing are Bangalore, Kolkata and Mumbai, including Pune and Delhi.

However, as Carmel (Carmel, 2003) notes, the relative attractiveness for graduates is first with large Indian companies as they supposedly can make a top career there, then the large IT players and then the other companies ranging third only, with at the other side even top talent in India is scares, as Pandey (Pandey, 2010) has witnessed.

What follows is that the top potential is more likely to go to the big services providers and other companies such as banks, often regarded in their home country as prime address only get second-class graduates, something they realize often quite late.

3.2.4 Advantages and disadvantages of India in a glance

As depicted in "Table 3-2: India key factors", India possesses some good factors that are suitable for setting up an IT facility there such as lower labor costs, a half-ways fitting time zone to Europe, a growing middle-class and an IT population coming new each year out of university.

In consequence, it is **the ideal** place for outsourcing services for probably the next decades. Even current language barriers, for example for French and German will be overcome if the business case does exist.

[7] What strikes is that that WIPRO with a similar employee amount than Capgemini only makes a third of Capgemini's revenues but about a similar absolute profit number.

[8] UBS has sold its operation in India to Cognizant end of 2009.

Item	Description
Population size	Greater than 1.2 billion inhabitants. A middle-class that emerges.
Factor conditions	Low labor costs at PPP because of a young population and result to no large payments for interest and retirement.
IT density	Overall, low but within the middle class and the IT centers such as Mumbai, Bangalore in an appropriate way.
Hofstede cluster	"Less Developed Asian"[9]
Language	Hindi and English as a main second language
Time zone difference to Europe	Three hours
Time zone difference to US East cost	Nine Hours
Constant feed of IT professionals from Universities	More than 3'000'000 people per annum, of which 500'000 from engineering schools. (Pandey, 2010)
Legislation	Has been westernized, still some difficulties with Intellectual property law
Labour cost in IT Services	About 15% of the Western European Cost.

Table 3-2: India key factors

3.3 Poland as an offshoring country

Poland has gone through a changing history over time and the country as such now exists since the Versailles treaty of 1919 and later on since the end of World war II in its borders of today. With about 38 million inhabitants, Poland has less than half of the inhabitants of Germany, however there are some good clusters and niches that provide opportunities for outsourcers to expand and grow.

3.3.1 Poland overview

According to the CIA, Poland has pursued a policy of economic liberalization since 1990 and today stands out highly successful amongst Eastern European economies. Because of an increased private consumption the GDP has grown by 5% per annum before the crisis of 2009, additionally EU subsidies and increased private investments helped spurt the GDP, still below the average of the European Union, but similar to Lithuania, Latvia or Estonia, aka the "Baltic Tigers".

Poland has become a member of the European Union in 2004. Since then, structural funds and the membership itself has helped the economy to skyrocket compared to neighbored countries such as the Ukraine. However, as the CIA notes, "an inefficient commercial court system, a rigid labor code, bureaucratic red tape, burdensome tax system, and persistent low-level corruption keep the private sector from performing up to its full potential".

[9] This might be revisited due to the age of the Hofstede sample, thirty years ago.

Figure 3-12: Map of Poland. Source: CIA

The GDP (purchasing power parity) is at $690.1 billion (2009 est.), and ranks Number 21 world-wide. At official exchange rate, the GDP is $427.9 billion (2009 est.). Despite the decline in Germany, the GDP was growing slightly in 2009 by 1.7%; in 2008 and 2007 it was in the 5-7% range of growth. Per capita, the GDP is at (PPP) $17,900 (2009 est.), and ranks number 68 worldwide.

Most business is being done in Services with 67.3%, industry 28.1% and agriculture with 4.6%; however, there are still disproportionally more people working in agriculture than in other sectors (17.4%). Poland is number 12 amongst internet users, relative to population with about 9 million internet hosts registered in Poland in 2008.

3.3.2 Poland's outsourcing landscape

Poland's outsourcing landscape is emerging. According to Business Week, Krakow is the main centre of outsourcing because of its big university, relative stability and lower labor costs compared to Warsaw, plus an affinity for the German and English language (Businessweek, Top Outsourcing places, 2009).

Figure 3-13: Capgemini Krakow, from company website

Besides some local players, there is an increase of western players who come to the country with the following main players around:

- IBM for software development and some services in Wroczlaw (2'000 people)
- Accenture for Business process outsourcing, Krakow and other places (1500 people)
- Capgemini with about 3'000 people, mainly in Krakow, Kattowice and Wroczlaw, as shown in Figure 3-14.
- Other companies include T-Systems, HCL, LogicaCMG, Hewitt and tobacco company Philipp Morris International.

The main universities are AGH University of Science & Technology and the Cracow University of Technology. As language skills can be noted English, German, Japanese and Polish. Capgemini itself notes that from Krakow, the company can deliver more than 26 languages in its service desk and call centre operations (Capgemini S.A. , 2008).

3.3.3 Advantages and disadvantages of Poland in a glance

As shown in Table 3-3, Poland has significantly lower labour costs than Western Europe, despite being Western European by a series of measures, the similar time zone, a well-educated uprising middle class, and very likely an almost Germanic culture. As a result, its value proposition for Outsourcing is clear: Western European quality at Eastern European prices.

Item	Description
Population size	Around 38 million inhabitants.
Factor conditions	Low labor costs at PPP because of a young population and in result no large payments for interest and retirement.
IT density	High.
Hofstede cluster	Not in Hofstede, it might be "Germanic" [10]
Language	Polish, High propensity of English and Some German
Time zone difference to Europe	Zero Hours
Time zone difference to US East cost	Six Hours
Constant feed of IT professionals from Universities	Estimated more than 40,000 people per annum.
Legislation	EU legislation, CIA still complains about insufficient adoption within commercial law and high bureaucratic burdens.
Labour cost in IT Services	About 30% of the Western European Cost.

Table 3-3: Poland at a glance

3.4 Chile as an Offshoring country

Located in South America, Chile has become democratized in 1990 after the dismissal of General Augusto Pinochet. As the CIA (Central Intelligence Agency, 2009, p. #CL) writes, "Sound economic policies, maintained consistently since the 1980s, have contributed to steady growth, reduced poverty rates by over half, and have helped secure the country's commitment to democratic and representative government". Chile has over time been appointed a south American but also global leadership role in international institutions, especially amongst the United Nations. This has also been the result by having become a democratic and stable nation.

3.4.1 Chile overview

According to the CIA, Chile has a market-oriented economy characterized by a high level of foreign trade. At the same time, the financial institutions are seen to be sound and the policy of the government makes the bond market the strongest in South America rating-wise. Definitely a commodity exporting country, more than three-quarters of the exports are commodities, such as copper and exports account for more than one-fourth of GDP.

[10] At the time of research, there was no significant presence of IBM in Poland for Hofstede to research on.

Figure 3-14: Map of Chile, Source: CIA

With Patricio Aylwin taking over from the military in the early 1990s, Chile's economic reforms were fostered and deepened the economic reform already started by the military government. Growth in real GDP averaged 8% during 1991-97, and later fell to half of this in 1998 because of the millennium-end financial crisis, mostly felt in Asia, where Chile already had good trade relationships. In February 2010, Santiago and Chile has been struck by a major earthquake, still affecting the economy.

With about 17 million inhabitants, the GDP at purchasing power parity is \$243.7 billion (2009 est.), Chile is the 46th richest country in the world; the GDP at official exchange rate is at \$152.1 billion (2009 est.).

However, the economy in Chile has started to decline in 2009 by 1.7%. Before, it was on a growth trajectory between 3.5 to 5 Percent. The GDP per capita is at \$14,700 PPP dollars in 2009, ranks number 78 in the world; by sector, 4.8% of the people work in agriculture, 50.5% in the industry, 44.7% in the services business. Of the 17.4 million inhabitants, 7.4 million people work, of which 13.2% in agriculture, 23% in the industry, and 63.9% in services. With an unemployment rate of 10% in 2009, Chile has labor shortage issues, and 18.2% of the people are below the poverty line.

3.4.2 Chile outsourcing landscape

Chile's outsourcing landscape is embryonic, mildly spoken. However, one main factor to outsource into Chile from a U.S. perspective is the same time zone, compared with a relatively low level of instability since 1990 – or as friends of the CIA say, since Pinochet in the 1970s.

In the meantime, the university and higher education system in Chile has developed. According to the German Foreign Office (Auswärtiges Amt, 2010), there are 61 Universities of which 36 are private Universities with in total around 800'000 students. This gives enough potential for outsourcers to tap on resources.

3.4.3 Advantages and disadvantages of Chile in a glance

Item	Description
Population size	Around 17 million inhabitants.
Factor conditions	Low labor costs at PPP because of a young population
IT density	Medium to High.
Hofstede cluster	"Less Developed Latin"
Language	Spanish, English
Time zone difference to Europe	-Seven Hours
Time zone difference to US East cost	One Hour
Constant feed of IT professionals from Universities	Estimated more than 30'000 people per annum.
Legislation	USA-friendly.
Labour cost in IT Services	About 30% of the US Cost.

Table 3-4: Chile at a glance

As shown in Table 3-4, Chile is a good place for US-originated outsourcing because of its similar time zone, a rather medium to high developed IT density, a network of universities bringing out ten thousands of well-educated graduates every year and of course a definitely lower labour cost than in the U.S.A.

It needs to be noted that Chile for U.S. measures is rather small in population; however, it can be taken as a good service delivery location at least for a certain time. Chile has been taken as example for the fast growing Latin American market for offshoring. A further thesis might just line out the differences between those Latin American places.

3.5 Romania as an offshoring country

Figure 3-15: Romania Geography, Source: CIA

Romania, as shown with the map on Figure 3-15, has about 21.5 million inhabitants. Romania was transitioning away from Communism in 1989 "with a largely obsolete industrial base and a pattern of output unsuited to the country's needs", as the CIA writes. In the year 2000, the country emerged from a punishing three-year recession due to a strong demand in EU export markets. Lastly it has become member of European Union in 2007.

3.5.1 Romania overview

According to the CIA (Central Intelligence Agency, 2009, p. #RO), "the domestic consumption and investment have fueled strong GDP growth in recent years, but have led to large current account imbalances." Since recently, the economic progress in Romania has generated a slight middle class and with this, it is believed to overcome Romania's high degree of poverty. Still, Romania according to the CIA and other newspaper sources, is said to be highly corrupt.

Romania's GDP is at $255.4 billion (2009 est.), number 44 to the world, and at official exchange rate, the GDP is at $162.6 billion. The GDP did contract by 7.2% in 2009 and with this Romania has become place 201 in the world of economic growth in 2009. Before, Romania was on a 6-7% growth trajectory. Per Capita at PPP, the GDP is at $11,500 (2009 est.), number 96 in the world.

12.4% of the GDP has been made in agriculture, 35% in industry, 52.6% in services. With about 9.33 people working, of which 29.7% in agriculture, 23.2% in the industry and 47.1% in services, and an unemployment rate of officially 7.6%, Romania belongs to the developing countries in the E.U. and a population of 25% below poverty line. The industry mostly comprises manufacturing for the west, by providing car assembly, electrical machines and euqpipment, a textile and shoe industry, mining, petroleum refining in the Danube delta, construction materials, metallurgy, chemicals and last but not least food processing.

3.5.2 Romania outsourcing landscape

Romania's outsourcing landscape is still embryonic. As with many countries, Romania also benefits from E.U. subsidies.

New outsourcers working in Romania are IBM, Genpact, Capgemini (in Iasi), some Austrian banks with processing centers in Bucharest (Erste, Raiffeisen et al), Accenture. However, as observers such as BITKOM argue, Romania has a future ahead in outsourcing because of the language proximity of the Romanian language to French and Italian and a burgeoning education system, especially in Klausenburg, Herrmannstadt, Iasi and Bucharest.

3.5.3 Advantages and disadvantages of Romania at a glance

As shown in Table 3-5, Romania has very similar metrics to Poland, being an EU member with the inhabitants being proficient especially in Romanian languages, such as French, Italian, but also German.

Item	**Description**
Population size	Around 21 million inhabitants.
Factor conditions	Low labor costs at PPP because of the fall of the east in communism and the abolition of retirement benefits thereof
IT density	Low to medium
Hofstede cluster	Not observed; might be "Less Developed Latin"
Language	Romanian, English, French, Italian, German
Time zone difference to Europe	One Hour
Time zone difference to US East cost	Six Hours
Constant feed of IT professionals from Universities	Estimated more than 10'000 people per annum.
Legislation	EU legislation, still some "red tape" and corruption.
Labour cost in IT Services	About 25% of the Western European Cost.

Table 3-5: Romania at a glance

The lower labour cost, combined with a constant flow of IT and other graduates makes Romania very attractive as a "second leg" for IT services companies in Central and Eastern Europe.

3.6 Key success factors in choosing the right offshoring country

Key success factors are specific factors influencing the company and its products or services (key success factors), firm- or industry specific factors critical to the success of the product or service.

The major key success factor – is cost of qualified labor in a sustainable and risk-contained way, as this is the main driver for going off-shore as described in Chapter 3.1.1.

In the services development area, additionally, these are the potential for continuous innovation and a human resource architecture that supports it. This has certain implications on how human resources need to be managed. Moreover, it has some cultural implications on where human resource practice as they already exist inside Service providers, it might be transposed/replicated best towards a country such as Saudi-Arabia, Brazil, India etc. In other words, it will become a too hard cultural shock if basic beliefs and principles of global players such as global diversity (gender, sexual orientation, race, religious belief and origin), or respect of the individual are very hard to implement in countries, in order to foster a high performance and innovation culture.

Thus, the culture that should be used is some along Hofstede with a low to medium uncertainty avoidance, perhaps some degree of individualism - which is always a moving trajectory as there is the tendency that with an increased education individualism grows - a lower degree of masculinity - a diversity allowance criterion together with individualism. If possible, medium power distance is also needed in order to allow cross-hierarchical participation because development activities involve a lot of empowerment of individuals.

Another key success factor is a supportive enterprise architecture - which boils down into operations and into the way the company works. It needs to be encompassed especially the external environment of the firm with vendors starting from the cleaning service to water and power supply until available communications systems that connect that subsidiary with the rest of the company. Last but not least, globally operating players need to install themselves in a country where there is room for more growth in its services development and research activities, first due to a growing middle-class and a growing engineering/information science culture and due to an emerging market that supports that.

If these three factors are encompassed, Japan has the same difficulties - with its limited availability of IT staff due to fierce labor market competition - as now Western European countries and the US do have. As a consequence, of all these thoughts above IBM should set up its development activities in India.

3.6.1 Recommendation Nr 1: India

As a consequence of the analysis above, India seems to be one of the most suitable countries for pursuing further product and software development activity. There is a good extent of available IT skill, the education system provides a certain degree of growth potential, local competition and competition from foreign countries towards workforce does exist but still the wages are five to eight times below United States rates and at least a third or comparable European rates. The climate towards foreign investment has changed from once negative about 15 years ago towards positive and still. This is despite the fact that the "brain drain" of Indian highly skilled workforce towards Silicon Valley indicate that even very high skilled workers prefer working in India if comparable personal growth opportunities allow.

3.6.2 Strategic limitation of globally operating service providers

Globally operating services providers by their nature of being western-dominated companies, there exists a strategic limitation that might impede the attraction of the best-of-breed developers to those companies in India. In particular, many US-based providers, such as IBM in some extent are systemically limited to allow for non-US participation into global development and strategic decisions. The systemic limits exist due to some inherent legacy of a US-company with strong US origins (von Gamm, 2001). Thus, in order to allow for innovation and the attraction of best-of-breed developers besides a larger amount of better-than-average developers, the work content itself needs to be self-fulfilling along international and Indian academic measures.

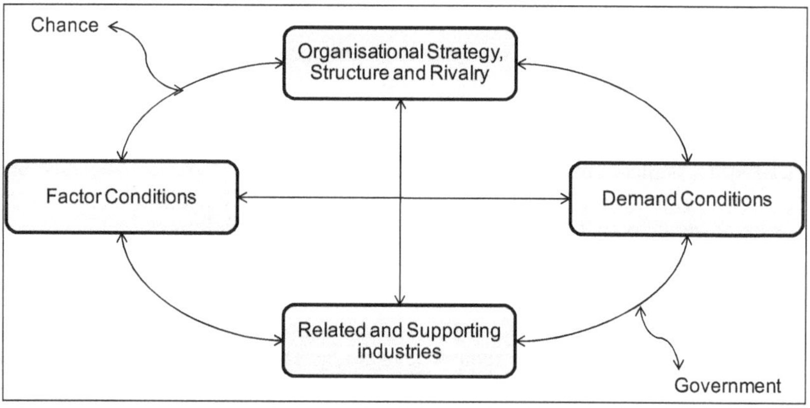

Figure 3-16: Porter's Diamond, (Porter 1990)

Using Porter's Diamond (Porter, 1990) as shown in Figure 3-16: Porter's Diamond, (Porter 1990), the following limitations can be explained: The organisational strategy, structure and rivalry as a US-centred company is very US-centric. Thus, an Indian installation will always be very Indian-centric.

Related and supporting industries that are setup in India will probably not be at the same levels than they are in the US. As a consequence, very often, a global services provider's installation in India then also needs to bring in related and supporting industries and cooperate with local players. Demand conditions are different, and thus the world view of developers who need to develop for a global market, probably. And of course, surrounding factor conditions are different too. These strategic limitations of global services providers by being a non-Indian-centric company need to be bridged or strategically stretched.

3.7 Implementing cooperation with global outsourcing companies

In order to implement a development site with a maximum population of about 10,000 developers in India, for example in India's IT capital Bangalore, there are two phases to be encompassed. First is an existing nucleus established in Bangalore with some limited development activity needs to be extended into a wholly owned subsidiary, then a running operation that acts with the rest of the provider's global development community together in a global team needs to be setup.

3.7.1 Entry mode: learning by doing

As a result, the best-fit entry strategy is to leverage upon existing resources that are already installed by the global services provider in the Indian market and to extend upon that. Some of the companies already have setup sales and distribution arms in India and a limited development arm, which is a partially owned service provider's subsidy.

Starting from the existing subsidiary, the service provider probably needs to expand and start hire additional workforce and then setup one or several more development sub projects that are not necessarily crucial for the survival of the company, like additional extra functions of a core database system or systems management tools (bells and whistle tools) for servers. With this, the service provider then can start learn how the HRM system needs to be installed and adopted towards Indian needs, how the services operation needs to be structured differently to other services sites in Western Europe or the U.S.A. After all, in order to enable learning and to take benefit out of such a development site maximally, it should be totally in control of the respective company, not a partner firm, not a partly owned subsidiary, not an agency. The services provider in every case needs to afford to learn and should take the controlled risk, thus it is the fastest way to embrace that development firm by having it as a wholly-owned subsidiary.

3.7.2 Make or Buy

A purchase of existing business only comes into question if either that existing business would bring a strategic global value-add to the global services provider, like a globally usable and not-substitutable product or if the human resources. Thus, the intellectual capital is very unique that the global services provider could not operationally live without it. It is believed by the author that both cases are not significant for an installation in India - there is no Indian global software or hardware product yet that cannot be substituted easily. At the same time, people are likely to be attracted by a development operation of the global services provider which provides interesting and rich employments.

A purchase of a service in consequence in the "package" would buy disadvantages of such a company, such as for global services provider's inappropriate human resources methods (i.e. Tariff systems, management structures etc.) that are not suitable for the services providers' global human resource system and model.

Thus, even though a "green field" investment might be initially the most costly one, it is probably at the very end the most flexible and most proven to be successful. A development lab needs to become a global team player in the provider's services development community.

3.7.3 Extending organizational relationships

The services providers' installation itself then should only formally report to an local i.e. India General manager, rather the development projects should be aligned globally within the vertical provider's divisions, such as IT Outsourcing for diverse business lines, Business Process Outsourcing, Software Development, Software Testing or other services lines. The projects then need to be financed and resourced and the project progress will be monitored, for example, a sub-product will be embraced into a larger product.

As a consequence, the Development lab might report into a global development executive of a hardware development unit or a software development unit. It even might be possible that one operating part of that development unit reports into a different person than the other. Only a remaining support and management staff (for HR, Finance etc.), might more strongly report into a Country General Manager. But even here, it probably makes sense to setup a matrix management system, where each functional manager has a global boss who provides direction from the US, and a local manager who consolidates these global views. Of course, this then would mean that every single manager might deal with conflicting messages and uncertainty, but it is probably the most effective way to tightly integrate a global development lab.

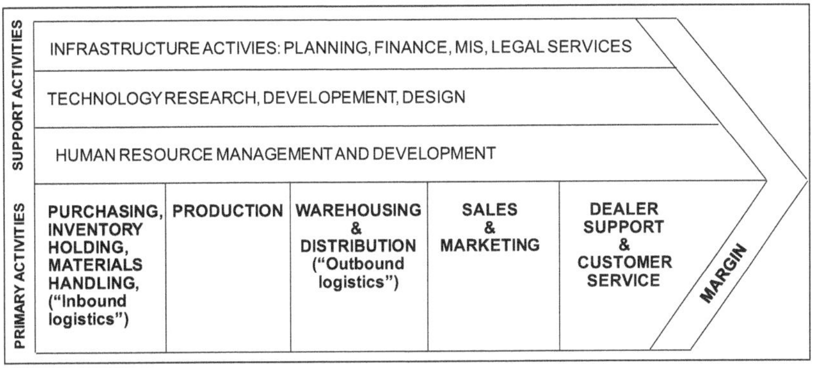

Figure 3-17: Porter's Value Chain (Porter, 1990, p.41)

3.7.4 Expanding external structures

In Porter's value chain model shown in Figure 3-17: Porter's Value Chain (Porter, 1990, p.41), a services operation in an outsourcing place, such India somewhat would be a separate systemic block in the middle - maybe equally to operations/manufacturing – from the view of the providers' organization. It should be noted that often services providers themselves provide so-called "support" processes for their global clients. Still, this is far from appropriate in today's highly customer-facing development organizations because externally cross-leveraging effects are put aside. This particularly brings a dilemma in Custom Software Development: Developers do interact in a self-directed way on project and on a first-of-a-kind base with key customers, sometimes provide in a "learning curve" after sales service and thus are closely interlocked into the entire value chain. As a consequence, as a follow-on to this value chain model, there also needs to be encompassed a more sophisticated model of that value chain, the value network, possibly with interlocking "T-shaped blocks of interaction." In a development organization, there are many side effects that stimulate innovation and thus at the end competitive advantage and profit margin, there is a set of co-determining variables that should be taken into account. Porter shows this with his diamond theory that might also be applied to parts of a company like a development arm: Local and factor conditions for example cause a development arm to start thinking into locally influenced directions, such as a tendency for "low-power" chips in areas of huge density or for mobile equipment, where non-mobile equipment is hard to deploy, such as India. Thus, it is extremely important that after an entry setup of a development organization, these developers find a way to attract customers or to get into relationship with customers - which - as many customers will be in other parts of the world than India - might become a location disadvantage, though.

3.7.5 Aligning functions strategically

The organization's functions affected by that implementation in the global services provider are several fold: marketing might have possibly some positive value-adds in India from "being Indian", on the other hand, India with a certain outside perception as a low-cost country might negatively affect the high value reputation of the services provider. Thus, in a global context, the marketing functions probably in the first instance should not place the Indian installation as a key value adds into their marketing concept.

Finance - Development is usually a cost-recovery activity. Thus, development activities will be funded out of a mission-based allocation of development resources into that specific country. Finance activities usually fund the activity offshore and to reimburse development labs for their efforts.

While all the functions discussed above are relevant, it is logical that at least one function will need to be emphasized as more important to the success of the expansion. That is in that case human resources, as training, recruiting and selection of such a development activity possibly lives and depends upon both the interaction and integration of the people involved both from India and from the home country.

3.7.6 Human resources strategy

Human resources strategy extends into two different branches. The first branch is to hire and to retain local workforce which is capable enough to execute development projects and put some sufficient innovation into it. Secondly, a limited set of expatriate workforce - be it formerly U.S.-based or former European - needs to be installed and retained. Figure 3-18 shows a model for international HRM as depicted by Morgan (Morgan, 1986, p. 44) which can be applied in an international outsourcing context.

The installation of this Indian subsidiary will be done in two steps. First, by sending a core set of entrepreneurial managers into India to setup, hire and install a core staff of people that manage the operation in the first instance; and second by hiring and retaining staff that then is actively pursuing development in a global team together with other service providing centers.

3.7.7 Hiring and retaining workforce

Hiring and retaining local staff: As most of development staff is recruited as young graduates from universities, relationships with universities need to be established in order to gain credibility already at the University for the Best of the best graduates and then to constantly get renewal from these universities and faculties. In order to install that development operation, it is highly recommended to start joint research/development activities with university professors, for example by partially funding these university installations. Alongside this, a commitment level of those co-funded university professors might be established to give incentive to the young graduates to move after their university time directly to the services provider.

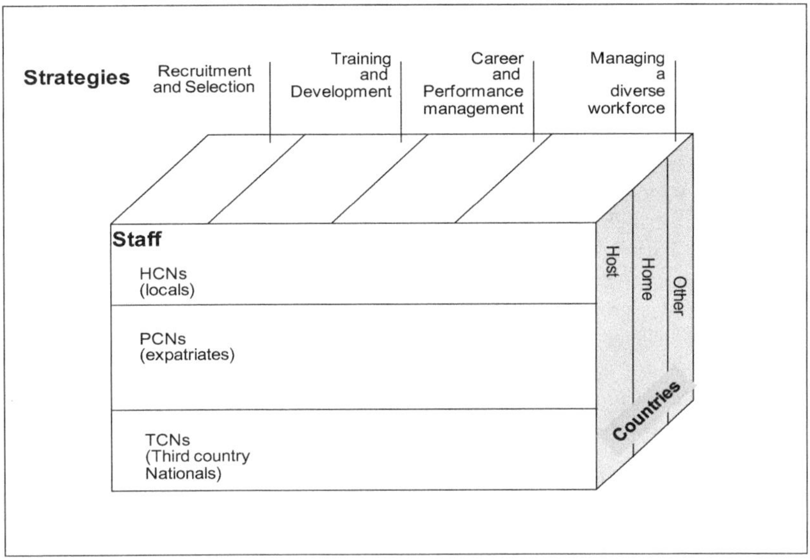

Figure 3-18: A model of international HRM - adapted from Morgan (Morgan, 1986, p. 44)

Retaining workforce: It is generally believed that competent service professionals only become productive after an average initial installment of about one to two years in a company. As a consequence, a key focus needs to be put on retaining workforce once hired, to keep attrition rates low.

In order to retain workforce, three factors need to be encompassed:

1. The services provider in the outsourcing country, such as India needs to provide a working climate in terms of degree of freedom, area of pursuance of self-fulfillment etc. that is at least equally interesting and challenging to the rest of the perceived top competition in country.

2. The services provider in the outsourcing country needs to be similarly attractive to those local best-of-breed talents than the European or U.S. based parent, in order to guarantee some longevity of their staff in India, first. This goes along with innovation culture and the perceived participation in global / international projects - thus, the services provider in the respective country needs to develop over time some leadership projects together with other development labs - they may not be in subcontract mode forever.

3. The services provider in the outsourcing country at least needs to be at least as attractive in pay and compensation as the best-of-breed local competition and simultaneously be at least that attractive in terms of pay that those employees

who recently have joined the services provider India do not tend to think that it would be more attractive to leave the country subsidiary and go to Europe or the United States to pursue a similar job. In other words, Capgemini or IBM in India needs to be the most attractive employer overall for an Indian in the IT industry in order to sustainably attract the best-of-breed people.

To focus onto India: As India tends to be a country with higher power distance, it is highly recommended to setup the structure of workgroups accordingly - more levels of hierarchy than in other countries and simultaneously a possibility for growth within these hierarchy levels. (In Germany, for example, there are usually less hierarchy levels than in the US in development in order to allow for more "democratic" participation and people empowerment). It must be possible for Indians both to climb in the hierarchy ladder as well as have self-fulfillment through intrinsic growth in their jobs. Thus, it is not appropriate at all to design and setup "IT slavery" jobs - it is even the question if these jobs that are currently setup by several software firms in India are sustainably appropriate, especially with the need for programmers and software developers that are able to manage complexity in a self-directed way.

3.7.8 Training and development

As most of the IT skills young graduates do have are rather generic, constant retraining needs to be encompassed. It should be foreseen an andragogic project based training that does allow for constant team-based rotations with US-based development labs.

Same happens with management development. Probably, one of the best way to perform management development would be to allow a constant rotation between those who setup and establish the development arm in India and skillful Indians from the US and back. Alongside, a growth of management by learning by doing is possible.

3.7.9 Career Management

There are two parts that need to be encompassed - the management of expatriates' careers and those of Indians. Indians' careers in country without global leadership tasks that are located inside India will probably limited in terms of growth - in a dual career path with a technical career and a management career these two variables will be affected both, probably (studies have shown that foreign development subsidies provide more technology career growth possibilities than management growth opportunities). As a result, the best-of-breed Indian developers might migrate to the western hemisphere, if a certain amount of global leadership is not given. Thus, after a successful startup of that operation, again, global leadership functions need to be installed.

3.7.10 Managing a diverse workforce

Diversity management and training amongst Indians and expatriates is probably one of the most important training besides all IT training. Indians in general have different views of the world and sometimes a diametrical attitude in Hofstede's dimensions, such as Power distance, Uncertainty avoidance, assuming controlled risks etc. As it can be seen, it would become fairly difficult then without a cultural training to expose each side into a global team. Thus, as a group process, inter cultural competence needs to be established in order to let people understand each other. As a result, an international multidimensional model of human resource management that encompasses all these factors needs to be setup towards this Indian development subsidiary.

3.7.11 Human resource Marketing

Marketing from a development location side is mostly a human resource marketing matter - as a consequence, to attract and retain the best and talented people in the industry in India, close linkages with education facilities need to be setup and established, perhaps with joint projects.

The provider in the Offshoring country, such as India also must develop management systems and capabilities to sustain that advantage and provide strategic flexibility in light of changing market dynamics, resource conditions, and competitor configurations. Central to this are multimarket sensing and border-spanning capabilities. In addition, development of mechanisms to facilitate transfer of information, experience, and ideas from one market to another becomes essential to stimulate organizational learning. Only by doing this can the firm use the diversity of experience and its rich base of resources to maintain a strong configural advantage in international markets.

3.7.12 Knowledge and Information management

Some words need to be lost on information and knowledge management – for example, IBM generally does provide a global system for information management, with globally accessible Intranet and Internet communications servers. These servers with the information stored herein of course also need to be accessible for the providers in India, same as the knowledge processes behind. Services and Development, as undoubtedly a very knowledge-intensive activity, live and breathe from a ubiquitously available knowledge structure. Knowledge processes not only enable individuals but also groups to group work and communicate probably might be a good recipe to capture the knowledge gathered in India and in the US in global teams and to make them readily available globally. In consequence, additional information technology needs to be installed in India as a hub to gather and collect knowledge locally and to empower local processes.

As a result of the thoughts around the MIT90s framework, as shown in Figure 3-19, it might be believed that technology will eventually overcome with structural and local friction that will exist in India by setting up a development operations is running. As Indians working with western culture on a day-to-day base, this culture eventually also might diffuse beyond the working environment and westernize India as a country, too, thus allowing to bridge the culture gap from both sides, internally within development and service companies and externally through a constantly renewed culture.

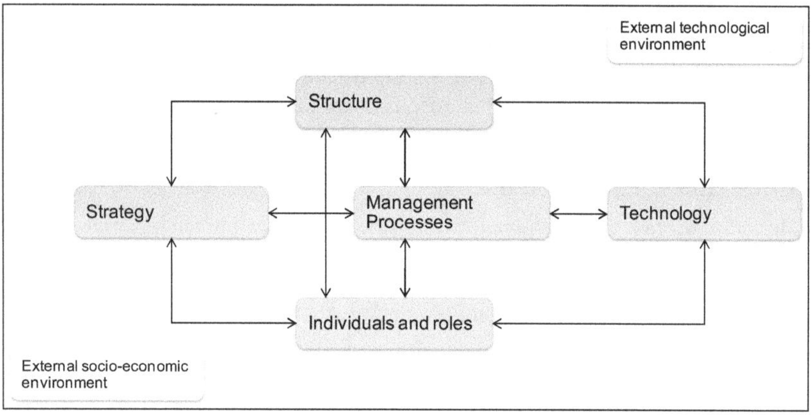

Figure 3-19: The MIT 90s framework (Morton, S., 1991)

3.8 Concluding this chapter

Concluding this chapter, there are many points to consider in outsourcing. Besides factor conditions, culture plays an ever-increasing role. Companies who start the outsourcing endeavor by themselves need be able to develop this capability on their own or – let the Outsource do a professional outsourcer, who already has gone through this experience curve. As a result, having gone through this experience curve is a rent-generating advantage to stay with Grant (Grant, 1999, p. 47ff) and a key success factor. All companies want to have low service production costs, many companies cannot achieve it. From a country perspective, there will be two sets of countries for outsourcing. First tier is off-shore countries, mainly India, maybe China later or Indonesia and Vietnam. The second-tier countries might be more suitable to provide offshoring for specific Geographies, such as Poland and Romania for Europe or Chile, maybe Argentina for the U.S.A and Canada.

4 Capgemini and its intercultural context

Chapter III deals with the company Capgemini, where the survey has been made within the sales management function of Germany, Austria and Switzerland. This chapter shows the history of Capgemini, analyses the competitive stance alongside the frameworks of M.E. Porter, aka Porter's Five Forces (Porter, 2008), gives an overview onto their internationalisation and the approach to work front-offices and back-office work and how Capgemini plans to win deals.

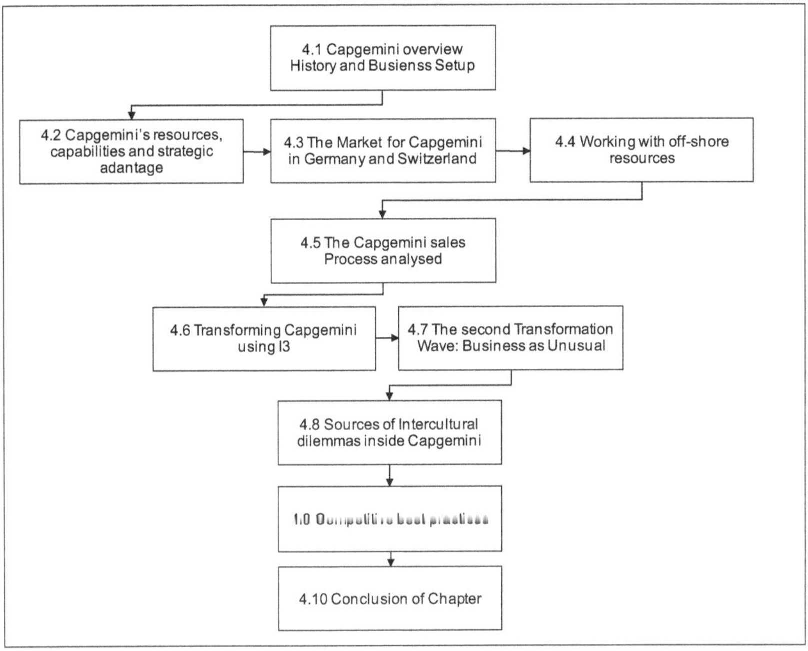

Figure 4-1: Chapter IV Overview

Figure 4-1 provides an overview over this chapter. Starting with the history of Capgemini, it will be discussed a resource-based view of Capgemini overall, then looked at the market using Porter's Five Forces and other tools especially for Germany and Switzerland before discussing the work with off-shore resources. Later on, the sales process of Capgemini will be investigated.

The discussion of two major waves of transformation of Capgemini towards a globally integrated enterprise are being discussed: "I3" and "Business as Unusual", whilst uncovering sources of often well-intended and unintended intercultural dilemmas. An outbreak will discuss competitive best practices before concluding this Capgemini-specific chapter.

4.1 Capgemini's history

Capgemini has gone through a moving history since its inception in 1967. As many companies, the strategy of Capgemini was not a "global master plan" that has been followed with scrutiny but rather emerged and has changed for years over time in an opportunistic fashion and adopted to both the market and labour conditions and its clients. As Capgemini is a live company, it might be clear that history is not ending and the next strategic change might already start to occur when this dissertation has been published. However; the following pages provide a snapshot of the context in order to better understand the chapters Six and Seven, specifically.

4.1.1 The History of Capgemini and its Organization

Capgemini, founded 1967 in Grenoble by Serge Kampf with Headquarter in Paris (Capgemini S.A., 2009), is a global provider for Consulting, Technology and Outsourcing services with European roots. The enterprise is listed on the Paris stock exchange under the name CAC 40 and on the Top 40-Enterprises-Index.

As one of the Top 5-Players, Capgemini has a high market penetration, notably in North-America, France, Great Britain, and the Benelux Countries and in Central Europe, according to company sources. The continuous growth and expansion of the Service-Portfolio have been and are the fundament of the presence in almost 40 countries since 43 years.

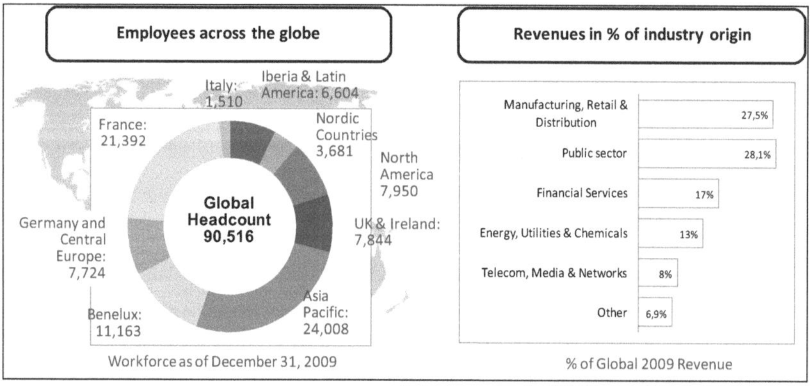

Figure 4-2: Market penetration of Capgemini, Source: Company Brochure

Capgemini has been founded out of a "chagrin d'être" (Gaston-Breton, 2007) by Serge Kampf who at time worked with a different company, Bull and found himself to revoke promises already made to clients (Gaston-Breton, 2007). Kampf apparently turned highly irate to lose its face towards his clients and in consequence, left Bull and founded his own company with a key notion of being independent. This independence is a key motivation and cornerstone of Capgemini and is also might be a key pitfall in building a joint account organisation, as displayed later on.

Capgemini describes its presence as a global one. Because of the internationality and the worldwide operative business-activity of Consulting, Technology and Outsourcing services, Capgemini has built processes and structures to serve the customers of Capgemini locally. Country-specific requirements are covered. At the same time Capgemini provides to the international customers all services around the globe from one hand. Capgemini advises governments, public authorities as well as Institutions of the public sector, international and national companies and medium-sized enterprises.

4.1.2 Organization

Capgemini worldwide presence extends over an area of almost 40 countries with more than 70 Service-Centres in North-America, Asia-Pacific and EMEA. Capgemini provides its clients all possibilities of a worldwide Service-Centre network. Self-evidently Capgemini provides on-the-spot support for clients locally, such as in Germany, Austria Switzerland and East Europe. Realising Outsourcings Capgemini uses a worldwide affiliate net of service centres. Organisation-wise, according to Minzberg (Mintzberg, The structuring of organizations, 1999), Capgemini has a setup a typical Matrix structure with region organisations and division organisations. Decision making is made centralized for major decisions and highly de-centralised for client related service activities. The local operating companies have quite a high degree of freedom to act, however they have to work within a framework of business controls guidelines.

For delivering services, the Capgemini Group relies on its global delivery model called Rightshore®, which aims to get the appropriate balance of the best and most cost-effective talent from multiple locations. Here, Capgemini has the philosophy – despite working on different locations, the teams are to be treated as working as one team to create and deliver the optimum solution for clients. Because the capability of Capgemini to build cross-nationals teams, the teams – according to company brochures - in the different locations are able to work directly and immediate together in projects.

Besides its locations in Western Europe with France – 22‘000 employees, Germany – 3‘000 employees, Switzerland – ca. 280 employees, UK – ca. 10‘000 employees, Capgemini's Nearshore and Offshore-locations are growing eminently, now to over 22'000 employees in India, alone. An overview is shown in Figure 4-3

Capgemini reported 2008 global revenues of € 8.7 billion and employs over 90,000 people worldwide. The percentage of the Outsourcing sector was 35.3% of the total revenue, of the Consulting sector 8%, of the Technology sector with

39% and others activities (local professional services) 17.7%. Circa 80% of the employees are engaged in Europe.

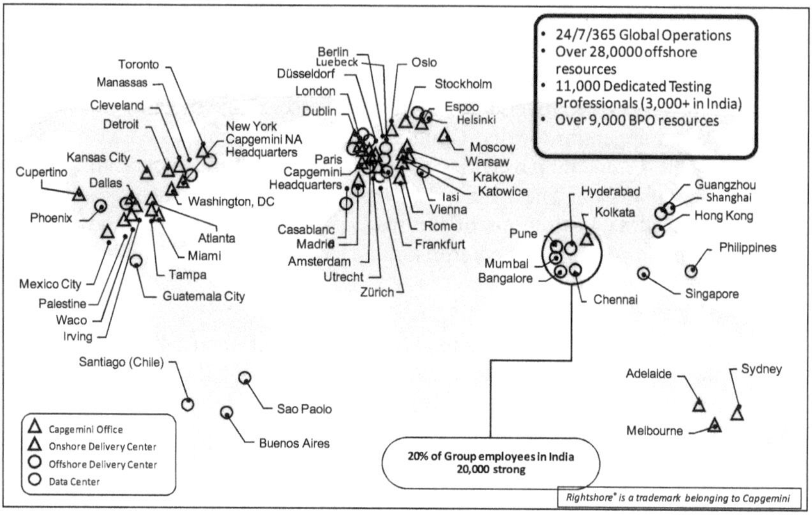

Figure 4-3: Service Delivery locations of Capgemini (Capgemini, 2009)

4.1.3 Core Competencies of Capgemini

Capgemini provides his customers an integral Service-Portfolio, shown in Figure 4-4: This includes the analysis and advice as well as Technology and an efficient service from one hand. Here a brief outline about our divisions **Consulting Services, Technology Services** and **Outsourcing Services**.

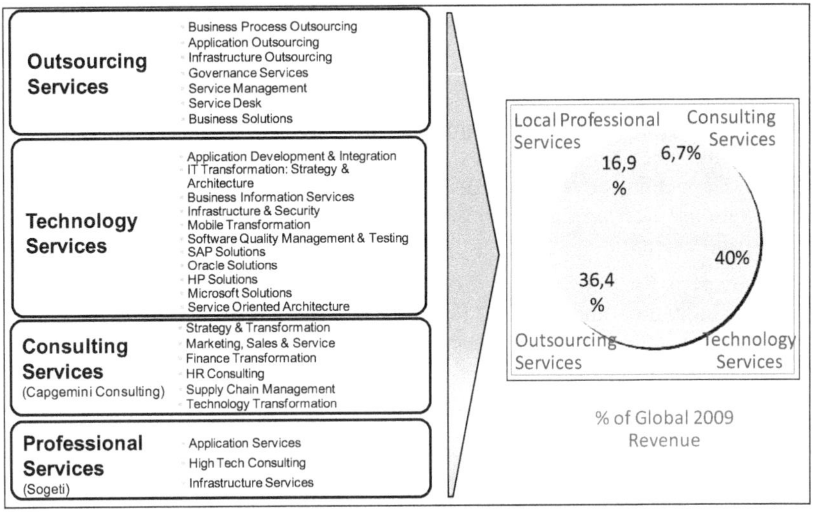

Figure 4-4: The Services Portfolio of Capgemini (Capgemini, 2010)

4.1.3.1 Consulting Services

Capgemini Consulting is the strategy and transformation consulting division of the Capgemini Group, with a team of over 4,000 consultants worldwide. Leveraging its sector and business expertise, Capgemini Consulting advises and supports organizations in transforming their business, from strategy through to execution.

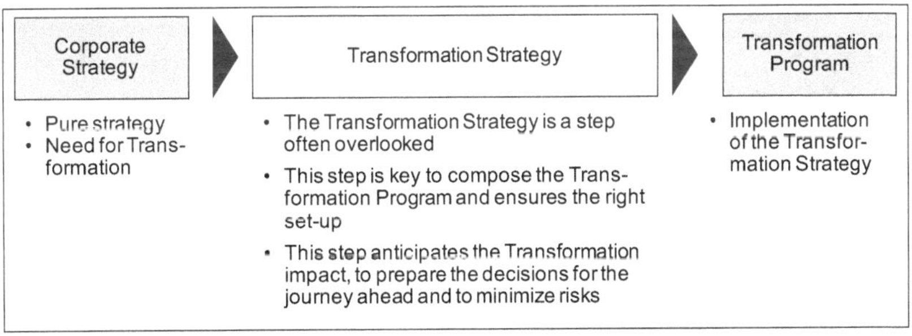

Figure 4-5: Capgemini Consulting Value Proposition, (Capgemini, 2009).

The core domains of Capgemini Consulting, depicted in Figure 4-5 is the support in strategy definition and the evaluation whether a need for a transformation of the existing business is needed. However, Capgemini Consulting sees its core competency in executing the transformation strategy and to compose a transformation programme with the right setup, thereby anticipating the impact of the transformation to systems, people and the environment of the company. Several successful transformation strategy examples are shown on Capgemini's website

4.1.3.2 Technology Services

Industry analysts have long recognized the exceptional technology expertise of Capgemini consultants, as an example being ASCO in Switzerland (ASCO, 2007). Capgemini consistently delivers technology services that exceed client expectations — from agents to SAP, application integration to web services, aerospace to retail.

A key expertise as shown in Figure 4-6 lies in the domain of Process and IT consulting, Individual and standard Software Solutions, Total Systems integration and the management of the applications throughout the entire lifecycle.

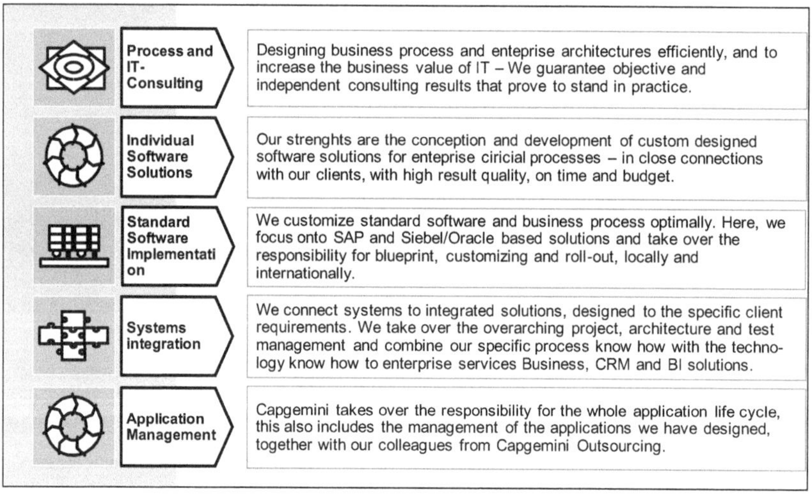

Figure 4-6: Capgemini Technology Services Value Proposition, from customer collateral

4.1.3.3 Outsourcing Services

With over 30 years' experience and a global workforce of over 25,000 outsourcing professionals, Capgemini is currently collaborating on some of the world's largest outsourcing contracts.

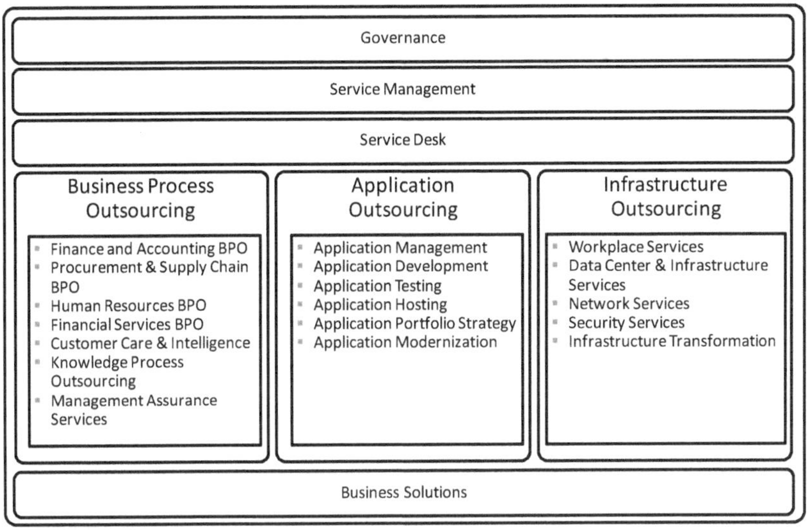

Figure 4-7: The Outsourcing Portfolio of Capgemini, from customer collateral

Worldwide, more than 400 customers are using the Outsourcing of Capgemini. The revenues of Capgemini Outsourcing Services were more than 3 billion euro for the year 2008.

4.1.3.4 Capgemini Outsourcing Services Domains

Application Outsourcing - Outsourcing application maintenance and development – here the labour arbitrage plays a bigger role.

Business Process Outsourcing (BPO) – Besides labour arbitrage, process knowledge is a differentiating factor in BPO. This can be achieved through assembling similar clients together in service centres and sharing process knowledge and ideas.

Infrastructure Outsourcing – Key levers of infrastructure outsourcing is the economy of scale effect plus labour arbitrage by putting repeatable and specialised labour to remote locations, i.e. in Poland or India, as already depicted in Chapter 3.1.1.

Local Professional Services by Sogeti

Under the brand name Sogeti, Capgemini provides "Local Professional Services", also known as "body shopping" for clients in domains such as: Testing, Microsoft Portals and Services, Java Programming. These local professional services, provided by around 20'000 people (Capgemini S.A., 2009) . Sogeti as a company is being left highly separately to the rest of Capgemini applying its own brand, having its own separate offices and having different marketing systems and the like.

4.1.4 Local implementation of Capgemini in Germany and Switzerland

Capgemini Central Europe, mainly consisting of Capgemini Germany and Switzerland, reported 2008 revenues of € 685 million with 7'500 employees, including a main delivery centre in Krakow and Katowice. Main locations in Germany are Dusseldorf, Offenbach am Main, Munich, Berlin, Stuttgart. In Switzerland, Capgemini is located in Zurich, Basel and Lausanne plus minor client locations with about 250 employees. In Austria, Capgemini has its main presence in Vienna with about 100 employees.

In Germany/Switzerland, Consulting Services, Technology Services and Outsourcing Services are organised each specifically – Here to date, the following organisation charts do exist:

- **Consulting Services** is divided by practice and less by region and has set up a quasi-matrix for its organisation. The following Service lines do exist: Strategy and Transformation and Organisational Transformation, plus organised by Sector: MALS (Manufacturing and Logistics), FS (Financial Services), EUC, TME (Telecom, Media and Entertainment) and Public Sector. Those organisations work together in a matrix, however this matrix is still in a flux at the current state of writing..
- **Technology Services** is mainly covered by the subsidiary Capgemini SD&M, as separate legal entity both in Germany and Switzerland. Capgemini SD&M has been re-named from S&DM in 2008, a former acquisition from the consulting arm of Ernst & Young. Same here, the organisation is divided by sector, however not by business practice. The sectors themselves are different to those of Capgemini Consulting, there is some overlap, but it appears that interfacing from one business unit to the next is not made easy. The Technology Services Switzerland function is a part of the "Financial Services" practice, even though 60% of their clients are outside of Financial Services.
- **Outsourcing Services** is organised as a globalised "seamless team", subdivided in matrix formed Regions, The Central European Headquarters are located in Germany, covering both Germany and Switzerland with a local outpost in Switzerland, then again integrated with the rest of Capgemini.
- **Sogeti** does operate loosely coupled with the rest of Capgemini, having its own processes and business priorities, however works together on some corporate support processes in the background.

4.1.4.1 Capgemini in Germany

Specifically speaking in Germany Capgemini entertains a local leadership team, called the Country Board with the mission of integrating those business units together. This country board consists of the heads of all business units, chaired by a country board leader, who is also part of Capgemini's Global Executive Committee.

4.1.4.2 Capgemini in Switzerland

In Switzerland, there exists neither a cross-discipline local leadership function nor a formal integration team; however there are sporadic meetings with the Business Development and Sales teams. Capgemini in Switzerland is trying to integrate the several arms of Capgemini in a "virtual manner", simply by cooperating and having regular team meetings amongst business developers. However, due to the nature of the organisational setup, this happens voluntarily and because of a belief that joint integration is needed.

4.2 Capgemini - resources, capabilities and competitive advantage

Using Grant's concept on Resources and Capabilities (Grant, 1999), Capgemini draws the following capabilities out of its differentiating resources:

Tangible resources:

- According to latest accounts, Capgemini holds around € 400 mln. of cash in its reserves. Besides this, Capgemini holds a series of assets, notably rented-in datacentre space for about 50'000 servers and office locations for about 90'000 people and is a major renter of a campus called Capgemini University in Les Fontaines, France.

Intangible resources:

- **Technology:** Capgemini holds resources – amongst other human resources and knowledge in order to manage and evaluate a broad set of technology and knowledge
- **Reputation:** Through a long-standing history of brand work, Capgemini has built up a reputation as "innovator", to be independent and show a competitive advantage to clients.
- **Culture:** The culture of Capgemini – albeit differing in many countries, is entrepreneurial with a high focus towards being an entrepreneur within an enterprise. Alongside with this, Capgemini leaders have structured their own little P&L with all its up- and downsides.
- **Values:** Capgemini does employ a set of strong values since the mid Honesty, Boldness, Trust, Freedom, Team Spirit, Modesty and Fun. These values are portrayed as core and essential. These are considered by company officials as key differentiating factors in order to win in the marketplace. Notably speaking, it is widely unknown of any other company which has also "fun" as its corporate value, as shown in Table 4-1.

Value	Explanation
Honesty	Particularly the refusal of unfair business practices aimed at obtaining a particular contract or advantage. In line with this principle, Capgemini has established clear rules with respect to commissions and gifts of all kinds.
Boldness	In the sense of an entrepreneurship and desire to take considered risks balanced by prudence and clear-sightedness, without which a bold manager can become reckless.
Trust	It implies a willingness to empower employees and teams, and to allow managers to experience the effects of their initiatives and decisions. Trust also implies an open mind and genuine transparency in the flow of information, and is at the heart of our Collaborative Business Experience®.
Freedom	It includes creativity, innovation, independence of mind and respect for others in their diverse cultures, habits, and customs, all of which are crucial for a company with a presence in more than 30 countries and that has over 100 nationalities among its employees.
Team spirit	With clients, employees, and partners; the ability to share in both good and bad times.
Modesty	In relations with others and in our approach to issues.
Fun	Without which any corporate vision is extremely difficult, if not impossible, to implement.

Table 4-1: Cagemini Values (Capgemini S.A., 2010)

Human resources:

- **Skills and Knowledge, in Consulting and Architecture:** Capgemini has human resources able to consult upon various matters, starting from strategy and transformation up to brand design or financial, manufacturing or human resource processes.
- **Communication and Interaction:** Having a "work hard, play hard" culture, Capgemini employees in most ways communicate openly and try to build up a common sense of teamwork and interaction, which appears to be a differentiator.
- **Motivation:** Similar to other service organisations, the motivation of people is of key importance. The key ambition of Capgemini, as described by Hessler (Hessler, 2009), is to be independent and to provide an independent view to its clients.

The aim is to combine business and technology towards the competitive advantage for its clients: Capgemini is combining business issues with technology solutions and capabilities to achieve a competitive advantage for its clients.

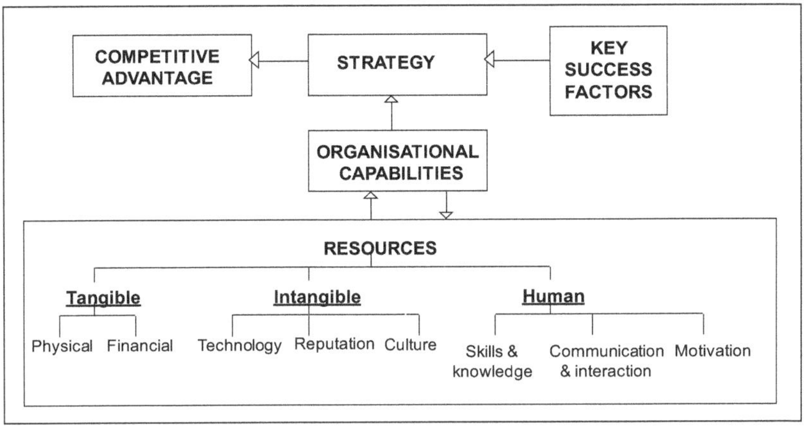

Figure 4-8: Resources, Capabilities, Competitive advantage (Grant, 1999)

Capgemini – according to company brochures draws its competitive advantage from the following key factors and differentiators, as depicted in Figure 4-9, which then can be depicted as capabilities.

- Technology Agnostic implementation for clients
- Low risk transition of services performed into Capgemini
- Choices and Flexibility
- Size, Speed and Complexity
- Collaborating to reach beyond, also known as "Collaborative Business Experience"
- Innovation for Economic value
- Proven speed to value
- End-To-End offerings.

These ambitions as stated by Capgemini are high and are to provide a competitive advantage for its clients and for Capgemini. These capabilities, together with a set of financial capabilities to manage risk and financial complexities derive Capgemini to charge a higher price for its services than it does need to take in order to produce.

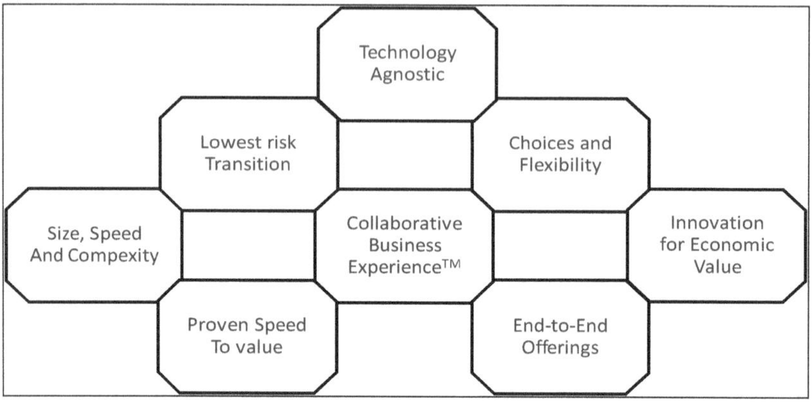

Figure 4-9: Capgemini Differentiators

At the same time, Capgemini tries to be both a quality leader – especially in consulting services and technology services and a price leader, especially in outsourcing. This allows Capgemini to realise a price premium above cost and thereof profitability out of its business system.

4.2.1 Sales implementation

Despite its cross-divisionalized setup, Capgemini tries to integrate for large accounts a certain corporate account management. This is being undertaken since 2008 at a selected group of accounts, called the Corporate Management Accounts (CMAs) (Capgemini S.A., 2009). Here, Capgemini is leveraging an account manager with certain seniority and joins this account manager with a "sponsoring executive", also known as Group client executive. Un-like in other companies such as IBM with Account Managing Directors having full Profit and Loss (P&L) responsibility (IBM, 2009), there are no special rights for account executives who report into the country board. The total share of the revenues is not known, yet it is estimated to be less than 20% in total.

4.3 The market for Capgemini in Germany and Switzerland

This chapter discusses market, market size and attractiveness of Capgemini and Switzerland and Germany using Porter's Five forces.

Germany – according to the CIA World Fact Book (Central Intelligence Agency, 2009) is the largest European economy and second most populous nation (after Russia), Germany is a key member of the continent's economic, political, and defence organizations. The German economy - the fifth largest economy in the world in PPP terms and Europe's largest - began to contract in the second quarter of 2008 as the strong euro, high oil prices, tighter credit markets, and slowing growth abroad took their toll on Germany's export-dependent economy. At just 1% in 2008, GDP growth was -5% in 2009. With a GDP of € 2'010 bln, Germany has a rich ground for an IT industry. The IT industry, entailing about 3.3% of the GDP in Germany, excluding telecommunications services, totals therefore to 66 (BITKOM, 2009) bln €.

Switzerland – according to statistics of OSEC and the CIA World Fact Book (Central Intelligence Agency, 2009) – belongs to the most globalised places on earth, having people from more than 180 different countries in Switzerland on a permanent base and incorporating four different languages plus one strong dialect into a national environment. Switzerland is called a "peaceful, prosperous, and stable modern market economy with low unemployment, a highly skilled labour force, and a per capita GDP among the highest in the world". According to the CIA, Switzerland's economy does benefit from a highly developed service sector, led by financial services and a manufacturing industry that focuses onto a high-technology, knowledge-based production. With a GDP of 210 € bln. (Central Intelligence Agency, 2009, p. #CH), Switzerland has is only a 10th of the size of the German economy, however, the IT industry, entailing about 5% of the GDP in Switzerland, is represented above average with about, totals therefore to 10 bln € or 15 bln CHF, according to SwissICT (SwissICT, 2010) and Ziegler (Ziegler, 2010).

Capgemini in Central Europe mainly consists of Capgemini Group companies in Germany, Austria and Switzerland. Capgemini in Germany currently employs 2270 employees, Capgemini in Switzerland, once a company of roughly 500 employees, has shrunk by half until 2009. With the dotcom boom and bust in 2001 (Florida, 2002), many of the consulting mandates have been lost and people had to be freed up to the market, and since then, no real sign of recovery has been shown.

4.3.1 The IT and IT Outsourcing Industry in Germany

Germany is the largest economy in Europe and with 82 million inhabitants and a high industrialization (Central Intelligence Agency, 2009), Germany has an IT and telecoms spend of € 129.7 bln. in 2009 with a slight prognosis for growth, according to the Germany industry association BITKOM (BITKOM, 2009). Same is for the sub-segment IT market with about € 65.4 bln. in 2009, after € 67.2 bln. in 2008.

The Germany IT industry is pressured by the following forces:

Immense **competition** within the existing players, such as IBM, T-Systems, HP-EDS Siemens IT Services, CSC, Accenture and Capgemini to name the largest. Due to the increased competition and a slightly shrinking market 2008 to 2009 and a stagnant market in 2010 there is a large tendency of mergers and acquisitions caused by price and scale pressure.

The **buying power** of clients is high. Clients can currently re-negotiate new daily service rates for services contracts, thus imposing pressure to suppliers to cut on rates. Same is to some extent with non-critical software licenses and since a longer time due to the productivity increase in the hardware area with hardware components. Here, according to Moore's law (Intel Corp.), the processing speed of hardware doubles every 18 months. Additionally, buyers increasingly concentrate and consolidate contracts and through this try to bundle purchasing power.

Suppliers have little bargaining power, except software vendors, if taken separately, such as SAP or Oracle, to some extent IBM and Microsoft and processor manufacturers, such as Intel. However, in a broader industry context, they can be seen as part of the industry.

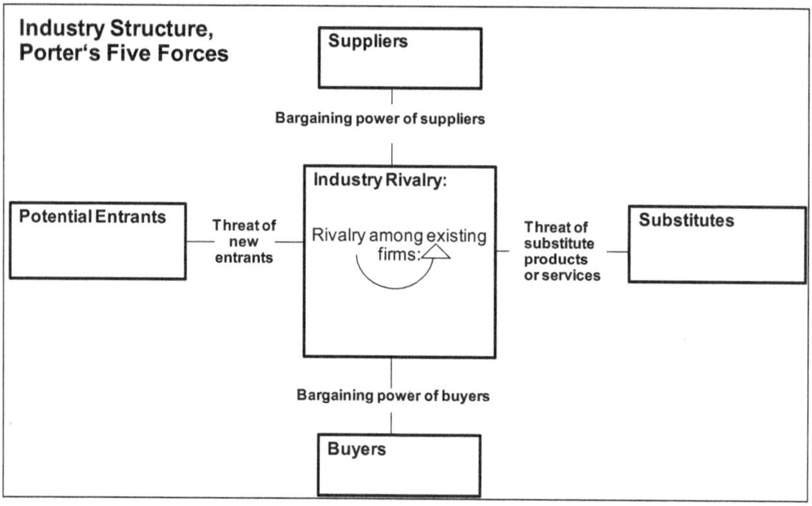

Figure 4-10: Porter's Five Forces, Porter (1980)

Potential new entrants come to the market especially from India, same as in other countries. Here, especially Wipro, Cognizant and Infosys try to enter the market with verve. Especially those new entrants do drive down prices for IT services through pressuring daily rates for consultants, professional services and application developers.

Potential substitutes for IT services only exist through manual labour or process rationalisation. This is often not possible and labour intensive. Therefore the IT market here is still growing, despite high buying power and potential new entrants. The German market can be considered as highly attractive, if special obstacles, such as local language (German), special customs and special labour legislation can be addressed in the selling and delivering of IT services.

4.3.2 The IT and IT Outsourcing Industry in Switzerland

From an industry analysis perspective, Switzerland is quite unique due to the fact that it has many advantages and disadvantages different to the rest of EU

Europe. As already mentioned, the market is sized to around 15 bln CHF, according to Ziegler et al (Ziegler, 2010). Ziegler then emphasises that the Outsourcing market entails roughly 3.0 bln CHF in Switzerland[11]. The IT implementation and integration market sizes at 1.1 bln CHF, the ICT consulting market does size at around 700 mln CHF, all numbers of 2010, as shown in "Figure 4-11".

Using Porter's Five Forces analysis (Porter, 2008), also shown on Figure 4-10, we can look at the Swiss outsourcing market in the following way:

Suppliers: Suppliers in the outsourcing industry are to 30% the hardware and software suppliers plus providers of real estate and energy. 60-70% is people cost (von Gamm, 2004, p. 28), means available resource to work on. Here, the biggest shortfalls do exist in Switzerland, not due to lack of skill in general but due to the lack of skill in large amounts. This is valid for virtually all outsourcing companies and IT and business process services providers, therefore the trend to go abroad with suppliers – i.e. Rightshore is an absolutely must in order to stay competitive. Rightshoring from Poland or India therefore is more than a must-do, it is essential.

Substitutes: There are two substitutes in the IT industry: Substitutes for outsourcing IT services is providing the services by in-house services providers or just not pursuing outsourcing at all. Many of this driving force increasingly falls away, simply due to professionalization of the IT services profession and a higher degree of specialisation.

Potential entrants: The entrants these days are not "potential" any longer. Besides the typical industry rivals, new players are on the block, from both a vertical side, providing entire vertical processes, such as Swiss Postfinance for Payments, Raiffeisen for simple securities transactions, or of course Indian pure players, who already have entered the market and have established – silently but surely a strong foothold in Switzerland, such for example Infosys now being a household application services provider for UBS. These players, notably Tata, Wipro, Infosys, HCL, Cognizant and Genpact according to IDC (IDC and Hedin, Marianne, 2009) and Arora et al. (Arora, Arunachalam, Asundi, & Fernandes, 2001) do play an increasing role in the IT Services provider market by directly off-shoring the work towards India, mainly.

Buyers: Buyers still can choose amongst a vast series of outsourcing services providers. Still, it is a buyers' market – or again a buyers' market.

[11] There is a certain debate as to how much the Swiss Multinationals as a "controlled IT Spend" can control. Examples are large banks which have a strategic spending authority from out Switzerland and then determine an IT budget, globally. This Gross IT Spend has been tried to count by several market researchers and differs by factors 2-5.

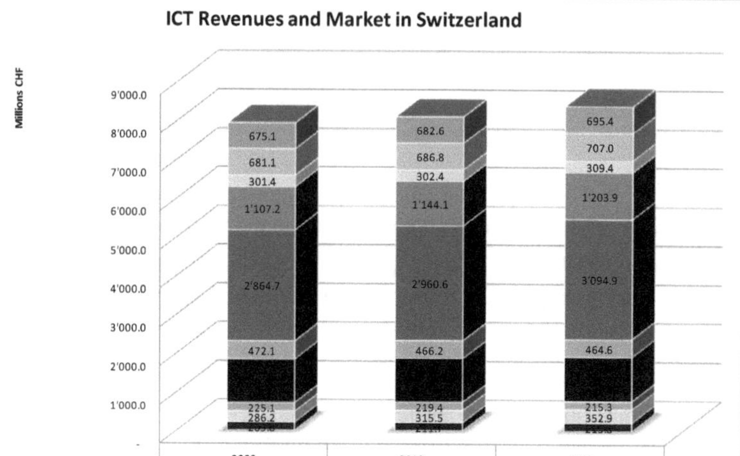

	2009	2010	2011
Custom Software Development	675.1	682.6	695.4
ICT - Consulting	681.1	686.8	707.0
ICT - Ausbildung	301.4	302.4	309.4
Implementierung & Integration	1'107.2	1'144.1	1'203.9
Total Outsourcing Services	2'864.7	2'960.6	3'094.9
Hardware Support & Maintenance	472.1	466.2	464.6
Standard Software Maintenance	1'119.1	1'121.3	1'136.6
Custom Software Maintenance	225.1	219.4	215.3
BPO	286.2	315.5	352.9
Sonstige Services	209.8	211.7	215.8

Figure 4-11: IT Services Market in Switzerland (Ziegler, 2010)

Industry Rivalry: Competition is tense, especially in a shrinking market. Due to increased industry rivalry, companies increasingly cut prices in order to win deals, thus change revenues for profits. With Swisscom IT Services, especially an outsourcing services provider is under way that is still very aggressive in the market and tries to leverage Swiss unique values by being a Swiss only company and some limited parts of internationalization (von Gamm, 2004). Besides this, the international players such as IBM, CSC, EDS/HP, Accenture and T-Systems, together with the new Indian Pure Players such as Wipro, Infosys, and Cognizant et al. are fighting to dominate the clients. In essence, the biggest fight is supposed to be in the banking area, yet at the same time, the large Western players seem to be shielded from this area to some extent.

The Swiss market can be considered as extremely attractive – even higher than the German market, if special obstacles, such as local language (Swiss German, French, and Italian), highly special customs and very different labour legislation from Germany and the EU can be addressed in the selling and delivering of IT services.

4.3.3 Market attractiveness –Strategic fit of client and Capgemini

Capgemini serves in distinct areas of IT outsourcing and business process outsourcing (BPO). Companies that appreciate the key uniqueness of Capgemini will be looked into first. Capgemini, according to its own view, fits very well with companies who value those differentiators, being in essence companies with an international background – i.e. a global clientele or supplier situation, global subsidiaries and a certain level of complexity. Here, Capgemini have decided that usually companies only larger than 1 bln € of revenues of an IT spend of more than € 50 million per annum might make sense to target. With this, Capgemini has then continued the market assessment one level lower for Switzerland.

4.4 Working together off-shore

As already mentioned, services become more and more not only a domestic play but do get imported into a specific country because of reasons such as labor cost or available resources.

Working off-shore, there are two types of configurations that can be found, especially in the IT Industry:

1. **Direct off-shore, also known as pure-play model**: The client then has to work directly with an off-shore service provider, i.e. in India. The client directly also has to handle cultural boundaries and the like.

2. **Front-Office, Back-Office configuration**, within Capgemini referred to as **Rightshore**. Here, the client interfaces with a front-office, as depicted in Figure 4-12. Here, the front-office works as a translator between the client, who often is used to his own cultural background and the back-office who performs the own original work.
   This goes along with Schröder (Schröder, 1998) who has emphasized that stereotyping typically generates intercultural contact situations that need to be bridged and overcome in order to gain efficiencies and avoid the building of stereotypistic losses by not having a "natural way of seeing the world". In that cases, the front-offices bridges this cultural and experience chasm between the client with his domain-specific knowledge and the service factory, often located in off-shore regions.

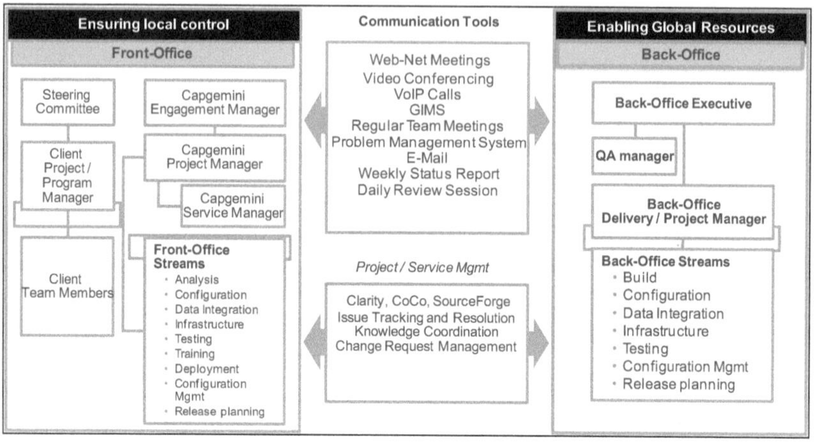

Figure 4-12: A combination of front-office and back-office, Source: Capgemini

Definitely, there might also be hybrids, such as front-office, middle-office and back-office, however; the original front-office – back-office configuration can be seen as a very classic one in outsourcing environments. Definitely, the front-office comes along with a price tag attached to it, same as a certain business value – the intercultural bridge – can be attributed to it from both sides. This price tag needs to be burdened as part of a deal and acknowledged as valuable in order to show a rent generation exceeding a pure-play model.

4.5 Opportunity analysis at Capgemini

In order to determine the size of the opportunity both of a market and then of a specific transaction, several methodologies are being used. Using the Holden (Holden International, 2009) Methodology, Capgemini examines the following elements within an opportunity analysis. Depending upon the size of the deal and executive focus, analysis does vary.

- **Opportunity Analysis** – Here, the overall scope of the opportunity will be analysed – what does the client want, can the supply organization add value, should Capgemini pursue it (geography, time frame, customer competence, risk assessment, profitability and future value for both sides), can Capgemini compete, is there an alignment to win. This then is plotted into a risk analysis chart (OARI) as shown in the picture.
- **Competitive Analysis** – who among the competitors are involved, can Capgemini differentiate, and whether neutrally speaking the opportunity analysis yielding for the competitors would add higher values on the Overall risk analysis than with Capgemini.
- **Value Statement** – Here, Holden suggests to state per buying zone – means decision maker - a clear value statement in the form of "what's in it for me".

This is based upon the agency principle as described by Jensen and Meckling (Jensen & Meckling, 1976) stating that if the person would have a personal [work] benefit, she would more likely support an opportunity than that without benefit and favors a supplying organisation compared to this competitor. Holden especially focuses on the business impact, a deal which can provide for a person and with this the credibility the buying organization can establish.

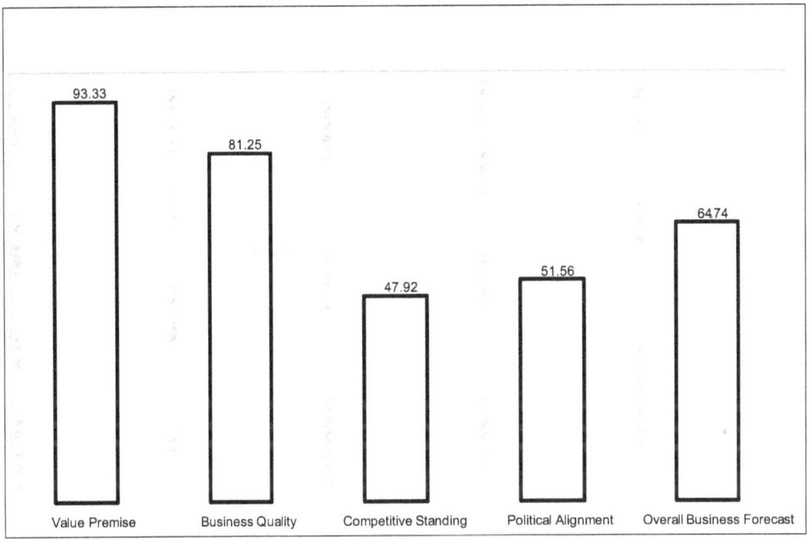

Figure 4-13: Overall Risk Analysis Chart – Sample, Source: Capgemini (2010).

- **Value Proposition** – Here, a concise and specific, timely value proposition for the whole organization is asked to be associated with this opportunity. Example: By End of 2010, the implementation of a system will save £ 20 M for the business in the area of finance administration, whilst costing only £ 5 M.
- **The sales objective** – Here, according to the value proposition, the value should be delivered and who it should be sold to, it also should describe a certain pricing mechanism, superficially.
- **The differentiation** – Clearly, in a competitive environment, a solution delivered should be better than the competition in terms of price, risk associated and value delivered. This best should be manifested on specific hard facts in order to enumerate this.
- **The competitive counter strategy** – Even if there is enough differentiation, competition can be rough and mean. Here, it should be noted whether to focus onto competitive weaknesses and put strengths of the own organization

against it. Same is of course; there are different strategies, such as a direct attack, containment, a flanking or an ignoring strategy.

- **The contact and political strategy** – Here, it is clearly described as to who from the supplying organization meets whom and with which message in order to provide the right value statements at that point in time. At the same time, it is being focused onto how the contacts help the prospective seller in establishing a priority access towards the decision making.
- **The "Fox" evaluation** – Here, the extent of which the people affected by the opportunity and in the powerbase have a positive influence towards moving the case in favour of the supplying company is evaluated. A set of questions, treats the intimacy of the contact and will generate a score by attributing to each question a value between +4 and -4. This summarizing then generates a contact score, a competitive contact score and a Fox score, contributing to the overall OARI value.
- **The powerbase and powerbase map** – shows the results of the "Fox" evaluation, by dividing people into supporters, non-supporters, allies and opponent. Depending upon the strength of the relationship, they are more closer to the center. Using such a powerbase map, a so-called "Fox", a person who has a personal and business interest to support a vendor-specific solution, might be identified easier.
- **Implementation plan.** – This implementation plan then should highlight the action plan in order to move the sale forward

4.6 Transforming Capgemini using I3

Capgemini has gone through several waves of transformation. In 2006, a transformation programme dubbed I3 or "I-Cubed" has been enacted after several years of recession and recovery.

4.6.1 Increasing win-rates and profitability at Capgemini using I3

In order to win better and to increase profitability, Capgemini has embarked upon a strategic transformation programme in 2006 called I3 (I-Cubed) with the following aspects, according to reports of Capgemini and various others, such as Cros, von Gamm and Hessler (Capgemini S.A., 2009), (Cros, 2007), (Hessler, 2009), (von Gamm, 2009):

- Innovation
- Industrialization and
- Intimacy towards the Client

On these three factors Capgemini has hoped to achieve superior results. Lastly, this has helped to spur some of the capabilities towards a better outcome, the company has stated in November 2003, when it discontinued the programme after three years of execution.

4.6.1.1 Industrialisation

Here, Capgemini tries to build global services delivery units from "craftsmanship to industrial operating models", as Cros (Cros, 2007) describes it. Here, besides building global templates for consulting works or technology services, global tools and processes for outsourcing, especially global delivery centres are to be built up that enable them to leverage upon labour costs thus being able to give in to price pressure imposed by clients, whilst improving measured quality (Capgemini S.A., 2009) through repeatable, controlled processes. Thus, work being conducted "on-shore" - means in the countries where the client is residing - will be transformed towards "near-shore" and "off-shore" work. Thus there are two parts: the on-shore-transformation with a transfer of "bench" and contractors offshore, an increase of sector and industry expertise, engagement, an improvement of management processes, architecture, functional design and innovation.

At the same time, the "offshore" transformation has the target to realize "stronger client and project management capabilities" and to move from a "capacity to a capability management logic", which can be best explained to leverage resources across the different client situations instead of just moving work 1:1 off-shore in order to gain cost benefits.

4.6.1.2 Innovation

Innovation is being seen as a prerequisite for competitive advantage in the Capgemini I3 program. After developing a "business and technology vision" for the next decade, Capgemini is trying to leverage and accelerate select technology bets and is trying to capitalize and industrialise those. Alongside with this, several innovation examples will be implemented, such as "RAIN" (Rapid Innovation) or TechnoVision. With this, Capgemini hopes to create a higher degree of independence from suppliers and gain a degree of freedom to deliver and consult.

4.6.1.3 Client Intimacy

Here, Cros (Cros, 2007, p. 16) emphasizes to advance the client relationship from a vendor situation towards becoming a "client partner", similar to the concepts of Christopher et al (Christopher, Payne, & Ballantyne, 1991, p. 87), by building group managed accounts for 10 to 20 strategic relationships by 2009. With this it is perceived to increase cross-selling across different Capgemini disciplines, as it is strongly felt that the cross-selling can be improved through inter-organisational alliances, as Carter (Carter, 1994) points out. At the same time, the strengthening of the sales discipline with the build-up of according tools and communities is to be fostered. The client intimacy domain is a key to enact sales leadership and to work with key account managers. It is ultimately believed that long-term client intimacy have a positive bottom-line effect for Capgemini, even though there is investment to be made (Kalwani & Narayandas, 1995). Lastly it is also imperative that sales people and the rest of the organisation understand the client, as it is often the case that there exists a gap in understanding (Sharma, 1999, p. 32).

The I3 programme has been abandoned in November 2009 and replaced with a new programme, called Business as Unusual (Capgemini S.A., 2009), however it is said that the program was a good start in focusing the organisation across three distinct initiatives for a long time ever. Looking at "1 ", it can be seen that most companies try to increase client intimacy through specialised "Hit-Teams" as Clutterbuck describes it (Clutterbuck, 1998) that gain domain specific knowledge. However it appears little things are done for industrialisation in the back-end and innovation.

4.7 The second Transformation Wave: Business as unusual

Besides a structural change towards the client end, a delivery change with the build-up of services offerings that fit more towards the clients' integrated needs are suggested to happen. Here it is important not only to show them as marketing programs, but to underpin them with real delivery offerings. If that is the case these offerings can have a real chance to turn around a divisionalized organisation into a market-based organisation, as Conant (Conant & J., 1999) observed, along with (Fiocca, 1982). With the launch of the Business Unusual initiative in November 2009, the following initial high-growth discipline offerings (Capgemini S.A., 2009) have been launched, some more might follow:

4.7.1 Business Information Management

Business Information Management (abbreviated: BIM) - The external launch took place in November, leveraging Capgemini's various sector points of view and differentiating us against the more generic, tools only, competitors.

The goal, as Capgemini (Capgemini S.A. , 2010) describes it is to "help companies manage the increasing volume and flows of information in order to generate maximum business insight".

The group sees their existing assets as follows:

- The overall vision of the information organization
- The technology expertise and
- The Organizational methodology for analysis of client's needs.

In order to do so, the company has technology partnerships with vendors in that area, such as EMC, IBM, Microsoft and others. To assemble the components, Capgemini utilises an in-house methodology, called Intelligent Enterprise to develop this offering that can be sold as a "service package". The strategic fit of the BIM initiative is shown on Table 4-2: Business Information Management – Map.

Disciplines Covered	Service delivered	Extent of Business Opportunity (Small, Med, Large)	Onshore/offshore
Consulting Services	Consulting on business integration	L	OnShore
Technology Services	Consulting and implementing on information integration	L	Analytics onshore
Outsourcing Services	Application Management Services, Datacenter Services	M	Application services offshore
Sogeti	Testing, Body shopping	M	Body shopping mostly onshore

Table 4-2: Business Information Management – Map

4.7.2 Application Lifecycle Services

Application Lifecycle Services (abbreviated: ALS) entails services of how to better manage the complexity of a large applications portfolio. It is designed to help clients to cut costs and gain flexibility "by handling their entire application lifecycles, from development to maintenance, including testing, integration and organisation".

Disciplines Covered	Service delivered	Extent of Business Opportunity (Small, Med., Large)	Onshore/Offshore
Consulting Services	Consulting on the right set of organisational structure and culture in order to reduce costs and improve revenues	M – L	Onshore
Technology Services	Application Services	L	Mostly offshore
Outsourcing Services	Application Services	L	Mostly offshore
Sogeti	Testing and Body shopping for specific services.	M	Mostly offshore

Table 4-3: Application Lifecycle Services vs. Capgemini Business Units

Capgemini writes (Capgemini S.A. , 2010) that it bundles the know-how and expertise of the main disciplines Technology Services and Outsourcing.

The goal is to maximise client application potential and utilise the following group assets:

- Business know-how
- "Numerous products"

- Industrial capabilities
- Original methods for rationalizing applications

The latter might be a critical asset, the other three points still need to be proven to be considered real assets or whether this is just marketing vapourware.

Application lifecycle services do consist both of an analytical part and a maintenance and development part. Many of the application maintenance and development parts will be performed out of India.

4.7.3 Testing

On testing services, the goal "is to assure the quality of the software used by companies through optimising the software testing process".

Capgemini here relies on its assets such as

- A tried and trusted testing methodology
- A set of product references, as noted more than 500 worldwide
- And the rapid mobilization of industrial capabilities

Capgemini sees this as a business opportunity in at least three areas: technology services, outsourcing services and mainly: Sogeti. At the same time, many of the testing facilities will be conducted out of India with a growing facility there.

Testing applications' internal launch is averaging around one €1-2 million deal per week, capitalizing on the strengths of the existing Sogeti and Financial Services testing capabilities.

Disciplines Covered	**Service delivered**	**Extent of Business Opportunity**	**Onshore/Offshore**
Consulting Services	Developing test strategies for business to minimize risks	M	Partly offshore
Technology Services	Testing of applications	L	More onshore
Outsourcing Services	Application Management Testing	L	Offshore
Sogeti	Testing	L	Offshore

Table 4-4: Testing - Mapping towards Capgemini Discipline Units

4.7.4 Smart Energy Services

Here, Capgemini wants to help companies, especially in the utilities sector – such as Energy Providers – to face the numerous challenges of smart management of energy. The value proposition itself is that using smart energy services (abbreviated. SES), utility companies can save in energy production and distribution and therefore reducing capital expenditure whilst providing the service to its clients at a similar or even improved level. Typically, without smart energy services the utility companies need to preserve energies for peak consumption, whilst letting idle capacities stand there for the rest of the day.

Capgemini (Capgemini S.A. , 2010) sees the following as group assets to develop this service:

- An extensive knowledge of the sector
- Smart meter and smart grid solutions that can be reutilized for every client
- Products in both North American and in Europe and a
- Dense network of technology partners.

Disciplines Covered	Service delivered	Extent of Business Opportunity	Onshore/Offshore
Consulting Services	Consult on the extent of smart metering.	M	Onshore, consulting design might be offshore
Technology Services	Develop and implement Smart-X Solutions for clients	L	Design on-shore, implementation offshore
Outsourcing Services	Outsource the operation of Smart-X installments	L	Infrastructure onshore Management offshore
Sogeti	Provide specific body shop Services for Smart-X solutions	M	Offshore

Table 4-5: SES - Mapping towards Capgemini Discipline Units

As this service theoretically applies to the whole energy sector as a globally replicable service, its chances of developing this as a "service as a product" might be very high, however there are existing energy consulting companies and suppliers that might also see this as a business opportunity.

4.7.5 Infostructure Transformation Services

In the infostructure transformation services (abbreviated: ITS) area, Capgemini tries to "rationalise organisations' IT infrastructures to help them to migrate to cloud computing", as the company writes in her annual report.

To say it more precisely and without marketing jargon, companies might utilise Capgemini as a service provider who provides to them IT services wherever they are, wherever they need it at a predictable cost with the technology that just might be at the right price-performance point in order for Capgemini to stay competitive in the market.

Capgemini here uses the following assets, as depicted in its annual report:

- Capability of mobilizing all of the Capgemini disciplines
- Partnership with major cloud providers
- The reputation for integrating cloud computing solutions.

Disciplines Covered	Service delivered	Extent of Business Opportunity	Onshore/Offshore
Consulting Services	Consulting on where an IT infrastructure can be transformed into an infostructure	M	Offshore developed templates, offshore consulting from remote
Technology Services	Tools and automation systems and consulting towards providing an infostructure	M	Mostly offshore
Outsourcing Services	Outsourcing an infrastructure and getting an infostructure provided	XL	High offshore components, infrastructure might be centrally localised onshore
Sogeti	Tools and body shopping to sustain a current infrastructure and to provide wisdom how to implement an infostructure, over time	M	Offshore, where possible.

Table 4-6: ITS vs. Capgemini business units

This infrastructure transformation services might have the longest standing heritage inside Capgemini. Therefore this initiative probably can draw upon more resources than the rather shallow text in the annual report is transporting. Several steps, however, are indicated:

1. Data centre optimization and consolidating and upgrading physical facilities
2. Virtualization by converting assets like servers, storage and applications into virtual environments
3. Unified communications, to accelerate and facilitate the interaction of individuals and organization entities with each other.

Cloud computing services: to extend the virtual environment towards a "cloud-based" solution.

4.7.6 "Business as Unusual" seen across disciplines and internationally

All of those initiatives have a cross-discipline element inside, thus they have a boundary-spanning role where a lead sales element is required in order to win.

The key is to make clear as to what extent the existing lines of business benefit from new initiatives, how they can support those initiatives and put targets against it. At the same time, by defining this set of business initiatives, the initiatives put forth with I3 continue somehow to live:

- **Innovation** will be packaged around five distinct service offerings which might be productized. By focusing around those service offerings, the innovation might be centred and clustered.
- By the **productization** of the service offering, an **industrialization** of those services will occur, whilst at the same time being able to move parts of this industrialized service production off-shore in order to reduce labor costs and increase the skill potential
- Client **intimacy** might also increase, as the offerings might be specific in solving certain clients' needs. Definitely, the chasm between being specific to the clients and having a standard offering will continue to exist.

With those initiatives, Capgemini also hopes to step up in terms of employee productivity and sales productivity. The chances do exist, as it is known that products with distinct features are more easily sold than custom developed services that need to be well-understood by sales people. At the same time, by having defined a product which might be a service offering, this service offering can be optimised, like an engine in a box.

4.8 Sources of intercultural dilemmas within the organisation

In a multinational, multidivisional company, intercultural dilemmas do exist from the following dimensional scopes of the company:

- **Division** – every division has a different business model and purpose – otherwise it would not be a division
- **Departments** within a division – for example Sales vs. Finance vs. Delivery vs. Purchasing. There are role-based goals which automatically generate their own goal conflicts. Sales for example are measured upon a (profitable) signing, delivery might be measured upon client satisfaction and profitability, and finance might be measured upon the overall profit rate of the company. Purchasing might be measured upon savings of the overall purchased volume.
- **Country** to Country. When working with different countries the country itself has its own culture, which has been described by Lewis (Lewis, 2007) and Hofstede (Hofstede, 2001) to a large extent.
- **Front**-office within Service Centre (**Back**-office).
- Management and employees.
- Headquarter vs. subsidiary

To show this at the example of the company Capgemini, the following empirical intercultural dilemmas are inherent.

- **Sales versus Delivery**: Sales tends to close the deal and will go after the sales negotiations are ended. Often, many deals need to be closed with promises of improvements, innovation and superior services. Those promises then need to be delivered. The services delivery teams need to take on the service once the deal is made and then work the client for the next years. Here, every innovation typically is causing more effort and costs. As a result it is of importance to bridge the expectation generated during the sales phase and at the same time define hard contractual obligations for the delivery team in order to execute the promises made.

- **Germany vs. Switzerland**: As with every multinational country in the D-A-CH region working between Switzerland and Germany, a certain part of misunderstanding and friction comes from the barrier between those two – highly neighbored cultures, Germany and Switzerland. As close sight, Germany has a higher power distance, a lower tendency for pragmatism generating a sense of harshness and stubbornness for the Swiss (Küng, 2007, p. 168f). When working with Swiss clients, this needs to be reflected, that Swiss often appear to be very friendly, however cool in their emotions.
- **Frontoffice vs. Backoffice (onshore vs. off-shore9**: With a client-facing front-office the pressure towards clients is high – at the same time a backoffice – located in Poland or India has different dynamics. They are less dependent upon client responsiveness but merely upon cost effectiveness, process adherence or people dynamics within this back-office. Therefore the systemic boundaries and functioning need to be understood and made clear to each other that there are differences in values and beliefs (Capgemini S.A. , 2008). This chasm between onshore vs. offshore will increase, as with an increased productisation of the services field, services will become industrialized and moved off-shore, resulting in a move of the center of gravity (power, control, profit and loss responsibility) over time from the front-end units towards the back-end units.
- **Tech Services vs. Outsourcing Services vs. Consulting Services**: With a multi-divisional organization, cultural gaps do occur between those divisions, often caused by the education-specific origin of the people and mainly by the different goals and business models of the divisions. Inside Capgemini, Technology Services is to take care of mid-term business that transforms a status quo using a software development methodology and tool into a new one. People often work in teams in order to achieve this goal- developing software together. Sharing knowledge has therefore become a common ground as the knowledge of the group is more than the sum of the parts of the individuals. Outsourcing services initially transforms a client by taking over its work, then the latter work needs to be taken over and executed flawlessly for years in order to adhere to the Service Level Agreements (SLAs) made with clients and in order to become profitable. Knowledge sharing amongst individuals happens – apart from the deal design phase – through controlled processes and procedures in order to become codified and replicable and – off-shorable into back-office centers. Consulting Services' business model mainly consists in advising and consulting clients as to how to transform their business or parts of their business, making assessments on the potentials and show plans in order to execute on the gaps of a strategic ambition (Capgemini S.A., 2009). Despite this, consulting refrains from the execution

of this transformation as this is not part of the business. Therefore the risk of execution – or reward – stays with the client. At the same time, the sharing of knowledge is detrimental for the individual's consultant's success – as her personal knowledge is an asset that needs to be accumulated. Due to the nature of these different business models the intercultural chasms when working together need to be acknowledged.

- **Management vs. Employees**: Certainly there is also a chasm between management and employees which comes from the nature of goals such as individual contribution vs. profitability of the entire operation etc. Much literature has been written about this topic which will not be repeated here.

4.9 Competitive practices of setting up IT Services sales forces

In order to understand better how to sell efficiently, it is worth looking at the competition. Not everything that works well with competitors works with the own company; however, there are a series of good practices that can be taken on as a template. Here, we will look at several aspects of the companies IBM, CSC and Swisscom IT Services.

4.9.1 IBM - Sales and Distribution Group as client integration layer

IBM has established a thin layer of sales force beyond its typical divisional specialised sales force for hardware, software and service. IBM calls this "Sales and Distribution Group" (IBM Corp., 2010) and is in charge of managing key accounts ("integrated accounts"), important major clients ("cluster accounts") and a broad variety of clients ("General business") through a unified way. This sales and distribution group then funnels and leads through a CRM system plus a personal interaction to the sales representatives of the respective business units, such as Systems and Technology Group, Software Group, Global Technology Services and Global Business Services. This method has proven to be effective to allow for synergies in base situations, however, it has proven by own experience far from successful to establish major new deals, as mostly new deals will be conducted with new or different stakeholders within the client that need to be identified.

Relationship Sales Career: As a result, IBM – due to the nature of its integrated business, has been on the forefront of implementing a relationship sales procession. IBM has formulated a view of the profession such as described below – according to IBM (IBM, 2009); the relationship professional, being part of an overall sales profession role (IBM Corporation, 2005) is in charge of being the key interface towards the client at a senior level and making sure that the business between the client and IBM flows and expands. However, the relationship professional does not necessarily need to do all the selling but rather enable an ecology that helps the rest of IBM to sell and work flawlessly.

IBM states, that the relationship sales career is founded upon the individual's capability to work with the client as a strategic partner. This follows the postulates of Holt (Holt, 2003, p. 26) and Rogers (Rogers B. , 1999, p. 60) as a boundary spanning leadership role. In order to do so, and by being a primary counterpart for a large account, the relationship sales processional needs to understand key business issues and requirements. For these, the relationship sales professional needs to map the right business and technology solutions of IBM in order to generate success.

In summary, as IBM (IBM, 2009), writes, the Relationship Sales professional has the "mission to build strategic relationships between IBM and their Client(s) and to attain IBM's business objectives". Their success is dependent on the value they bring to their clients, ultimately.

SVCT – Strategic Value Creation Team: However, new opportunities of larger size need to overcome existing relationships or perceptions. In order to overcome this, IBM has built a special sales force called the **Strategic Value Creation Team,** piloted in Europe. In 2006, IBM Europe has setup a team of cross-divisional deal makers and solution experts directly reporting into the European Head of Sales (Pop, 2009). This team, consisting of roughly 50 senior executives has had the mission to identify, develop and drive further large scale engagements and by the nature of their leaders be able to put resources behind the best of the best deals. The value creation teams are organised European-wide by Industry, such as Banking, Insurance, Oil and Gas, Telecoms and others. IBM has organised the whole as a "virtual team" with mostly letting the people residing on their original places and geographies. A major effort was needed to bring the people in organisations together. Key for IBM especially is to pre-qualify any leads through a value analytics team that writes Blue Books, as Pop elaborates.

4.9.2 CSC and its Global Sales Hub

For larger scale engagements, Computer Science Corp. has setup a global "hit team" of senior deal leaders, bid managers, architects and experts (CSC, 2007)[12] that work from deal to deal regardless of European Geography. However it is said that with the on-going maturity of a country, the country organisations are gaining more weight in moving deals forward. This is a typical example of a hit-team organisation, as described by Clutterbuck (Clutterbuck, 1998).

4.9.3 Swisscom IT Services and its vertical business units

An example of a domestic contender is Swisscom IT Services.

Swisscom IT Services is a leading Swiss IT Services company which has setup vertical special business units to focus around solutions for special verticals such as health care insurers, private banks and other industries. Several business unit acquisitions of smaller Swiss firms have complemented the portfolio. In order to execute on this, Swisscom IT Services has purchased subsidiaries, such as Comit

[12] Several colleagues of the author have joined from CSC, thus some word-of-mouth experience has been spread about this organisational setup.

(Swisscom IT Services AG, 2005)[13] for Banking and thus verticalized the business where possible. Here solution leaders and domain experts are to be assigned in a "stable team" around a solution and an existing market. The big advantage of Swisscom IT Services is its clear presence in Switzerland with a big Swiss brand name. The big disadvantage is the lack of global execution. In other words, as soon as Swiss International firms want to go abroad – and with an export ratio of more than 70% of Swiss GDP (OSEC, 2009) which is often the case – Swisscom IT Services does not provide an integrated value proposition. As a result, its strategic space is limited.

4.10 Conclusion of chapter

Capgemini in its very nature is amongst the Top-10 leaders of the IT services and consulting firms worldwide. Capgemini has a strategic space by both being globally integrated and locally present and has its key advantage from being independent from any franchise – such as geography, key major clients, key legacy product or service platforms or any other type of limitation. However at the same time this makes the company risk-averse, all-too-often too much risk averse.

In order for Capgemini to achieve growth both in terms of revenue and margin it needs to keep its cost structure competitive and find new areas of success other companies cannot copy quickly. The biggest threat both for revenues and margins will most likely not come from the "old" players such as IBM but rather from the Indian-originating service providers as they too at a large extent have already mastered the Indian Delivery earlier than others.

However, the big chance of Capgemini is to be both present on the Indian shore and combine this with a local delivery and sales execution arm that provides more proximity and intimacy for the clients.

For Germany and Switzerland, Capgemini still has a need for improvement in market share and needs to re-address its go-to-market approach if it really wants to become as successful as for example in France or the U.K.

[13] The author has worked with Swisscom IT Services as a key account director from Sept 2003 to Dec 2005.

5 Research Methodology

This chapter details the research methodology employed for the base research to refine the theoretical framework that was developed from the literature in Chapter 2.

The purpose of the base research is to see how an integrated services organisation can increase its market share by refocusing its capabilities and by actively pursuing sales management as a discipline in its own right. This chapter shows the methodology, as shown in Figure 5-1.

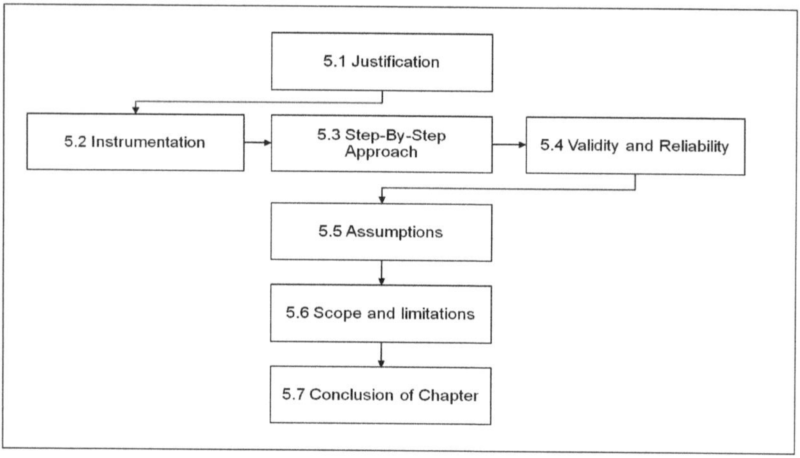

Figure 5-1: Chapter Five Overview

5.1 Justification of survey methodology for this research

This section justifies the methodology used in this research, describes the approach to theory construction and, lastly, it depicts the research design of this research.

From looking at the status quo of the organization of Capgemini in Germany and Switzerland, the research will compare organizational setups of several competitors and then look at the gaps to analyse what ingredients of the organizational setups with respect to sales organizations might make a company more successful.

5.1.1 Research paradigm

The paradigm for this research can be classed as behaviouristic positivism or realism (Mises, 1951), because it rejects metaphysical speculation and attempt to reduce statements and propositions to pure logic. This reality can only be explored by empirical research because of limited human understanding of the complexity of people who can change their behaviour (Schunk, 2008, p. 48).

The issue regarding limited knowledge of external reality was addressed in two ways. Firstly, data was acquired through exploratory research across multiple sources (Chapter 2) and the survey study (Chapter 6). Secondly, the conceptual model was employed to test survey data in this research to discover relationships among variables.

5.1.2 A two-stage research design for this research

According to Bryman (Bryman & Bell, 2007), research design plays an essential strategic role in the choice of the data collection methods, but has more tactical decisions involved, such as the scaling of answers or the formulation of ambiguous and unambiguous questions.

An exploratory research will be initially carried out in order to gain background information and to generate hypotheses toward the research problem. More specifically, the market of Capgemini has been identified and its sales management practices have been described using academic literature to help identify various practices, like territory and account planning, sales measurement and structuring. Bryman and Bell (Bryman & Bell, 2007, p. 326) propose that a good examination of available secondary data is a conditio sine qua non prior collecting primary data and to avoid duplication which has been done here.

Descriptive research will be performed after having conducted a solid review and analysis of available secondary data in order to test and to answer specific research hypotheses which were derived from secondary data. The survey method was chosen as it has been the most useful technique in descriptive research which is able to gather primary data, especially in order to verify opinions, attitudes and beliefs (Knorr-Cetina, 1993).

5.2 Instrumentation

Questionnaire Step	Activity
1.	Decide the information required.
2.	Define the target respondents.
3.	Choose the method(s) of reaching your target respondents.
4.	Decide on question content.
5.	Develop the question wording.
6.	Put questions into a meaningful order and format.
7.	Check the length of the questionnaire.
8.	Pre-test the questionnaire.
9.	Develop the final survey form.

Table 5-1: Nine Step Approach for Questionnaires

According to practitioners, such as the UN organisation FAO (FAO, 2008) and academia like Bryman and Bell (Bryman & Bell, 2007), there are roughly nine concrete steps involved in the development of a questionnaire, as Table 5-1 shows.

5.3 Step-By-Step Approach

5.3.1 Step 1 - Decide the information required

The questionnaire for this study served a number of functions by coding research objectives into a series of questions. All questions and formats were standardised so that all respondents faced the same stimuli. Due to the online format, the questionnaire was designed in a way to ask comprehensible questions to motivate respondents to cooperate and accurately complete all the questions asked. Simultaneously, it facilitated and simplified administration and data processing.

In order to overcome the issue of non-response (Bryman & Bell, 2007, p. 245f), this survey carefully designed a process of require permission, provide reward, and follow-ups. First, the company's permission was required before questionnaires were distributed, next it was made clear of the importance for further sales research.

5.3.2 Step 2 - Sampling considerations – Define the target respondents

Another crucial area in conducting a field survey was to determine which subjects should be surveyed and to achieve proper class groupings (Minto, 1996, p. 91) to obtain the appropriate information for the research problem (Bryman & Bell, 2007, p. 257f). The steps in selecting the subjects for this research have been derived from Davis and Cosenza (Davis & Cosenza, 1993, p. 120f) and Desarbo & Zikmund (Desarbo & Zikmund, 2009, p. 46f). It was determined inside Capgemini by the following frame limitations:

- All Business Development personnel in Outsourcing (n=17)
- All Vice Presidents in Consulting Services except Enabling Services VPs (Finance, HR, Legal) (n= 22, originally 23)
- Select Vice Presidents and Area Leaders in Technology Services (n=10)
- Countries covered: Germany, Austria, Switzerland

Some parts of the survey – especially around sales management - have originally been published at von Gamm in the realms of a Sales Management thesis (von Gamm, 2010) and was resampled, because in one area – TS SAP or badged here TS AM - had to be excluded for this dissertation, as the area leader wanted to have a highly distinct level of confidentiality and on top of this specifically asked to query two named people. In the sample drawn, the respondent who self-identified himself as being working within this area was therefore excluded. From the other areas, the leaders had no objections on this research.

5.3.3 Step 3 - Defining the target respondents and the survey method

Being an IT company, the most appropriate survey collection was through an on-line tool, called thesistools.com. The relevant people to be surveyed were identified through corporate directories. Beyond this, the data analysis tool behind was able to provide the graphics and statistics in Chapter 4. The survey has been brought active by putting it on-line on November 3rd, 2009 using an Email to all invitees, and then sent with reminders two times on November 15 and November 23.

5.3.4 Step 4 - Choose question content

The next step in questionnaire development was to draft the questionnaire with the knowledge of the research objectives, characteristics of respondents, the communication method and approximate length of the questionnaire. Principles of good questionnaire design were adopted to minimize measurement errors.

5.3.5 Step 5 - Develop the question wording

The scale questions were all close-ended following a simple structure that is less demanding from respondents. The format of responses determines the ease of answering for both sides – researcher and surveyed persons – as well as validity and reliability of the survey (Bryman & Bell, 2007). Close-ended questions were used wherever possible due to the large scale survey approach, and were kept as simple and short as possible. Five-point Likert type scales, with all points labelled, were used for collection of most of the data.

5.3.6 Step 6 - Put questions into a meaningful order and format.

Questions were ordered from the most interesting and topic related at the beginning to personal information at the end. Also, questions with similar structure were grouped together.

5.3.7 Step 7 - Check the length of the questionnaire.

The questionnaire has a total length of 52 questions, of which 90% are multiple choice "Likert-type" questions. Three questions were text-based questions, where people had to express with their own words regarding suggestions on how to improve specific points inside the firm.

5.3.8 Step 8 – Pre-Test the questionnaire

As mentioned in ***Section 3.3.4,*** the validity and reliability of the questionnaire were reflected in the pre-testing stage. Then minor changes to the wording and content were made to the questionnaire based on the feedbacks from academic staff and respondents.

5.3.9 Step 9 – Distribute and administer the survey

After pre-testing and re-testing, the survey was administered through the tool thesistools.com – This tool has been proven to be successful with other academic surveys inside Capgemini and therefore was a tool of choice because of its intrinsic reputation. The response rate was very high with a response total rate of roughly 50%. Generally, there are three approaches to encourage responses: minimize social costs, provide rewards to respondents and establish trust that the reward will be delivered (Bryman & Bell, 2007). In order to establish trust, an e-mail explaining the identity of the author, the nature and importance the survey, the guarantee that this survey has been approved by the Capgemini board and steps taken to ensure anonymity and privacy was sent out with every questionnaire. Social cost reduction has been achieved by e-mail response and rewards are intrinsic.

5.4 Validity and Reliability

In order to depict the current sales situation, this survey will be conducted on consulting and sales leaders. The validity of the content therefore is of prime importance, same as the validity of the construct itself. Validity will be proofed with the accuracy of measurements, as well as how well a specific research method is useful in claiming to measure (Davis & Cosenza, 1985). A reliable measure is considered as one which provides consistent results and where the random error is limited (Schrüfer, 1989). The survey itself has been validated by both the University of Portsmouth from an ethics perspective as well as by the board of Capgemini Central Europe. However there is a validity risk because asking sales leaders about their business might effect in an optimistically-biased ("half-full") response, whilst at the same time people might answer in a way that they stand there as a hero even in objectively unfavourable situations.

5.5 Assumptions

Based upon the hypotheses as outlined in Chapter 1.6, the following assumptions are being laid out:

- Execution of a sales management function is of benefit for selling and will outweigh the costs of the sales management function.
- A sales management function will enable a services organisation to achieve client results faster.
- Measurement of the outcomes can be executed
- A linkage between a reason of loss and an improvement plan to avoid a loss can be drawn upon.
- Ex-post reviews are half-ways fair and accurate and can depict – despite all organisational hiding after lost deals – a path for improvements.

- Losses and wins are not just statistical but based upon splendid sales and delivery excellence. Learnings can be drawn out of won and lost deals, implying that the reality of deals is not an isolated, un-repeatable event.

5.6 Scope and Limitations

Budget constraints: The whole research is to be set up in free time without disrupting the business from running and at low budget. As a result, the sample had to be limited to a medium size of influential people.

Limitations from structured observations: Bryman and Bell (Bryman & Bell, 2007, p. 297) point out that all post-bid interviews tend to be biased and subjective. Here it shows that even as people are learning from losses more than from wins, experience shows that they probably will keep those learnings on lost deals rather for themselves in order to keep their jobs protected.

Time constraints: An ideal to-be-state of an organization might not easily be implemented without major disruptions. Therefore, any changes in the plan needs to encompass the given status quo, the future state and the on how to get there.

Research deficiencies: As Plouffe et al (Plouffe, Williams, & Wachner, 2008, p. 80) point out, sales researchers "should continuously challenge themselves to consider the strategic nature of their work". In this research, the strategic nature is being maintained by looking not only at the tactical interaction of won and lost deals but also how the sales system can be modified into a broader context of the organisation embedded in a specific market place.

It also needs to be noted that senior executives need to be self-reflective about the possibility that the organisation might be limited, thus the survey is biased by nature by the executives' experiences. In order to test this, a counter-group theoretically would be needed to be set-up; however then the domain-specific knowledge queried in a series of questions is effectively nil.

5.7 Summary of chapter

To conclude the research conducted is a positivistic, realistic and behaviouristic two-phased research. It investigates into behaviouristic and belief patterns of senior sales leaders inside Capgemini. The results of the research might give an indication where beliefs need to be changed and behaviour must be changed by invoking a turnaround in order to sell more (Slatter, 1984, p. 127).

Despite having its limitations because of sample size and the bias of the colleagues being actors and reactors within the sales process itself, the research can be taken to draw conclusions for the improvement of the intercultural work and the sales process.

6 Capgemini Sales Survey Results and Findings

This chapter discusses the results and findings of the sales survey, including the text questions. It will first discuss all questions that had either on-off or "Likert" scales from Chapter 6.3 onwards and then draw from Chapter 6.4 into the four multi-text questions, where a more filigreed and subtle approach towards improving main imperatives of Capgemini – structural issues – client intimacy, innovation, industrialization have been asked. One of the main deductions then is the distil of the survey into the Hofstede dimensions, this is then discussed in Chapter 6.4. The structure is shown in Figure 6-1.

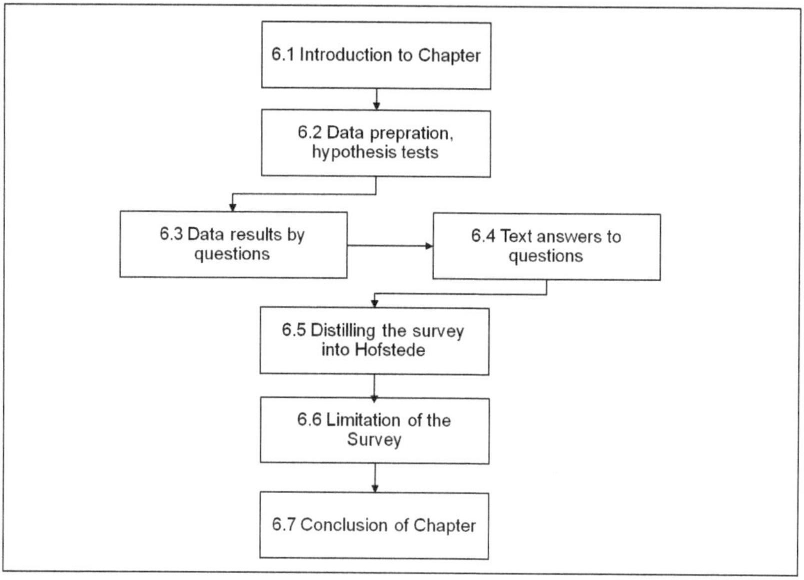

Figure 6-1: Chapter Six Overview

6.1 Introduction

The survey designed provided a series of results which has been grouped into clusters of answers and graphed via Excel.

The survey did consist of the following key areas:

- Basic Questions
- View of Performance
- Client facing activities
- Opportunity development
- Border-crossing activities

- Reasons of loss of opportunity
- Planning territories
- Planning accounts and opportunities
- Key account management
- Payment models for key account managers

6.2 Data preparation

The data then has been prepared using thesistools.com and an EXCEL table and a HTML version of the graphics has been downloaded.

6.2.1 Data Cleansing

Data cleansing has been provided by the tool – there were two versions available, one by extracting the non-responses and one by including the non-respondents into the percentage sets. For accuracy reasons, the non-respondents ("no answer") have been excluded. The respondents who were from the group "TS AM" (Question 2) have been excluded for data privacy reasons.

6.3 Data Results by questions

In the survey, about 50 people have been queried. The answers have been grouped by complex, basic questions, view of performance, reasons of winning, reasons of losing, on account management, payment models and on account and territory planning. The answers to text questions (n=49) have been analysed, distilled and condensed.

Because of the small sample size (n=23) more advanced or additional statistics could not be performed. Besides sampling by research group, averages and medians both per population sub-group – i.e. Technology Services or Outsourcing Services have been calculated. Despite the small size, the reliability and validity of the research can be taken into account, as a vote of those sales and consulting leaders do entail a high degree of experience from their field of expertise.

6.3.1 Basic Questions

As shown in Figure 6-2, the distribution of participants is almost equally distributed between Consulting services, Technology Services incl. Capgemini SD&M and Outsourcing Services, according to Q1.

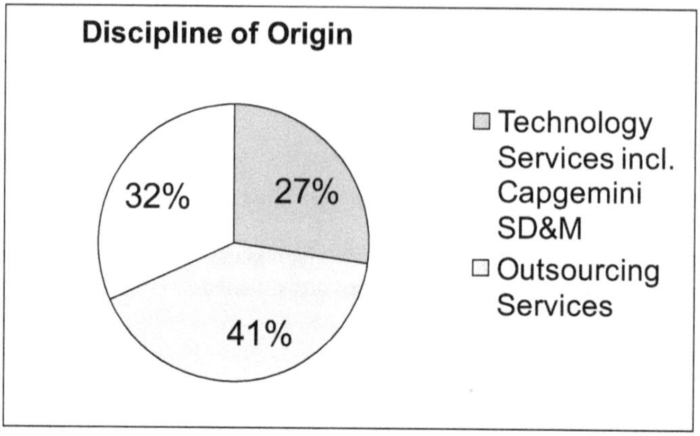

Figure 6-2: Discipline of Origin, n=22, Question 1

Most people see themselves being in "Business Development" roles, says Q2, depicted in Figure 6-3. This means they see themselves: Developing or closing sales situations. As there were seven people from Consulting services, but only one defining oneself as a consultant, the people queried apparently have a higher focus towards business development – means selling consulting services than consulting themselves.

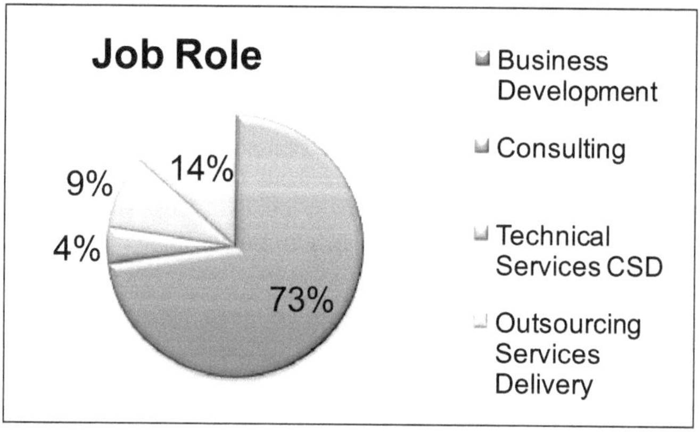

Figure 6-3: Job role covered, n=22, Question 2

This might correlate with the higher grade levels queried. As already indicated in the previous chapter, the people indicating themselves with "Tech Services AM" have been excluded from the survey, as the area leader did insist on a too far-reaching confidentiality clause.

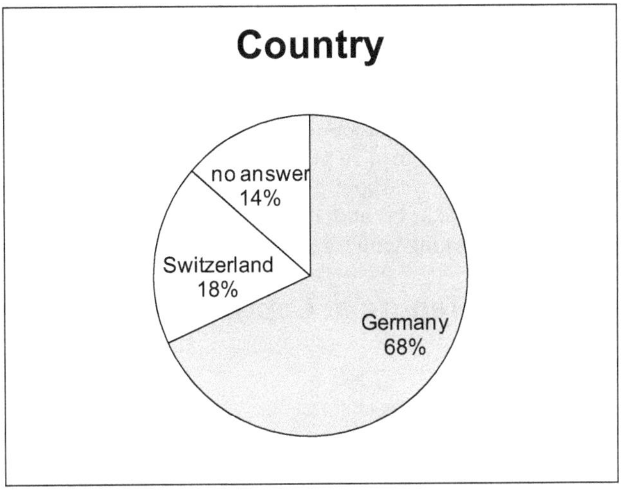

Figure 6-4: Country of origin, Question 3, n= 22

Q4 tells that despite the fact that people from Austria and Poland have been queried, no apparent response came from there or has been kept anonymous. Thus as Figure 6-4 shows, most respondents are from Germany, followed by Switzerland.

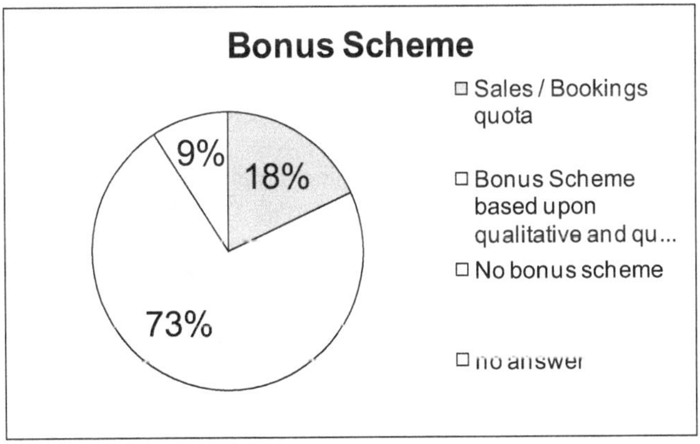

Figure 6-5: Bonus Scheme, n=22, Question 4

In Question 4, shown in Figure 6-5, 73% of all respondents did indicate that their bonus element – up to 33% of total salary - is based upon a bonus scheme and qualitative and quantitative elements. Here, the bonus payment is not directly correlated from one's individual sales success but rather from group performance. 18% of the respondents did indicate they have a sales/bookings quota solely related to personal contribution.

6.3.1.1 Question 5: Tenure

In this sample group, there is an interesting mix: 30% of the respondents did belong to Capgemini for longer than 10 years, and another 48% did belong to Capgemini between less than a year and up to three years, see Figure 6-6. Apparently – either in the sample or because of longevity reasons – there appears to be a gap between people working with Capgemini in the range of 3 to 10 years.

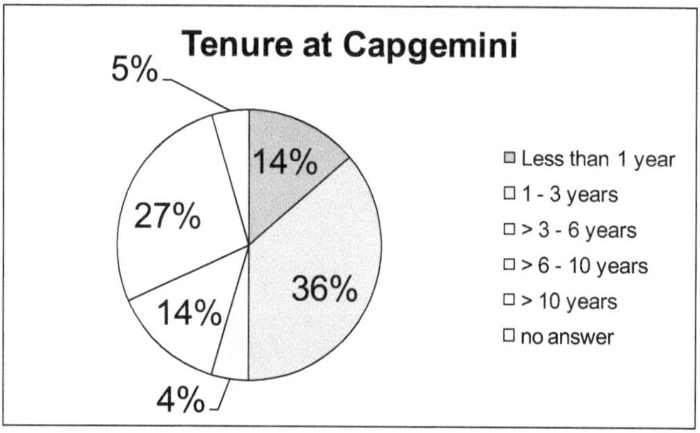

Figure 6-6: Tenure at Capgemini, n= 22, Question 5

6.3.2 View of Performance

Subjectively the performance of Capgemini group is being perceived as good to fair by 78% of all respondents, says Figure 6-7. Only 17% perceived the performance of Capgemini as below average. For research purposes, this question was designed as a biased question in order to sense a mood expression. What is striking here is the slight disassociation of Question 6 (left and middle graph) and Question 7. Apparently, only 56% of the respondents perceived the performance of the own business area as good to fair, whereas 13% of the sample perceived the performance of the own area as "bad" and 22% as "below average", meaning 35% did see a below-the bar performance of Capgemini. A big discrepancy is between the respondents of Tech Services versus the others.

Interestingly enough, combined with Question 7, most respondents did realize that Capgemini is performing opportunity misses, whereby 43% of the respondents think this is "sometimes" the case. It is a bit surprising that people apparently do not respond more often with "often" if market shares are considered (Capgemini S.A., 2009).

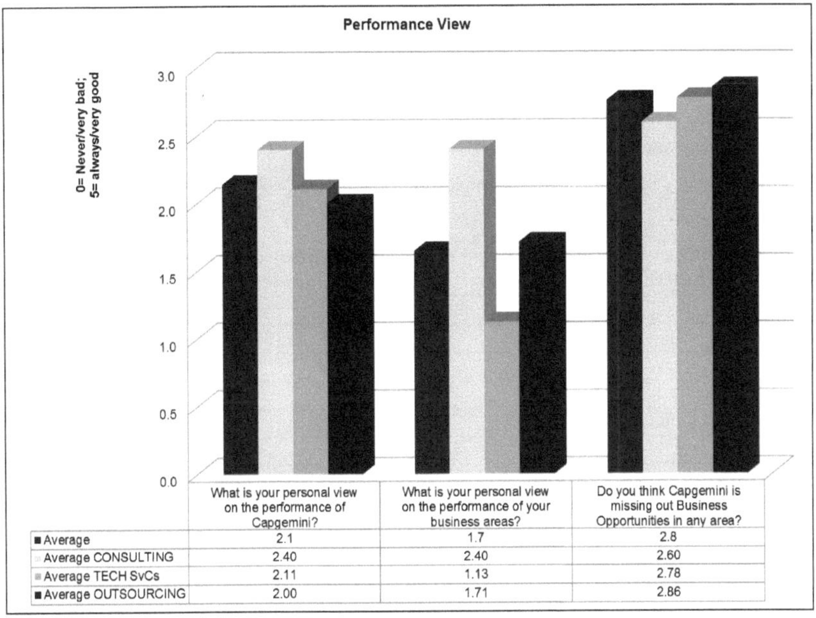

Figure 6-7: Performance View , Question 6 (a and b), Question 7 (third graph)

6.3.3 Client facing activities

The next set of questions did discuss client facing activities. It was especially surveyed as to how often the sample group surveyed were visiting clients, which type and variety of clients it was and what ought to be done in order to work better with clients.

6.3.3.1 Question 8: Client facing time

How often do you have (external) client contact (all contact counts, like phone calls, face to face visits, e-mail etc)?		
Every day	#7	32%
1- 5 times per week	#12	55%
1- 5 times per month	#2	9%
Less than one times per month.	#1	5%
no answer	#1	5%
n=22		

Table 6-1: Client contact, Question 8

It appears that most people (87%) meet clients at least once per week and 32% of all respondents appear to have client contact every day. However it is felt that the responses are biased as there is a huge push to “be in front of clients”.

Question 9 was a text question which will be treated in Section 6.4.

6.3.3.2 Question 10: Rightshore delivery model

Capgemini is utilizing a so-called Rightshore®[14] delivery model to deliver services from the best possible place. In Question 10, 79% of all respondents do feel that the Rightshore delivery model applied by Capgemini is helping people in their personal business goals.

Questions 11, 12 and 13 were allowing text comments which will be treated in Section 6.4.

Capgemini utilizes Rightshore as a means to promote a distributed delivery model How do you believe Rightshore helps you to achieve your business goals?	
A lot	#10 45%
A bit	#8 36%
Neutral	#4 18%
Is contra productive	#0, 0%
Is very contra productive	#0, 0%
n=22	

Table 6-2: Rightshore, Question 10

6.3.3.3 Question 14: Client encounter variety

Client encounter: In terms of client encounter, is your client encounter rather the same client or different clients	
Always the same	#2 10%
Mostly the same	#4 20%
Quite the same	#1 4%
Some varying clients	#8 14%
Many different clients	#5 25%
n=20	

Table 6-3: Encounter variety, Question 14

In terms of client variety, most respondents do meet different clients all the time, which means they are working on varying projects. For the validity of the survey this is of somewhat importance, as then the respondents can share views of different client activities in the following questions, thereby adding credibility

6.3.3.4 Questions 15: Client desire and fit when offering a solution

Client encounters in business development do have the ultimate goal of selling a service in Capgemini. If the question 15b is being rephrased into Question 15c, the respondents then uncover what is needed – a custom-made service for the clients, as otherwise, clients do not buy the service if it only fits "half-ways" well.

In diving deeper into this subject, it shows that if the service is only fitting half-ways, clients are more likely to seek alternatives from competition.

[14] Rightshore: Offshore vs. Onshore

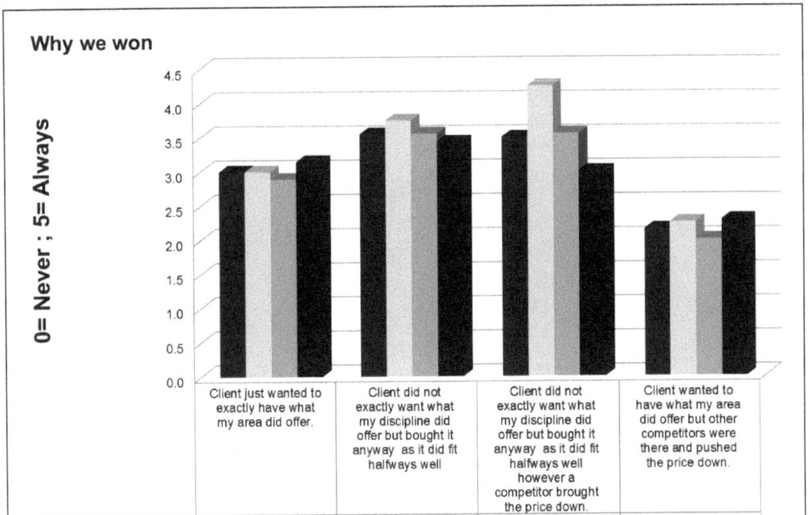

	Client just wanted to exactly have what my area did offer.	Client did not exactly want what my discipline did offer but bought it anyway as it did fit halfways well	Client did not exactly want what my discipline did offer but bought it anyway as it did fit halfways well however a competitor brought the price down.	Client wanted to have what my area did offer but other competitors were there and pushed the price down.
Average	3.0	3.6	3.5	2.2
Average CONSULTING	3.00	3.75	4.25	2.25
Average TECH SvCs	2.89	3.56	3.56	2.00
Average OUTSOURCING	3.14	3.43	3.00	2.29

Figure 6-8: Client desire and fit, Question 15

Competitive price action seems to be paramount, as even if clients do exactly get what they want from Capgemini, they query competitive offers in order to bring the price down. All of the respondents have experienced this during their career. In this set of questions, there is no big discrepancy between the disciplines found, except question 15c. So apparently the scope definitions of the clients go a much more rigid way in outsourcing than in other disciplines.

6.3.4 Opportunity development questions – Q16

This set of questions has dealt with how Capgemini sales leaders develop opportunities. Q16a indicates that most people do combine resources into new capabilities in order to provide extra value for the client, however there is one business unit – Consulting, that brings in the most "wild ideas".

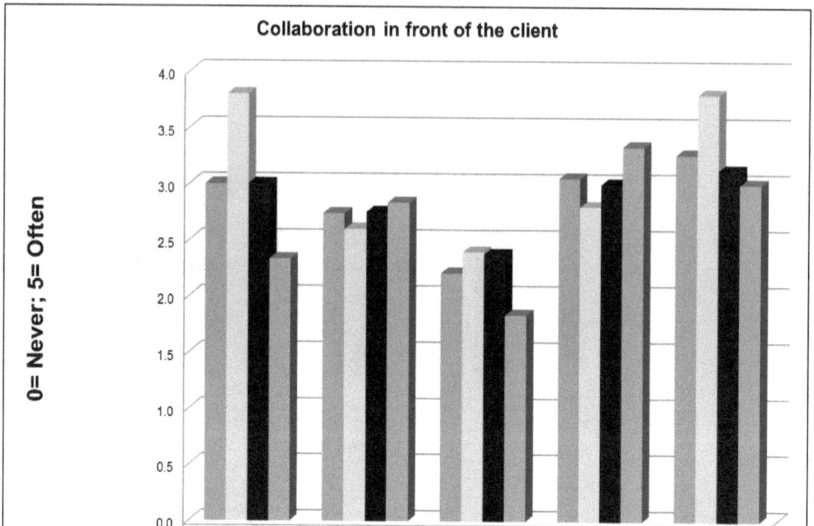

	Wild ideas	New and useful people	Bringing along other disciplines	People from other geographies	Bringing in third parties
Average	3.0	2.7	2.2	3.1	3.3
Average CONSULTING	3.80	2.60	2.40	2.80	3.80
Average TECH SvCs	3.00	2.75	2.38	3.00	3.13
Average OUTSOURCING	2.33	2.83	1.83	3.33	3.00

Figure 6-9: Client-facing Collaboration, Question 16

On Q16b, most people do encounter opportunities that apparently are of benefit to take colleagues from other business areas to the client. There is not a single answer that says "never" and at least more than 56% of the respondents do take this opportunity more than a single time.

Despite being a global company apparently taking colleagues from other geographies into their opportunity development discussions is of lesser significance.

The respondents do reflect a similar picture when bringing along third parties, i.e. suppliers, to the client opportunity development discussions. Thus, apparently what comes out of Question 18, 19 and 20 is that they are well connected at a merely local level with each other but as soon as it comes to the outside the involvement is kept more limited.

Question 17 was a text question which will be treated in Section 6.4.

6.3.5 Reasons of loss of opportunity: Questions 18

In terms of not winning, means: losing, the first answer to the Question Set number 18 was: **Price**. Clearly, most sales people do want to get the price down in order to have one disadvantage less in the game besides other factors, such as solution, political fit or risk. In comparing this with other factors, a further losing factor was a home-made one. It is being fully acknowledged that apparently the sales personnel was not able to bring the whole picture of Capgemini together – reasons here now left apart – and therefore quite often, the competition appears to "change the game". This implies that competitors are more capable of altering the decision process than Capgemini is capable of doing.

Question 18d shows that in most cases a reason of loss was not a lack of available references. Apparently though, in most of the cases Capgemini business developers sell services and solutions those are "proven and tried" with existing references. This combined with Question 16 – "Wild ideas" the rate of innovation does not appear to be very high, as otherwise the loss reason "lack of references" would appear to be much higher, especially on outsourcing services.

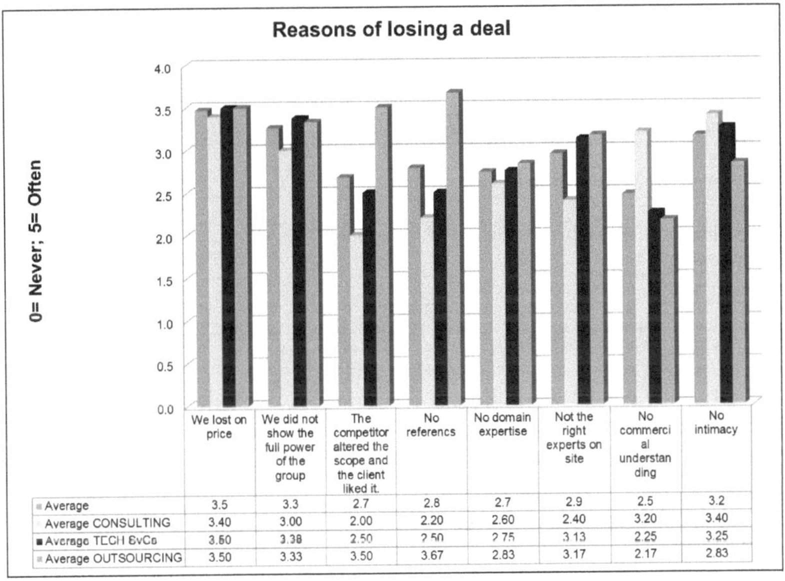

	We lost on price	We did not show the full power of the group	The competitor altered the scope and the client liked it.	No referencs	No domain expertise	Not the right experts on site	No commercial understanding	No intimacy
Average	3.5	3.3	2.7	2.8	2.7	2.9	2.5	3.2
Average CONSULTING	3.40	3.00	2.00	2.20	2.60	2.40	3.20	3.40
Average TECH SvCs	3.50	3.38	2.50	2.50	2.75	3.13	2.25	3.25
Average OUTSOURCING	3.50	3.33	3.50	3.67	2.83	3.17	2.17	2.83

Figure 6-10: Reasons of losing a deal, Question set 18

Same is the case in question 18c. The solutions sold are covered with a solid domain expertise. Answers to question 18f – a refinement of Q18e – show that there is somewhat a domain expertise available, but – when push comes to shove – the experts are often simply not available for a specific client situation. The group surveyed has a strong view that they do understand the client quite well in its commercial behaviour – solution appetite, risk taking and reward (Lemke, 2009). Thus, it appears even if lost, that the commercial behaviour was understood in most of the cases at 69%.

Looking at the results of Question 18g, people rather feel a lack of political intimacy of the client buying cycle. This is often the case. 48% of the respondents here feel that this is often the case, and an additional 13% feel that this is quite often the case.

It needs some further exploration what "political intimacy" might imply and then – why this is so often a reason of losing, especially in consulting. Looking at the last five answers to the questions then the main reasons of losing deals are price, lack of political intimacy and competitors in return being able to "change the game".

6.3.6 Planning accounts and opportunities

A series of questions have dealt with planning accounts and opportunities.

6.3.6.1 Question 19: Account Planning

Did you ever participate in one of the following planning activities:		
Account planning for one account with your business unit	#5	28%
Account planning for one account with more than one business unit	#9	50%
Territory planning for a multitude of clients with your business unit	#1	6%
Territory planning for a multitude of clients with more than one business unit.	#1	6%
Account planning with an external partner	#2	11%
n=18		

Table 6-4: Participation in planning sessions Question 19

On Q19, some people did complain that they were not given a multiple choice type answer for this question. However, this was made by design so that people were forced to answer what they were answering the most likely.

More than 60% of the respondents did participate at account planning sessions, and a multitude of them at account planning sessions with more than one Capgemini business unit.

However, the planning of the entire territories is more of a rare concept, same as performing account planning sessions with partners.

6.3.6.2 Question 20: Integrated account Management

Here, this basic introductory question has been designed to lead the people queried towards the account management and planning ideas.

Many people have heard of the concept of integrated account management, key account management or client account management and can use it.

On the concept of Integrated Account Management / Key account Management / Client Account Management:	
I heard of it and I think I do use it	#12 55%
I heard of it but I cannot apply it	#4 18%
I heard of it and I do not believe into ...	#0, 0%
I do not understand what you mean	#1 5%
no answer	#5 23%
n=22	

Table 6-5: Integrated Account Management, Question 20

6.3.7 Key account management: Question 21

A similar percentage of respondents as with Question 20 are able to see benefits for Capgemini to help coordinate activities for the client across multiple disciplines. Both key account managers and non-key account managers were asked and to a large extent – 70% of the people disagreed heavily or slightly that key account management would not add unnecessary overheads. What most people agree here to is that key account managers are capable of capturing more opportunities otherwise lost.

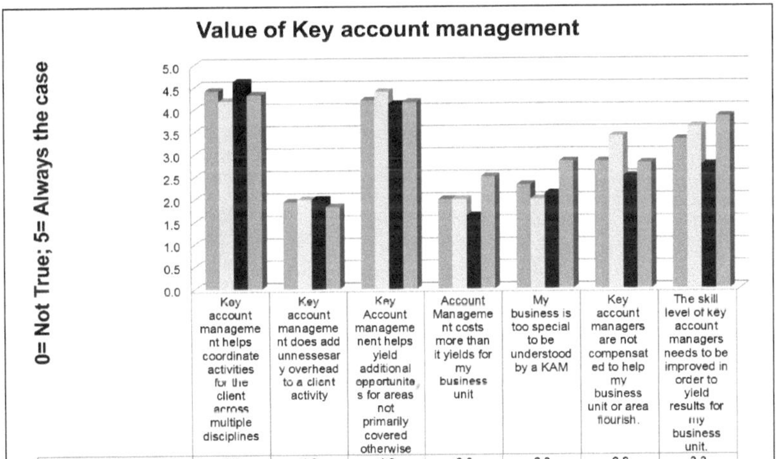

	Key account management helps coordinate activities for the client across multiple disciplines	Key account management does add unnessesary overhead to a client activity	Key Account managenent helps yield additional opportunites for areas not primarily covered otherwise	Account Management costs more than it yields for my business unit	My business is too special to be understood by a KAM	Key account managers are not compensated to help my business unit or area flourish.	The skill level of key account managers needs to be improved in order to yield results for my business unit.
Average	4.4	1.9	4.2	2.0	2.3	2.8	3.3
Average CONSULTING	4.20	2.00	4.40	2.00	2.00	3.40	3.60
Average TECH SvCs	4.62	2.00	4.12	1.63	2.13	2.50	2.75
Average OUTSOURCING	4.33	1.83	4.17	2.50	2.83	2.80	3.83

Figure 6-11: Value of Key account Management, Question Set 21

Question 21e, together with question 21d which in essence is the counter-question shows that respondents feel that key account management yields more and it also does cost less than it provides as results. Only one respondent has a different view. Nevertheless, it is felt that account managers often might lack the skills necessary to perform; therefore they would be needed to be highly integrated into one's business unit.

However, account managers do not seem to be compensated appropriately to help individual's business unit or area flourish. On 21g, it shows that the respondents feel that the specific skill levels of the account managers identified are not sufficient enough to perform and in order to yield results. No big discrepancies have been found between the different disciplines here.

6.3.8 Payment models for key account managers: Question Set 22

The following set of questions has dealt with paying for performance of key account managers. On 22a, people surveyed agree that the variable element is to be linked with the overall success of the business area the key account manager is serving. Most people do agree on Q22b that it is only to a certain extent that the variable element should be linked to the individual contribution of the sales person.

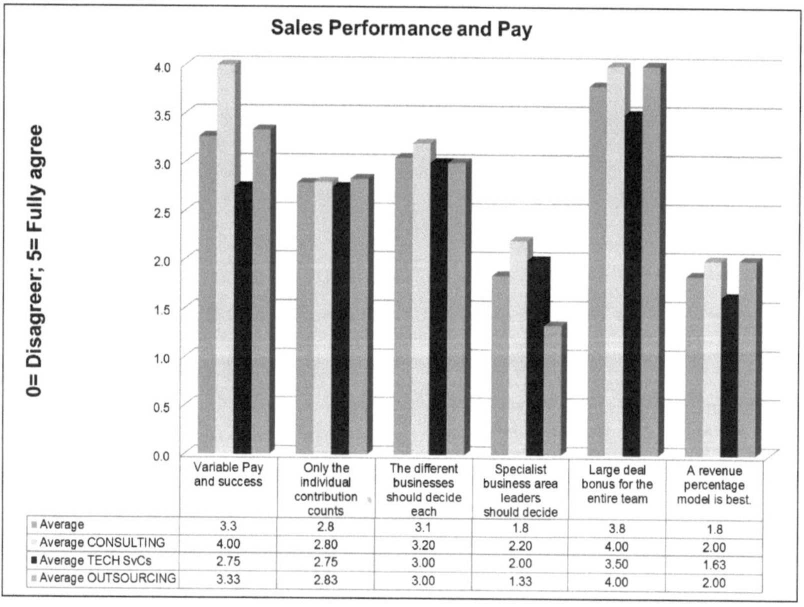

	Variable Pay and success	Only the individual contribution counts	The different businesses should decide each	Specialist business area leaders should decide	Large deal bonus for the entire team	A revenue percentage model is best.
Average	3.3	2.8	3.1	1.8	3.8	1.8
Average CONSULTING	4.00	2.80	3.20	2.20	4.00	2.00
Average TECH SvCs	2.75	2.75	3.00	2.00	3.50	1.63
Average OUTSOURCING	3.33	2.83	3.00	1.33	4.00	2.00

Figure 6-12: Sales Performance and Pay, Question Set 22

It might be implied that people feel contribution is very difficult to measure and feel that even if the individual contribution is being achieved under dubious aspects or, despite all best will, was not achieved, the variable pay should be paid anyway.

A slight agreement does exist in Q22c that the contribution expectation of key account managers should be decided upon by the different business units and pre-agreed at the beginning of the year. A majority of the people do agree with this largely (66%). On the other hand on Q22d, the specialist business areas should only decide as a team upon the pay of the key account managers. Here, especially outsourcing services has a different view.

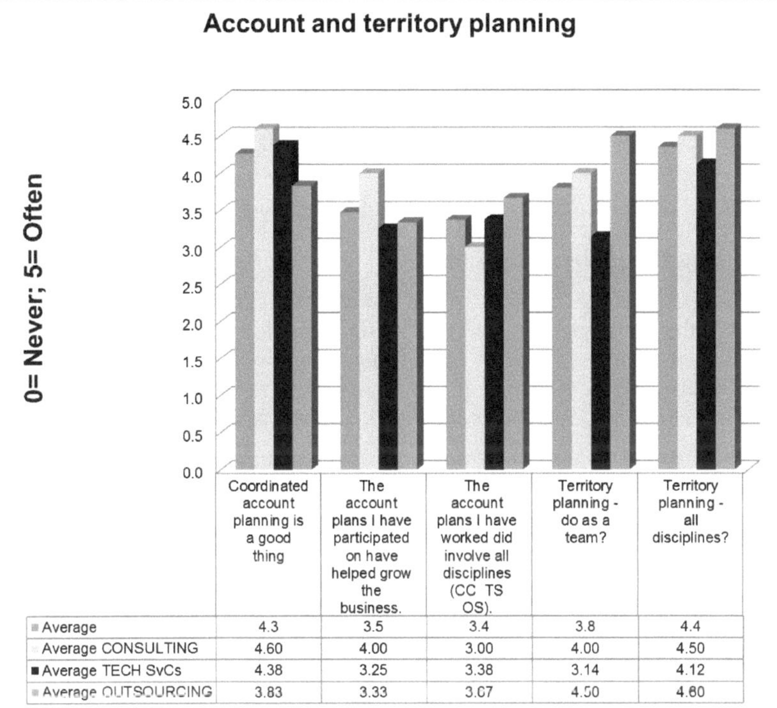

	Coordinated account planning is a good thing	The account plans I have participated on have helped grow the business.	The account plans I have worked did involve all disciplines (CC TS OS).	Territory planning - do as a team?	Territory planning - all disciplines?
Average	4.3	3.5	3.4	3.8	4.4
Average CONSULTING	4.60	4.00	3.00	4.00	4.50
Average TECH SvCs	4.38	3.25	3.38	3.14	4.12
Average OUTSOURCING	3.83	3.33	3.67	4.50	4.60

Figure 6-13: Account and territory planning, Questions 23 and 24

When it comes to a large deal as asked in Q22e, people agree that a pool bonus should be defined and be decided upon by the business unit leader as to how to distribute this deal bonus to all members according to contribution. This is being felt strongly by 30% of the respondents, and to a large extent by 60% of the respondents. What it implies is that people believe that a large deal in many ways is a team effort and usually cannot be achieved by a single individual. On the otherhand, account managers should not simply receive a certain percentage of the revenues – (Q22f) independent of their individual contribution. Thus, people do see contribution and work related to performance and not necessarily results related to performance.

6.3.9 Account and territory planning Q23 and 24

On Q23a a large amount of people responded that account planning is worth the time, indicating that they have positive experience out of the account planning sessions they have participated into, it is answered in Q23b. On Q23c, a repeat to Q19, many people did realize that account planning might involve more than one discipline. This is the same as territory planning in Q24a. It should be performed by a team and not so much top-down by a single individual. Interestingly enough, there are 8 people who did not respond to this question.

Q24b, being the last likert question of the survey is a forward-looking question to Question 19 and 23a. It is strongly felt that territory planning is to be conducted by a multiple of business units and rather less by individual business units.

Question 24 was a text question which will be treated in Section 6.4.

6.4 Comments by Colleagues

Besides the good participation of the surveyed sample (n=22 of 50) a striking fact was the good quality of comments supplied along with the survey. There were four dimensions in terms of text questions supplied – one was about the organisational setup of Capgemini, one was more specifically towards how to foster client intimacy, one about innovation and one about industrialisation.

The text answers were short – a one-line reply was only possible, however it was a good result in terms of what was delivered.

All answers have been edited for typographic and orthographic errors. It is also to be noted that mostly all of the respondents were not English native speakers but German or French Native speakers.

6.4.1 Comments on the organizational change:

This was a free text flow question on how to change the organisation of Capgemini in order to increase performance. It was a one-line question in order to let the questioned persons focus onto the essential.

Interpretation of descriptive statistics: Apparently, there is a lack in cross-discipline cooperation. It is felt that – unlike practices from Accenture or IBM, an alumni network is apparently not really being taken – or the activity is not known. It appears that there is duplication or an "unclean" org structure.

Apparently, a coherent sales plan is not known. People feel a certain disconnection between personal targets and personal responsibility. Further, what a commenter here shows is that outsourcing is more a matter of delivering through a globally integrated enterprise and not through a small set of franchises.

Text answers – "Organizational change"
Work more aligned towards clients, de-stack in the delivery organisation.
Foster cross-discipline cooperation
Build and manage Alumni network - attract and retain ""best people"" through a human-centred company culture.
Clean up the org structure. Give people right personal objectives so they will collaborate.
Develop and execute a sales plan
Explicit structure (= team, BDV budget, etc.) for Enterprise deals
"Think local, act global"; Sectors as first line dimension"; "build up a centralized, cross-discipline business development department and an according marketing support function. The BD/Sales directors should get cross-discipline goals and should sell the complete service portfolio of Capgemini (CS-TS-OS-LPS).
Focus on implementation of end to end delivery models over the whole organization (a lot is still just paperwork). Consequent use of same tools, processes methods over the matrix organization. Delegation of appropriate responsibilities and competencies to sales managers
Clearer focus on a defined portfolio - Follow the portfolio plan and bring it to mastery"
Define a cross discipline collaboration model including incentivation",
better background functions and support, like research, accurate client contact data, client org charts
better incentivation of team work and creating a spirit of team work
better tailored personal targets
In the outsourcing area it is necessary to act as one company with one global delivery concept. The advantage of CG in Consulting and Technology service (act on a regional, local bases, be flexible, do sometimes the same in all service lines and see, who performs) is here detrimental.
More solution sales via demand generation and stronger sector teams developing this solution in a global team
collaboration between CS,TS,OS and Businesses, select cross discipline business development activities", foster collaboration internally, motivate collaboration through competitive sales bonus, focus on major opportunities/large revenue instead of small/selective people related "own person selling", Big Deal Incentives
Integrate / get rid of disciplines. Global clients want *one* global supplier, not independent acting disciplines, cannibalizing its business more eager than the worst competitor.
serve clients on a global basis and cross disciplines
Adjust operational (governance) procedures to objective needs

Table 6-6: Answers: How should Capgemini improve its organisation?

The same applies in this section, it is asked to develop solutions more in a "pre-canned" variant, so that it can be deployed more rapidly. In some ways, this comment is paramount across several comments in several text questions. This appears to be a common trait. People want to work together in a more flawless way but apparently are impeded by systemic boundaries. Here, the question is whether there should be made a difference whether it is a big deal or a small deal to give incentives.

Clearly, management does not walk the talk. It talks about collaboration, the measures being taken are not enough however. Same here, it is asked to develop solutions more in a "pre-canned" variant, so that it can be deployed more rapidly.

6.4.2 Comments on improving client intimacy

This section covers the question "What is your specific view to improve client intimacy at Capgemini?" It was a one-line question in order to let the questioned persons focus onto the essential.

Text answer – "Client intimacy"
Work joint account planning
appropriate trainings and schools for all people with client contact
More focus on Account Management.; walk-out-talk as currently practiced
encourage staff (goals, bonus plan); Regular exchange of experiences (round tables)
Put sectors as first line dimension; set up a business development activity management with a proper controlling
Intimacy is a question of trust. If we deliver "OTACE" intimacy and if the client is interested in more "intimacy", the governance model is a profound method to work on that. Nevertheless collaboration with TS and CS could additionally help.
Build up a strong and effective back office that keeps track of daily operations to free up client time.
Be prepared to invest and systematically work with selected clients for a significant time period
More studies with the client. The senior management within outsourcing should get more involved towards the client (and not got stuck with a lot of internal stuff and reports)
stronger involvement of top management of Capgemini
More midterm thinking a real account teams not only one exec
Aligned and coordinated client contacts; put more emphasis on quality of services instead of focus on sales volume; Follow up on the I3 program; ... assign right skills to right clients
Focus on Rightshore references

Table 6-7: Answers: How should Capgemini work on client intimacy?

Interpretation of descriptive statistics: Apparently, account planning sessions are being conducted by line of business more. Additionally, some people complain about training, which might indicate a perceived lack of training. Apparently, the control and performance feedback loop does not exist. Obviously, it is felt that people working in front of the client are too much burdened with back office activities. Additionally, some respondents believe that the top management of Capgemini is disconnected. Here one respondent thinks that the quality of the services needs improvement. As it appears, the I3 program is not being followed up. The I3 Program has been discontinued in November 2009, in the middle of this querying period and has been substituted by a program called "Business Unusual".

6.4.3 Comments on improving client intimacy

Most account planning sessions are more conducted by the line of business. Additionally, some people complain about lacking training whilst the control and performance feedback loop does not exist. Moreover, it is felt that people working in front of the client are too much burdened with back office activities. Lastly, some respondents believe that the top management of Capgemini is disconnected from the front. One respondent thinks that the quality of the services needs improvement.

6.4.4 Comments on improving industrialization

This section does cover the question "What is your specific view to improve industrialization at Capgemini?" It was a one-line question in order to let the questioned persons focus onto the essential.

Text answer – "Industrialization"
Setup a product management organisation for services, work templates
That's going ok; develop more standards
simply speaking: professionalize it while start using it (KION)
that is taken care of and not the primary task for the near future
Regular exchange of experiences, consequent usage of existing knowledge tools
target setting & rewards; good example: new outsourcing services portfolio
see point 9 operating model; one ERP system; improve and automate processes within disciplines;
Create own unit for setting up joint and common consulting tools
improve knowledge management tools and processes to be able to industrialize
Get a real Global Delivery Model; build solutions
aligned education and sharing of knowledge; more knowledge sharing and less sales credit allocation
Follow up on the I3 program; We still are struggling to use standards at our own delivery, which the clients use for years now. Example: Ticketing System in OSCE

Table 6-8: Answers: How should Capgemini improve on industrialisation?

Interpretation of descriptive statistics: Interestingly enough, despite being an industrialized services company by its corporate DNA, people had the biggest issues in providing meaningful responses on industrialization. It is very likely that people do not really understand the concept of industrialisation in services and still need some more education around it (von Gamm, 2009). However, there are some good examples, such as that of processes in order to foster industrialisation that need to be established, like team meetings or to get a "real" global delivery model, whatever the adjective "real" means.

Apparently there are only a few people here who thought of an innovation in terms of providing organisation capability change, such as "providing a product management function for services, work templates".

Some people apparently do not even see a need to act and respond "that's going ok", which means that industrialisation of services might be less of an issue or an issue too big to be really discovered, yet inside sales-near functions within Capgemini.

6.4.5 Comments on improving innovation

This section does cover the question "What is your specific view to improve innovation at Capgemini?" It was a one-line question in order to let the questioned persons focus onto the essential.

Interpretation of descriptive statistics: Innovation is high on the radar screen with Capgemini being an innovation company. Even though one respondent also utters "we are innovative" but apparently does see the transfer of innovation missing. There are many people who see that listening to the clients and working together across boundaries might be of greater benefit in order to stimulate innovation.

Text answer – "Innovation"
Listen to the clients; take the best what the competitors have.
There is enough innovation; problem is we don't share it enough. So: Increase collaboration.
stronger 3 D and cross country approach
thought leadership survey (Global After sales)
support and enforce market orientation of staff (see answer to 9)
Regular exchange of experiences, focussed enhancements for employees
globalize innovation & distribute actively
Set up a small innovation team. Example can be the "Turn the lights on" project at Capgemini OS CE where some good examples are available for improvement of innovation inside our organization.
leverage knowledge between TS, CS, OS in a formal way
Think Tank / Board, Conduct innovation fairs in employee events; give SL clear tasks what to develop
invest in an infrastructure which enable innovation - make innovation a goal of everybody but also empower and enable everybody
More crossover initiatives (CC, TS, OS)
Regular client ASE and RAIN session on this innovation side
More emphasis on thought leadership generation instead of focus on sales volume
Follow up on the I3 program
Set incentives, link to outside research / faculty
That's not the point, we are innovative. The point is to get delivery bringing innovation to existing clients.

Table 6-9: Answers: How should Capgemini improve innovation?

6.5 Distilling the survey into Hofstede's Culture dimensions

Hofstede's dimensions have been reviewed in chapter 2.3.4 in detail, where it has been critically researched and reviewed with regard to the current literature and scientific debate. Definitely other models, such as the Lewis model, presented in 2.3.3, could have been taken to present the research findings, however results using Hofstede dimensions – masculinity and femininity, power distance, uncertainty avoidance, longer versus short-term view as well as individualism versus collectivism can be derived rather linearly by calculating a translation formula out of the questionnaire as shown in the figure.

In order to understand the intercultural dependency between sales management, teaming and the way Capgemini handles its divisions, a connection had to be made between the research, primarily intended to depict sales management attitudes and the dimensions of Hofstede. This is one of the key originalities of this research. To understand further, the survey results then have been analysed and distilled into the dimensions of Hofstede thus showing the difference between different divisions in their cultural attitude.

The following cross-relationships between questions and Hofstede dimensions have been drawn by using a multiplication between the areas.

Hofstede Dimension	**Questions drawn**	**Rationale**
Power Distance	My business is too special to be understood by a KAM Variable Pay and success Only the individual contribution counts	Collaboration is effected better when the power distance is lower. Pay differences co-determines power distance. Individual contribution related in pay generates a power distance.
Individualism vs. Collectivism	Large deal bonus for the entire team; Key account management helps coordinate activities for the client across multiple disciplines; Bringing along other disciplines; People from other geographies; Bringing in third parties	Collectivistic working and reward imply for example that people should then also be paid as a team. If key account managers are accepted, a collectivist function helps the other people to serve for them. If people from other geographies are accepted, same as third parties there is more likelihood for teaming.
Masculinty vs. Femininity	No intimacy; Key account managers are not compensated to help my business unit or area flourish; Variable Pay and success; Large deal bonus for the entire team	Pay and masculinity have a high correlation, same as a saying about having intimacy with a client or not. If large deal bonuses are preferred, typically this implies a higher degree of masculinity.
Uncertainty avoidance	Wild ideas, New and useful people Bringing along other disciplines People from other geographies	Avoiding uncertainty is effected for example by avoiding bringing new people to a client or by not trying new ideas.
Longterm vs. Short-term	We did not show the full power of the group, Key Account management helps yield additional opportunities for areas not primarily covered otherwise; The skill level of KAMs needs to be improved in order to yield results for my business unit.	Long term thinking requires investment, i.e. bringing in the full power of the group, investment into skills and to think of additional opportunities.

Table 6-10: Relating the survey questions to Hofstede

In order to provide a linkage between the survey questions and the Hofstede dimensions, "Table 6-10: Relating the survey questions to Hofstede" depicts the correlations chosen between. As the survey itself has been designed specifically at that point in time to work on the differences of teaming and the concept of

Hofstede overshadowed the question generation, only a set sample of questions have been chosen.

Item	Formula
Power Distance:	$PD(div) = I_1(div) * I_2(div) * I_3(div)\frac{1}{5^3}$
Individual-ism/Collectivism:	$Ik\ (div) = I_4(div) * I_5(div) * I_6(div) * I_7(div) * I_8(div)\frac{2}{5^5}$
Masculini-ty/Femininity:	$MF\ (div) = I_9(div) * I_{10}(div) * I_{11}(div) * I_{12}(div)\frac{2}{5^4}$
Uncertainty Avoid-ance:	$UA(div) = 1 - (I_{13}(div) * I_{14}(div) * I_{15}(div) * I_{16}(div)\frac{1}{5^4})$
Longtermism:	$LT(div) = I_{17}(div) * I_{18}(div) * I_{19}(div)\frac{1}{5^3}$

Table 6-11: Transformation Formula between Sample and Hofstede

The transformation formulas between the survey results and the Hofstede matrix used are shown in Table 6-11. All input factors, numbered $I_k(div)$ representing the input values shown in Table 6-10 by division or Capgemini entirely, have been assigned values between Zero and Five, they are multiplied together and thus can result in a value between Zero and Five powers the numbers of questions.

In order to norm it therefore the numeric result has been divided then by the Maximum possible number, for example 5^3 = 125, thus resulting into a value between 0 and 1.

This value then has been translated into equal steps and displayed into the tables.

6.5.1 The total Capgemini Sample

The total Capgemini Sample is quite average, which to a large extent was expected so. As it shows, the total Capgemini sample as depicted in "Table 6-12: Total Capgemini Sample and Hofstede" has a medium power distance, a higher degree of individualism than expected, a medium degree of masculinity and a medium degree of uncertainty avoidance whilst also being medium in its short-term to long-term thinking.

Dimension	Very Low	Low	Medium	High	Very High
Power Distance			x		
Individualism vs. Collectivism				x	
Masculinity vs. Femininity			x		
Uncertainty Avoidance			x		
Longterm vs. Shortterm			x		

Table 6-12: Total Capgemini Sample and Hofstede

6.5.2 Technology Services and Hofstede

What it shows at Technology Services in "Table 6-13: Technology Services and Hofstede", the population apparently depicts a lower degree of power distance than average, a high degree of individualism, a lower degree of masculinity, a medium degree of uncertainty avoidance and a medium-term thinking.

Dimension	Very Low	Low	Medium	High	Very High
Power Distance		x			
Individualism vs. Collectivism				x	
Masculinity vs. Femininity		x			
Uncertainty Avoidance			x		
Longterm vs. Short-term			x		

Table 6-13: Technology Services and Hofstede

Linking this to the business goals of Technology Services it appears that the business goals, by driving midsize systems integration projects, often times and material base, less often at fixed price situations determines the outcome of this survey, all other things left equal.

6.5.3 Consulting Services

Consulting services – as depicted in "Table 6-14: Hofstede Dimension and Consulting Services" shows a medium degree of power distance[15] - a very high degree of individualism – often consulting stars play a larger role than consulting teams, a higher degree of masculinity, and a lower level of uncertainty avoidance and shorter term thinking.

Comparing this with the typical consulting mandates in an average of three to five people on a project, billed on time and material base which bears no larger risks for the provider with individual knowledge application plays a certain role and the engagement itself typically not lasting longer than half a year, the Hofstede results are quite coherent with the business demands. In other words, Consultants are suitable for the Consulting business.

Dimension	Very Low	Low	Medium	High	Very High
Power Distance			x		
Individualism vs. Collectivism					x
Masculinity vs. Femininity				x	
Uncertainty Avoidance			x		
Longterm vs. Shortterm			x		

Table 6-14: Hofstede Dimension and Consulting Services

[15] The phenomenon of the paramount „Sich-Duzen" inside Capgemini comes originally from the consulting services division of that company.

6.5.4 Outsourcing Services

Outsourcing services typically has long-term contracts with its clients for over five or more years. Once an outsourcing contract has been made, there is little room for manoeuvre to alter or change the contract into higher zones of profitability[16]. After the service take-on and the transition towards the provider, the service should run more or less on "auto-pilot", meaning: without large modification of the service design as such, as modifications are cost drivers and typically cannot be charged back to the client.

Dimension	Very Low	Low	Medium	High	Very High
Power Distance			x		
Individualism vs. Collectivism				x	
Masculinity vs. Femininity			x		
Uncertainty Avoidance				x	
Longterm vs. Shortterm			x		

Table 6-15: Outsourcing Services and Hofstede

As a result there is a huge business focus on uncertainty avoidance, risk control and long-term planning. Interestingly enough, this also turns out to be the case with the respondents of the outsourcing services population, shown in "Table 6-15: Outsourcing Services and Hofstede". There exists a higher power distance amongst this group compared to others, a higher degree of collectivism, a medium degree of masculinity which results in the questions as to how to appropriate bonuses and a high degree of uncertainty avoidance. At the end, outsourcers appear to be long-term thinkers and therefore do appear on the left hand side of the scale.

6.6 Limitations of this survey

Nearly all research collects demographic information, thus it is the same for this research. The biggest challenge of this survey is that factual experiences are belief and perception-biased, thus facts and perception need to be differentiated. The null hypothesis of the original survey is that no sales management will either not augment or further deteriorate the market shares of a company like Capgemini in Switzerland and will likely end in annihilation from the market. The further null hypothesis of the conclusion drawn into the Hofstede dimensions is that different divisions create a different organisational behaviour and attract and retain a different breed of people over time.

At the same time, it needs to be shown that often people answer what they think they ought to answer and not what they truly think. Therefore, a good amount of test and counter-test questions had to be put in place in order to dissect biased survey answers from unbiased.

[16] Especially in contract design and negotiation, the focus is on the profitability of the contract.

One also needs to accept that despite the fact that there were 23 respondents to the survey, this simply implies there were about seven or eight per division. This sample can be only be seen as marginally and statistically significant, however it entails a majority of the senior sales leaders of Capgemini Germany and Switzerland.

6.7 Conclusion of this chapter

This chapter did present the survey results thoroughly. On this survey, 2600 data points came together that give an indicative view on how Capgemini sales professionals in Germany and Switzerland perceive the performance of the company, the market and how the performance can be improved and that it must be improved, too.

Notably, there is a certain but not striking difference in cultural attitudes and beliefs between the groups of Consulting, Technology Services and Outsourcing. Most differences can be explained by the different nature of the tasks and it is very likely that with a common account management approach those differences can be used to promote diversity and a multi-faceted view of a client.

Letting the divisions work together appears to be doable and worth a try as there exists a certain overlap in how the respondents express their cultural behaviour. It also shows that from the responses indicate that people are willing to work together and see it as a prerequisite for success. The question therefore remains: How to perform the cooperation in the best way possible?

7 Conclusion, Change Recommendation and Implementation

This chapter deals with the conclusions of Chapter two to six and puts out a recommendation and action plan plus a measurement and tracking recommendation for success, as shown in Figure 7-1.

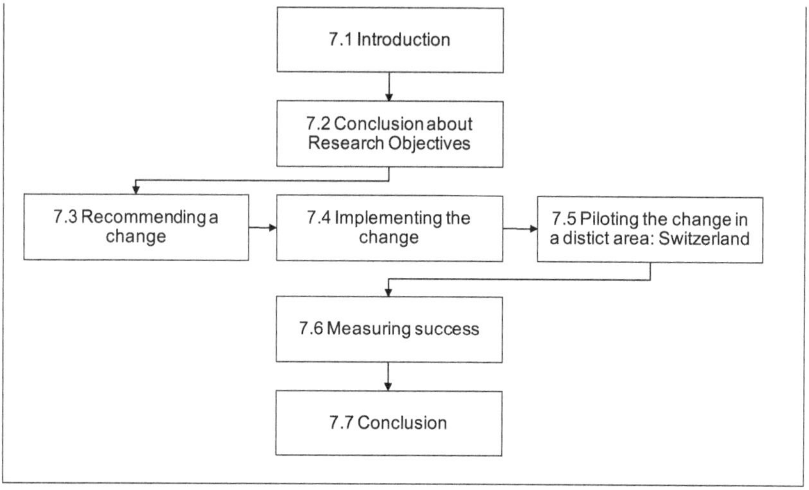

Figure 7-1: Chapter VII Overview

7.1 Introduction

Here, it will be concluded whether the findings show that a sales management function will improve the organisation of Capgemini Central Europe in order to win international big deals and how the Capgemini organisation can be leveraged. First, this chapter shows the conclusion about the research objectives then recommends a change and gives hints on how to implement this change. Here, a pilot in Switzerland is recommended. To finalise on this chapter, a measurement of the success is suggested by introducing and installing a "light" balanced scorecard.

7.2 Conclusion about the research objectives

The following conclusion out of the research objectives can be drawn:

- First: Would Cross-Discipline collaboration generate more results than the efforts it requires? Conclusion: Yes it would.
- Second: Does intercultural awareness yield sales success? Rather yes.

- Third: How should account management be conducted inside Capgemini? Conclusion: In an integrated way.
- Fourth: How should a common account management function be designed and steered? Conclusion: Measurably lean.
- Fifth: What are the elements of a measurement, payment and scoring model? More than just trailing financial indicators, the focus should go to leading indicators.

The Research Objectives (ROs) are being laid out in the following three points.

7.2.1 RO 1: Does cross-discipline collaboration yield returns?

The answer is a big YES. Drawing upon Grant's (Grant, 1999) resources and capabilities model, the gaps apparently exist in providing a full-scope value chain picture to clients, where they either demand it or demand it but apparently not speak it out yet.

Cross-discipline collaboration is seen as beneficial, but apparently the system of the company impedes it. According to sales mantra "what's in it for me?" (Duncan, 2002), sales leaders need to see a both intrinsic and extrinsic - monetary - reward for their actions. However, the rewards are too remote because of the systemic boundaries.

There are five major conclusions out of the research:

- **Culture**: People have a strong view of independence and because of that, the systems are built around fiefdoms. However people are very likely and willing to team up.
- **Skills & Knowledge**: It is viewed that there is not enough knowledge to show the "full spectrum" of Capgemini.
- **Communication and interaction**, also dealing with **structure**: The structure of the company is not designed to collaborate towards the clients across disciplines.
- **Motivation**: There is a common feeling that there is a need to "do something", to work together and to change the systems, however, the financial rewards are counterproductive.
- **Financially**: The whole financial system is built around divisions – meaning: cost ends and not around where the money is coming from, such as revenue sources.

Consequently, the capability to up-sell and cross-sell virtually does not exist, same as there is a lack of viewing even larger accounts holistically on a senior relationship level.

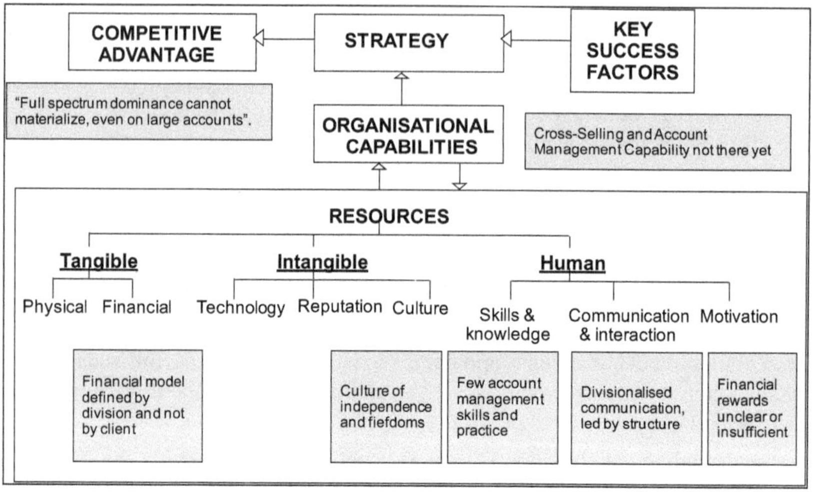

Figure 7-2: Resource, Capability, Competitive advantage gaps.

As a result, due to the missing lack of intrinsic resources, combined with a structure that impedes the collaboration, a strategic capability gap exist which, at the end, turns into a strategic disadvantage to reach "full spectrum dominance" at a client. Cross-discipline collaboration is seen as beneficial; however the system of the company prevents even the better people to perform. According to the old mantra in sales "what's in it for me?" (Duncan, 2002), sales leaders need to see both intrinsic and extrinsic - means monetary - reward for their actions. And this reward is considered being too remote because of the systemic.

7.2.2 RO 2: The intercultural sales success

The research objective was to find out how the intercultural aspects of working in a multi-divisional and multinational company can leverage the sales success, especially in working together with international clients. The answer is short but simple: As multi-divisional companies have different divisions – or as Capgemini calls it "disciplines" by purpose, they will always have conflicts of interest when working in a similar area, like a territory or customer environment. Overlaps do exist and will continue to exist. However, a small coordination function, like a sales management core, directed to the client can help bridge those gaps.

International conflicts are unavoidable, here – an ambassador function, i.e. a services delivery manager, working on "both sides of the fence", can work wonders. Here, an implementation proposal is made in Chapter 7.4, as to how to bring global value to local clients.

7.2.3 RO 3: How should account management be conducted?

Territory planning, account planning and account management across different divisions and disciplines would overcome this as it would entail a band of mutual trust and relationship, but it is not implemented yet. Too few joint account planning meetings with people from other disciplines happen to exist, left alone account planning meetings as a global sales and delivery team.

In order to dissect this, a gap analysis by using Holden's sales process model (Holden International, 2009) has been performed. According to the answers found, the following key gaps exist in executing the Holden sales process in Capgemini, as shown in Table 7-1. Per sales step, there are other mis-steps that occur. However, as a common trait an increased level of cross-discipline coördination and collaboration across the sales process is highly recommended, even though it generates some overhead – and clearly not only sometimes this overhead might not generate incremental revenue.

7.2.4 RO 4: How to steer a common account management function?

Sales Stage	**Finding of gap**	**Recommendation of improvement to be made**
1- Market planning	No cross-discipline market or territory planning	Have joint territory planning sessions.
2- Account Planning	Not enough cross—discipline account planning	Setup cross-discipline account planning schedules.
3 - Identification	Identification of deals for other disciplines gets often discarded	Setup cross-discipline account planning schedules
4 – Qualification	Deal is then qualified too often as a "single-discipline" deal, thus power of the group cannot be leveraged	Have ambassadors from other disciplines in qualification meetings of each other disciplines.
5 – Solutioning	Too little involvement from other disciplines and geographics, content therefore too thin.	Institutionalise "Flying Squad" for larger deals, include all disciplines.
6 – Final Pricing	Pricing is often too high, has too many iterations.	Global overview on marketable prices, especially for standardised "catalogue services".
7 – Closing	Relationship is lacking on superior levels for closing deals.	Key relationship manager in charge of multiple brands. Senior leader required in front of the clients.
Q – Qualifying out	Too many deals are qualified in, carried through the pipeline and lost then at a higher cost and a later stage.	Hard qualification-out-criteria to be observed.

Table 7-1: Gaps by Sales Stage and Recommendations for improvements

A common account management for Capgemini Group should be designed and steered in a measurable and lean way (Kellen, 2002), (Duncan, 2002) and (McDonald M. H., 1999). This is the major conclusion out of the survey and of best-practice findings.

People are willing to give up power if there is a material return for it. The account management discipline should be designed in a half-autonomous way, to steer the discipline teams to the right opportunity, but not without a certain touch point of control. Same goes with compensation of account managers or client unit sales leaders.

For the measurement and payment, a simple and accountable measurement system is desired, where on large deals, team members are compensated on the gain according to their respective contribution. Account managers should receive targets as a sum from the supporting business units.

7.2.5 RO 5: How to measure, score and pay?

The fifth objective was to find out what elements a measurement and scoring model should include in order to yield additional success. The scoring model should encompass several views and not only be focused on past financial views alone. "Working just with revenue numbers is like steering a car through the rear mirror", Kaplan & Norton (Kaplan & Norton, 2009) have written. It is therefore recommended to have implemented a small but useful Balanced Scorecard that tracks success and gives indications of future developments. This will be explained more in Chapter 7.7.

7.3 Recommending a change

A change is required, and as shown from the results out of this survey, it is clear that change does not happen overnight.

Two major changes should be undertaken to spur growth inside Capgemini:

- More accountability towards the client end – a structural change end.
- More integration of offerings that fit to the client at the delivery end.

A structural change should be put in place, by grouping the currently scattered client-facing resources across one **key core of revenue source: the client**. Here, the building of clusters around clients might aid in focusing around a common objective.

In order to implement the change, a series of standardised, industrialised and cross-fitting offerings should be put in place in order to give more freedom to the teams in front of the client to work together using those offerings like Lego stones. Thus, it is highly recommended to do the following to get in synch with the "CCM" postulates of Ryals and Rogers (Ryals & Rogers, 2006) of Communicate, Change and Measure.

Communicate

- First of all, communicate on the Capgemini Strategy more often and more concisely. They need to be lived by example.
- Demonstrate by communicating positive results as to how cross-discipline collaboration has yielded results for every participant – either in more revenues or less effort.
- Foster collaboration where possible through both intrinsic as well as extrinsic measures.
- Make collaboration easy for all participants.
- Put Cross-Collaboration targets into the personal goals of all affected employees.
- Put cross-selling and collaboration discipline into the sales process by implementing checkmarks into the Holden Sales Staging Plan.

Change

- Perform sales leadership job rotations across the disciplines.
- Build up a key account management system around "clusters" which are similar in terms of industry, client size and geographic spread.
- Align sales and delivery according to those clusters; industrialize the cluster-centrism back into the Rightshore delivery centres.
- Have a hard-line dual reporting of the sales teams from the disciplines – including the consulting VPs to the Key account manager.
- The sales teams should be given functional and target guidance by the Key account manager or cluster leader, same the key account managers should be given business guidance by the executive committee in terms of targets.
- Build high-growth cross-discipline service offerings that can be re-sold and industrialized and thus show by example that cross-discipline collaboration makes business sense.
- Perform the change within one year.

Measure

- Build up a team quota element for client facing members within this cluster plus an individual or business unit led quota, i.e. according to the model in Section 7.7 below.
- Make people accountable for their actions. Measure success and make success visible.

In order to see whether the recommendations do result in growth, it is suggested to perform a pilot in a distinct area, i.e. Switzerland, and check and monitor results.

7.3.1 Structural change: Team structure

According to Clutterbuck (Clutterbuck, 1998), the team structure is heavily dependent upon their membership and tasks. In net new sales, the team requirement is to have a hit team on new deals but at the same time some repetitive stability in order to understand and learn the roles in a team setup, as shown in Figure 7-3.

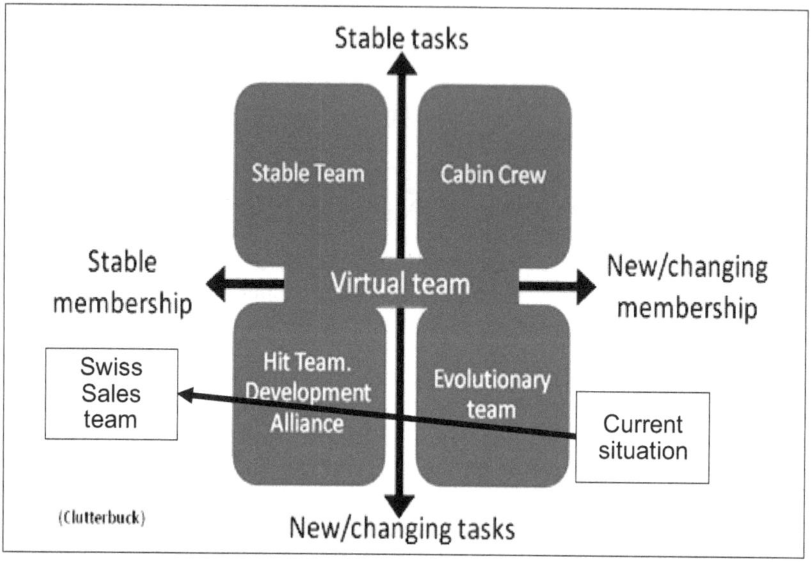

Figure 7-3: Team structure (Clutterbuck, 1998)

Therefore, a current situation with a high degree of fluctuation should be changed towards a more stable team membership. A structure is wished where experienced professionals know what they do and what they can expect from others. The hit team structure with new and changing tasks, resulting out of new deals, with at the same time having mostly a stable or only slightly evolving membership therefore might be the best approach to form such a team. In order to bring one key component of I3 (Capgemini S.A., 2009) - Innovation into this team is suggested, therefore the intent is to strongly cooperate with international groups – such as KAMS and KIMS (Capgemini S.A., 2007) and the Global Deal hub, as well as Rightshore® (Capgemini S.A. , 2008) centres in the world.

7.3.2 Building of clusters

Clusters should be built around the source of revenue – the client. The revenue source should be dis-coupled by the service providing disciplines, in order to give each side distinct targets, following the postulates of Rogers (Rogers B. , 1999), shown in Figure 7-4.

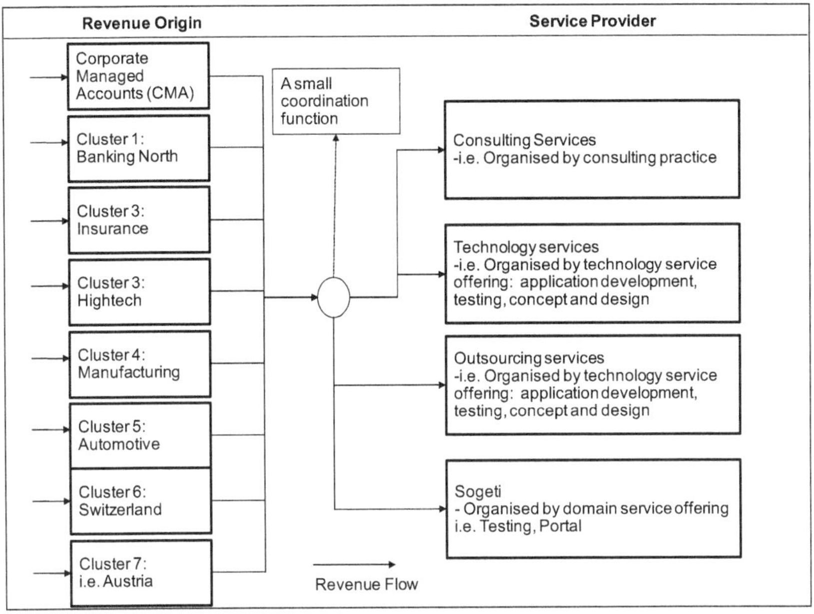

Figure 7-4: Cluster concept model

This then, alongside with the flow of revenues and the translation into cost through the delivery units, the cluster in the sales area should then assemble all revenue opportunities within one area and then distribute – using sales experts towards the right cost and value providers.

The big advantage of this concept is:

- Client centrism, thus building domain-specific whilst;
- Keeping the focus of the organisation towards the service disciplines.

A Cluster should be built around certain gravity, this might be – in larger countries such as Germany – a set of similar clients, such as in one industry, i.e. high-tech or banking – for smaller countries it is the country. For large above a certain clip-level of e.g. 100 M€ revenues a cluster can be a single client. A small coordination function might provide guidance and adjustments.

The funding for those clusters should be a percentage of revenues or TCV, so whilst having revenue, profit and signing targets, the benchmark is measured upon cost of selling.

7.3.3 Cluster Setup – Base layout

The following team per cluster is suggested:

- 1 Cluster leader per cluster, adjoined by a team consisting of account managers or solution architects, depending upon the discretion of the cluster leader. This person should be able to be a counterpart towards C-Level contacts and to act like the CEO of her own company. The cluster leader has the role of Kotler's Chief Revenue Officer (Kotler, Rackham, & Krisnavany, 2006).
- 1 Technology Services Leader, full-time or part-time aligned
- 1 Consulting Vice President, full-time or part-time aligned, both depending upon revenue and potential identified
- 1 Outsourcing Engagement Manager – for existing outsourcing engagements or one Business Development Director for new deals. The allocation depends upon the booking potential.
- 1 Sales Assistant – desired to off-load repetitive internal and preparatory work from the rather highly paid Vice presidents and leadership persons.

This team should be complemented by global resources both in the services delivery and in the business development area, as shown in Figure 7-5. Reason for the build-up of a local team is the expectation of the clients: The team needs to be present in market locally in order to perform and sell. From a Global Player like Capgemini, clients do expect internationally networked resources. In order to give this team some autonomy, changes in approval behaviour also might occur thus local decision capability up to a certain level can materialise.

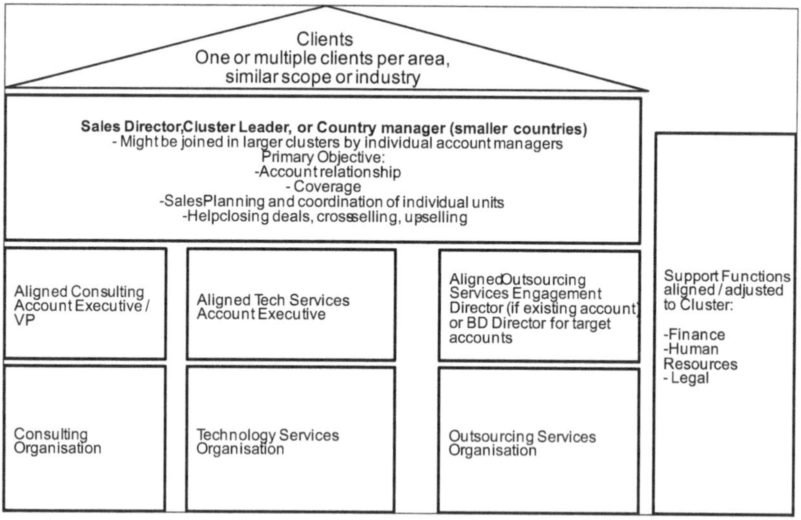

Figure 7-5: Proposed Cluster setup concept

The following advantages, following the models of McDonald (McDonald M. H., 2000) can be leveraged:

- Accountability towards both ends – the delivery end of the discipline – such as Consulting Services, Technology Services and Outsourcing Services – and towards the revenue end – means: the client.
- A thin layer of adoption. Only the resources that are needed will be drawn into a cluster.
- The system grows dynamically. If the cluster yields more revenue and profits, the cluster can be extended or – if it becomes unmanageable for one cluster leader – split.
- The cluster can even be spread – if the client set requires it – across multiple geographies. For example, a cluster covering "Global Exchange Markets" might make sense due to the nature of the replicability of the business, globally.
- No major change of the underlying discipline model is required, disciplines that leverage this model benefit from it the most.

7.4 Bringing global value to clients

In order to provide the value of a global organisation, including resources from for example Poland, Germany, Romania or India directly into a country such as Switzerland, a strong linkage between those countries need to be established, as shown in Figure 7-6.

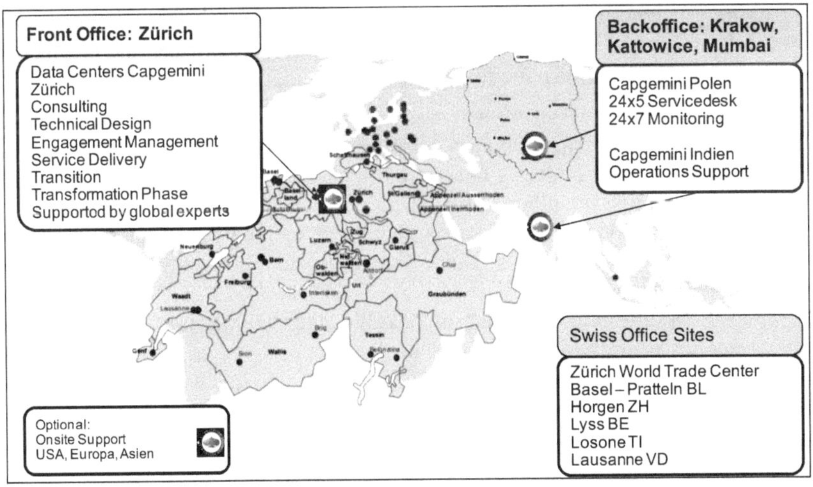

Figure 7-6: Providing Value to a client from the global organisation, locally, source: Capgemini, 2010

This then implies, that the frontoffice-backoffice interplay needs to be understood, people need to know each other and the processes such as ITIL in order to collaborate need to be established and also learned without "dialect" on either side.

7.4.1 Organisational setup

From an organisational setup, the organisation in Switzerland should be "self-similar"[17], meaning – from a general perspective the organization should not be that much dissimilar to that one of for example in the Netherlands, Germany or in France; however it should encompass the special conditions a country does face. Thus, the typical key features of an organization that works in a country, such as a country General Manager (CGM), Head of Finance, Head of Human Resources, Head of Business Development, all together in a way that makes the country organization as lean as possible should be there. However, everything else is left to a global disposition on a "need" basis or better yet, on an "if the customer pays for it" basis.

7.4.2 Inclusion of global resources in Switzerland

Key is to include global resources in Switzerland in order to come close to the concept of a "globally integrated enterprise", as postulated amongst other by Palmisano (Palmisano, 2006, p. 127). As he writes: "The globally integrated enterprise will require fundamentally different approaches to production, distribution, and work-force deployment… ", however he adds that, "a challenge will be to figure out how to maintain trust in enterprises based on increasingly distributed business models." Therefore – along with the concepts of Mintzberg (Mintzberg, 1999, p. 238) the following client facing organization blocks should be looked at:

1. Strategic apex: In a country-organised services company, there are two strategic apexes: One is the "core brain" in the headquarter, here Capgemini in Paris, the other is the "local brain" in front of the client facing organization. This strategic apex should be located highly in front of the client. In that respect, a country-based services company might be compared with an octopus[18].
2. The Middle line: As much as possible, the "middle line", consisting of people near the client should be located in Offshore delivery centers. Those delivery centres still should communicate in a well-organised manner with the front-office that helps them steer the market.

[17] The concept of self-similarity has been introduced in mathemathics by Benoît Mandelbrot and extended for example to financial science, here the term is coined for business structures (Mandelbrot, 2009) .

[18] An octopus interestingly enough has nine brains, communicating through the core brain with another. Compared to manufacturing companies where as some writers believe "one brain" might suffice, services companies need more than one brain.

3. Support staff: In a country organization, as little support staff as possible should be located: If possible all support staff should be located off-shore.
4. Technostructure: Typically, the technostructure has to come out "of the cloud" from the rest of the company and should be placed where it is the least expensive and most effective place.
5. The operating core of the company in a country might be threefold, following the rule: "when the client pays for it, he gets it". This implies that: Firstly, Local professional consultants might be definitely placed with or in front of the client. Secondly, Service delivery centers which provide continued service level based value can be placed off-shore or where the most cost-effective place is. Thirdly, data centers and other infrastructure – should be placed locally in order to avoid high network costs when communicating with the clients' organizations.

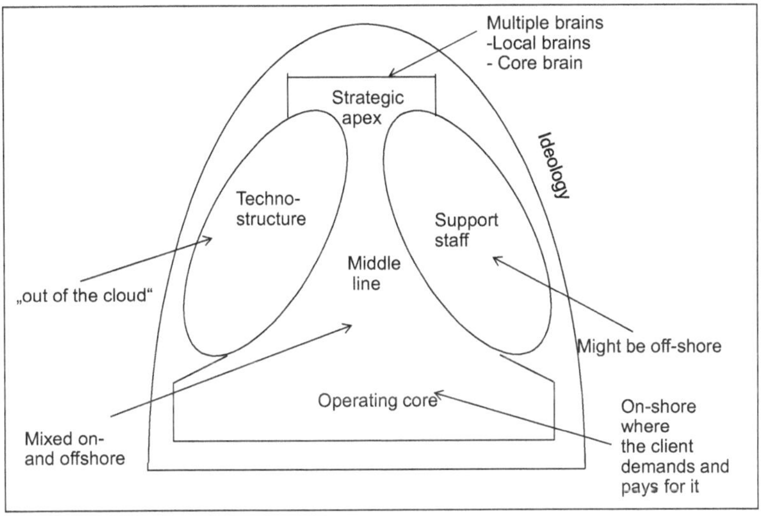

Figure 7-7: On- hand off-shore position of organisation parts (Mintzberg, 1998, pg. 239)

Using the Mintzberg model, as depicted in Figure 7-7, a highly cost-effective mixture between client proximity and global integration can be achieved. The communication flows follow the concepts of Rightshoring as already seen in Figure 4-12, by combining communications tools that enable the communication between front-office and back-office.

7.4.3 Key relationship managers – intercultural ambassadors

However, there are intercultural dilemmas, especially with remote cultures, such as the Indian culture. Here, the relationship needs to be established and maintained by "domain experts" with knowledge of both on cross-culture and on the specific, often technical domains. These might be people with sufficient knowledge of the culture i.e. by having already worked in India on this specific domain, such as application management and then returning on-shore. An alternative might be for example to assign Indian nationals themselves on-shore by relocating them for a while and then bringing them back into the Indian services and delivery centers. Both should be exercised and applied, however due to cost reasons often the less expensive – bringing lower-cost Indian nationals to Europe is widely practiced.

7.5 Implementing the change

We definitely see that changing the whole environment towards getting this sales team in place and making Switzerland for Capgemini has some driving and restraining forces. At the same time, we do foresee some path valleys of adoption towards the new situation.

7.5.1 Communication of Strategy

Key is to communicate the strategy and the strategic imperatives of working together continuously. A shift of working from a line-of-business organisation towards cross-discipline collaboration will not happen overnight.

7.5.2 The steps of change

Using Kurt Lewin's (Lewin K. , 1943) Field Force Analysis, we can analyse driving and restraining force towards a change. As a result, as Lewin suggests, the driving forces can be strengthened and the restraining forces weakened in order to enact the change. Key is to drive the change and to use the driving forces to eliminate the restraining forces. To then further enact the change several writers, such as Lewin (Lewin K. , 1943), suggest utilising a three-staged change model.

- **Unfreezing:** First by unfreezing the current situation where the majority of Capgemini in the select area – Switzerland – is still residing.
- **Changing:** Making the change happen and burn the bridges to the former stage and then;
- **Freezing:** Freezing it back into the new stage with a higher level of performance desired.

Between the current situation and a new situation, it is very likely to experience an implementation dip, also known as the "valley of tears" (Rayner & Adam-Smith, 2005). Key here is to avoid or to reduce the implementation dip. Typically, the implementation dip will happen unavoidably. However, it can be managed through open communication about the desired progress vs. the progress felt, about communicating the scorecard of the achievements so far and about continuously fostering the messages about the future state.

Barriers to change: However, it should be noted that there will be hurdles and barriers for this change, such as a "Not invented here" syndrome by some of the areas – despite a clear realisation that change needs to happen, an overcome of the fiefdoms by every leader and of course the fact that breaking old habits is not easy.

7.5.3 Enacting the Change

In order to change businesses towards the better, it needs to be observed that there are many forces which try to maintain a business at a certain status quo. Definitely, there are forces that help drive those forces, however; there are typically at least as many forces that keep a business situation where it is residing at a certain point in time. If that would not be the case, change would happen virtually without resistance, or automatically. It is therefore of importance to understand the process of change and to examine the ways how change can be accelerated.

7.5.4 Field Force Analysis

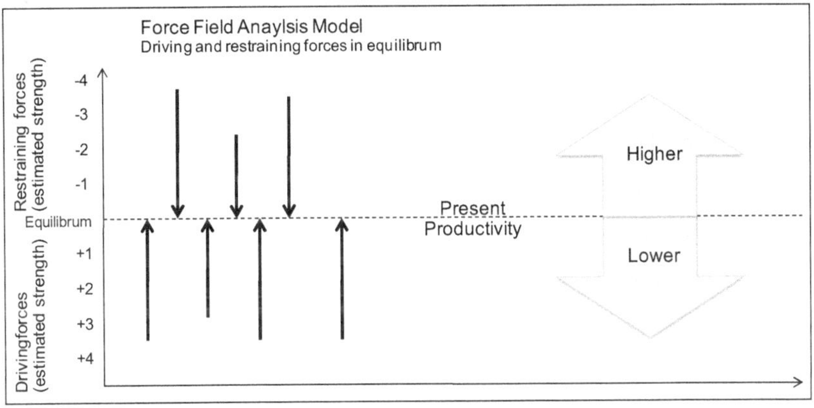

Figure 7-8: Field Force Analysis according to Kurt Levin (Lewin, 1943)

Using Kurt Lewin's (Lewin K. , 1943) Field Force Analysis, we can analyse driving and restraining force towards a change, as shown in Figure 7-8. As a result, Lewin suggests, the driving forces can be strengthened, the restraining forces weakened in order to enact the change.

7.5.5 Driving forces

- **The numbers**: A 50% decline of the business is a 50% decline. With this, many well-loved behaviours cannot be maintained. At the same time, this imposes drastic change onto the residual delivery organization, which comes under pressure to cut down sites.
- **The changing market**: The market expects from Capgemini in Switzerland to be present with its global reach and scale and to provide the services in this "Rightshore" global model. At the same time, changing attitudes of Swiss

companies towards offshoring can be leveraged as a driver for change of implementing a new sales and delivery culture.

- **Increased competition**: Capgemini in Switzerland has lost many deals due to increased competition. The new setup is a key driver to be more cost-effective whilst being ready to attack competition.
- **Executive pressure to change**: This buy-in of senior executive sponsors is important for success, as in the first year especially as Capgemini writes out a loan to the team to start the performance.
- **Part of the services delivery team**: Some people simply realize that change must happen and already work towards it.

7.5.6 Restraining forces

- **Individually, parts of the existing team** have the following restraining factors: Loss of Status, Some Inertia and The Fear of Unknown, as well as the loss of some friends who had to let go. The team, including their leaders, is aware of the financial situation they are in and the implications, yet they are not yet willing to change.
- **Organisationally**, the current Capgemini culture takes a long time to acknowledge organisational facts as facts – often, the wish for harmony supersedes a clear and fact-based discussion, thus hinders progress.
- **Sunk costs:** Typically, an organisational setup has cost money to produce. Therefore, big restraining forces are sunk costs, for example people who are there but do not really work.

7.5.7 Driving the change towards a new model

Key is to drive the change, here several writers, such as Lewin (Lewin K. , 1943), suggest utilising a three-staged change model:

- **Unfreezing:** First by unfreezing the current situation where the majority of Capgemini in the select area – Switzerland – is still residing.
- **Changing:** Making the change happen and burn the bridges to the former stage and then;
- **Freezing:** Freezing it back into the new stage with a higher level of performance desired.

Stage 1 - Unfreezing: The Unfreezing stage is one of the more important stages to understand in the world of change we live in today. This stage is about getting ready to change. It involves getting to a point of understanding that change is necessary and getting ready to move away from our current comfort zone.

This first stage is about preparing the employees and the leadership team before the change and – ideally making sure that there is a situation where they want to change. It therefore needs to be made sure that the employees feel that change is necessary.

Here, in order to unfreeze the change, it is clear to

- Set a clear deadline of change
- Make clear to the people about the change needed – in terms of collaboration and cooperation
- Communicate the measurement model
- Install the resources, i.e. the leadership team accordingly.

People will weigh the pros and cons; however it needs to be made clear to the participants that the change is inevitable.

Stage 2 - Change or Transition: The transition towards the new model is not an event but rather a process for most of the participants, as Lewin stated it, it is a "transition". During this transition, it is of key importance to take the people along and burn the bridges towards the former state.

It needs to be made clear that people are unsure or even fearful about this change transition. Therefore it is important not to look back but forward during this transition.

Additionally, it is important to let people develop their own solutions in order to manage their personal transition, whilst communicating a clear picture of the end-state of the change, meaning: communicating the strategy and the effective benefits out of it, as Rayner & Adam-Smith point out on leadership of people (Rayner & Adam-Smith, 2005).

Stage 3 - Freezing (or Refreezing): Kurt Lewin (Lewin K. , 1947) refers to this stage as freezing. As the name suggests this stage is about establishing stability once the changes have been made. The changes are accepted and become the new norm. People form new relationships and become comfortable with their routines. This can take time.

As Lewin stated (Lewin K. , 1947): "A change towards a higher level of group performance is frequently short-lived, after a "shot in the arm", group life soon returns to the previous level. This indicates that it does not suffice to define the objective of planned change in group performance as the reaching of a different level. Permanency of the new level, or permanency for a desired period, should be included in the objective." – Therefore it is of importance to make the changes permanent and to communicate about progress and success.

7.5.8 Shortening the implementation dip

Between the current situation and a new situation, it is very likely to experience an implementation dip, also known as the "valley of tears" (Rayner & Adam-Smith, 2005). Key here is to avoid - if possible - or at least to reduce the implementation dip. Typically, the implementation dip will happen and is virtually unavoidable. However, it can be managed through open communication about the desired progress vs. the progress felt, about communicating the scorecard of the achievements and about continuously fostering the messages about the future state.

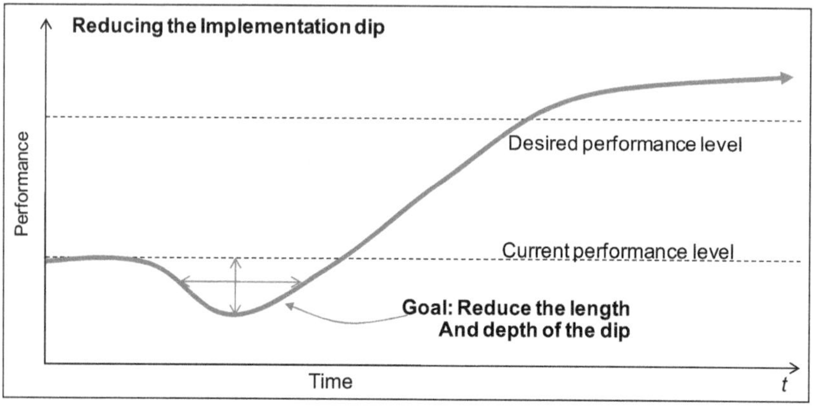

Figure 7-9: Shortening the implementation dip (Rayner & Adam-Smith, 2005)

There are several dimensions in the implementation dip:

- **Perception-wise** – Future pipeline of projects. The future pipeline of projects that has a positive impact needs to be communicated and highlighted in a special way. New and bright examples need to be demonstrated and fostered.
- **Fact wise** – Actual revenues and bookings. The actual revenues and bookings from existing projects might still occur, however they might fall off a cliff.
- **Felt change at people** – The change felt hardest at people who lose existing systems, existing behaviours and existing business relationships. People are typically used to work they were used to, thus learning a new behaviour costs additional energy.

However, it is important to reduce the implementation dip as much as possible to achieve this new performance level fast enough. What might happen is that the implementation dip occurs in phases, i.e. first there might be a behavioural dip, later a strategy dip and a systemic, technological dip. These dips might overlay themselves either in a counter-correlating way, thus letting the total "implementation dip experience" perceive lighter, or in a cross-correlating way resulting in a "valley of tears" " (Rayner & Adam-Smith, 2005), as shown in Figure 7-9.

7.5.9 Changing the behavior

Key in this whole change process is not only to change the systems and the processes whilst hiring and finding the right people, it is also about changing the behaviour of the people into the new way of Capgemini's I3 mode: Innovation, Client Intimacy and Industrialisation.

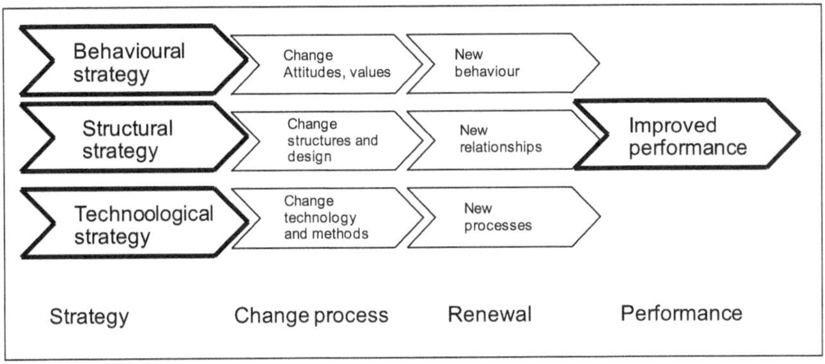

Figure 7-10: Key is to change Structure, Tech and Behaviour (Rogers, 2006)

Here, the following key methods, as depicted in Figure 7-10 are needed in order to change those dimensions:

- **Structural Strategy**: Here, setting up the new team is of paramount importance. It needs good leadership and here, learning from the best people needs to be fostered and implemented.
- **Technology**: Here, the need for change is slim but also important. A key focus of the sales teams towards g such as SharePoint tools, Office Communicators and others is important in order to foster and stimulate a collaborative behaviour.
- **Behaviour**: Key of I3 is learning from each other as best as possible, therefore key to internationally successful projects from across the world is important. Behaviour is the hardest thing to change and requires a longer breath.

7.6 Piloting the change in a desired area

With this dissertation, a design template towards a higher degree of success of Capgemini in Central Europe might be possible. Key is to start with a nucleus and in a foreseeable time, and therefore a pilot for a "healthy corporation" can be established as Dobbs et al write (Dobbs, Leslie, & Mendonca, 2005). Currently, the business conditions to setup and implement cross-selling are favourable as clients increasingly see this holistic view.

Key is to build-up a cluster along Figure 7-11 and to integrate this with the current organisation of the pilot area, Capgemini Switzerland, as shown in Figure 7-11. What is clear, in the country the organisational setup should be a replica of the overall organisation, with only a small apex in order to keep the organisation lean.

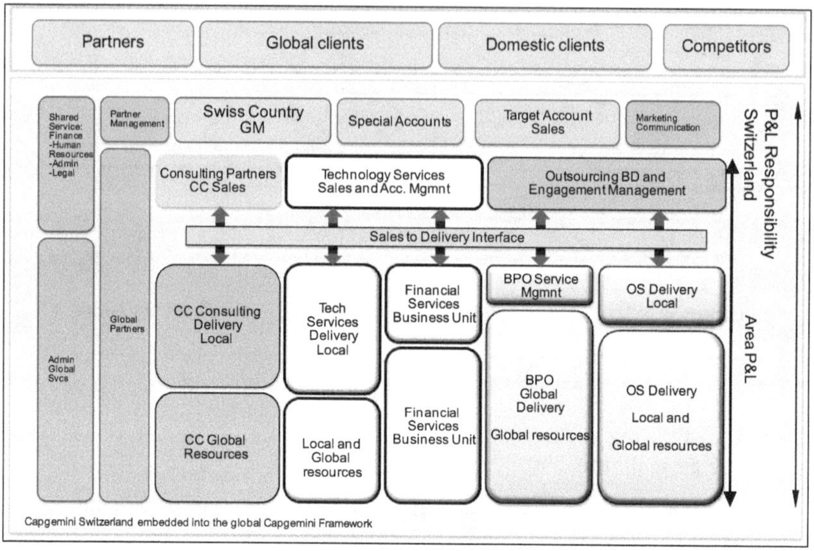

Figure 7-11: Proposed To-Be-Setup of Capgemini Switzerland

Besides changing certain parts of the system, changing the behaviour at Capgemini in Switzerland, to be ready for I3 – Innovation, Industrialization and Client Intimacy is a must and it will be difficult. Here, the biggest value for Capgemini clients then can be brought to bear. This then can be the nucleus for a new Capgemini Switzerland and a new era of success, providing more shareholder value and client satisfaction than ever before and work along the models of a "healthy corporation" (Dobbs, Leslie, & Mendonca, 2005).

7.7 Measuring success

In order to be clear upon the direction taken on, the measurement of success is a mandate. Success in sales can be measured in several ways:

- New Market share vs. old market share, measured by independent analysts
- Revenue growth, discounted for inflation of market and/or monetary base
- Profit growth if the profit comes from net new projects, thus derived from revenue growth
- Sustainable new projects: As these new projects might initially be of small revenues but have a potential for growth – sowing the seeds of a larger project – a special care might be taken upon these projects.

However, for starters, a pipeline view might suffice. What would be beneficial in order to see whether this distinct change has caused success is to have a controlled group. For example, a similar country where this change will then not be implemented – Austria – might serve as a controlled counter-group.

7.7.1 Target and measurement

A simple dashboard, based upon the SPADE / Siebel CRM entries as shown on Figure 7-12: Dashboard sample based upon CRM systems entries of the deals in progress, the deals signed and the deals in development should be implemented and monitored.

Weighted Bookings Pipeline for Cluster	Stage 2-3	Stage 4-7	Weighted Pipeline	Sold	Total Forecast	Weighted Pipeline Target Incl. Sold	Sales Target	Pipeline vs. Target	Forecast minus Target
Consulting Services	2'800'000	150'000	635'000	820'000	1'455'000	7'000'000	2'800'000	- 6'365'000	- 1'345'000
Technology Services - CSD	1'200'000	700'000	590'000	220'000	810'000	3'750'000	1'500'000	- 3'160'000	- 690'000
Technology Services - SAP	22'000'000	40'350'000	24'575'000	145'000	24'720'000	20'547'500	8'219'000	4'027'500	16'501'000
Outsourcing Services	52'095'000	50'000'000	35'419'000	1'500'000	36'919'000	57'500'000	23'000'000	- 22'081'000	13'919'000
Total Cluster	78'095'000	91'200'000	61'219'000	2'685'000	63'904'000	88'797'500	35'519'000	- 27'578'500	28'385'000
Pipeline Weighting Factor:	0.2	0.5							
Identified by Cluster Leader	15'970'000	9'683'000	8'035'500	100'000	8'135'500	10'000'000	23'000'000	- 1'964'500	- 14'864'500
Sum Engagem.	15'970'000	9'683'000	8'035'500	100'000	8'135'500	10'000'000	23'000'000	- 1'964'500	- 14'864'500
Sum Total Cluster	94'065'000	100'883'000	69'254'500	2'785'000	72'039'500	98'797'500	58'519'000	- 29'543'000	13'520'500

Figure 7-12: Dashboard sample based upon CRM systems entries

The following metrics should be monitored specifically:

- **Identification** of pipeline by individual team members and closure of pipeline by teams.
- **Weighted pipeline** – a probability heuristic of weighted pipeline by stage should be taken into account in order to measure a forecast per discipline and cluster.
- **Weighted Pipeline target**. This might be a target derived out of the signings / bookings target as an intermediate target.

This simple financial scorecard has two advantages:

- It is **simple to implement** and tracks pipeline progress over time, thus adding a level of sustainability into the controlling equation.
- It gives an **individual indication** per team member, thus adding granularity into the system.

However, this scorecard might be refined into a balanced scorecard, as described by Kaplan and Norton (Grant, 1999, p. 43), using not just a financial perspective, but also a learning perspective, a business process perspective and a customer perspective.

7.7.2 Balanced scorecard to track sustainability

Measuring sales success only upon a pipeline perspective might be a good start, however it will not show the underlining efforts and progress made in order to move the organisation forward. Therefore additionally, in order to track the hidden changes in behaviour and culture, reporting and steering based upon the following parameters, based upon Kaplan and Norton's Balanced Scorecard. Grant points out that balances Scorecards should be top-down in order to be really effective.

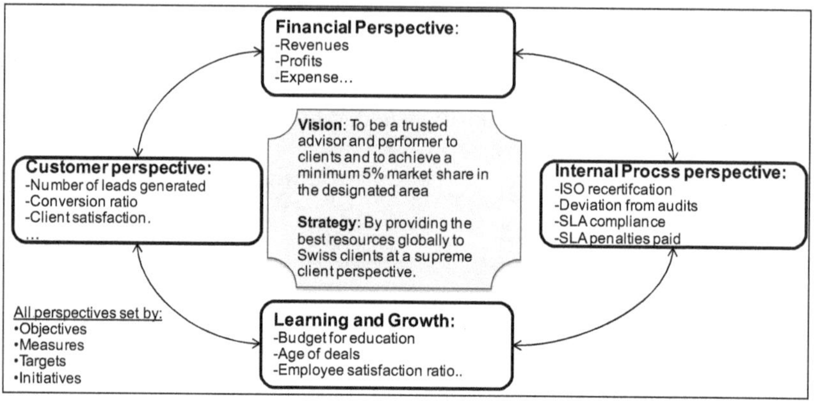

Figure 7-13: Balanced Scorecard applied to Capgemini in Switzerland

However, we believe that at least measuring success of such an emerging business unit might make sense to be scored separately, anyway, as long as it fits into a larger framework. The balanced scorecard, shown in Figure 7-13 suggests that the organisation is being looked at – besides the overall vision - from four measurement and analytics perspectives (Kaplan & Norton, 2009), and to develop metrics, collect data and analyse in regards to those four:

- Customer perspective
- Financial perspective
- Internal Process perspective
- Learning and growth perspective

Overshadowed by a vision and strategy as the centrepiece of the balanced scorecard development. The following example measurements for a scorecard are suggested to be implemented and monitored for the pilot area and can be shown in the following sections.

7.7.2.1 Customer or Client Focus

Table 7-2: Client Perspective Measurements shows a usable set of indicators for the client perspective. It needs to be noted that some of the elements also might be used for the process perspective, however in this example as they are to do with the client process; they have been grouped into the client focus.

The following elements are proposed to be used to measure the client perspective:

- **Leads generated Pipeline Target for full year**: This is a so-called "Leading indicator", as it might pre-indicate using a probability entry heuristic a future sales volume. Only measuring this leading indicator might generate pipeline "bubbles", means – it would over-emphasize deals. It is clear that setting a pipeline target will incentivise people to look for deals which generate a certain bookings volume. Not every deal will materialise and some deals that initially turn out to be a "big deal" would not be qualified for such a deal in any way. However; not measuring this item would then only yield to further deals.

Client focus	Target
Leads generated: Pipeline Target for full year	xxx M€
Total Conversion ratio	Percentage %
Conversion ratio "Qualification" to "Sold"	Percentage %
Total Cluster TCV Target incl. Upselling and Cross-Selling	yyy M€
Leads Generated - by Business Unit	Number
Client satisfaction (OTACE) of existing clients	Measurement Number (1-5)
Brand perception survey result of future clients	Measurement number

Table 7-2: Client Perspective Measurements

- The **total conversion ratio** is the ratio of deals converted from early stages of the pipeline into latter stages. The following logic applies: If the conversion ratio is high then sales people would only go after "sure deals" and potentially underperform in trying out new ideas in the market, new clients or new services. If the conversion ratio is comparatively low, then there might be an issue of focus. The art is here to find a good balance between low and high. Same here it is a trailing indicator, as conversion ratio only can be measured after the facts.
- **Conversion ratio Qualification to Sold**: As the Qualification stage a la Holden or Kotler is the stage where the biggest amount of resources is put into place, such as a deal team, contract team, technical architects and so on, a special consideration should be established to measure this special conversion ratio, also known as a trailing indicator. Not every deal engaged can be won, there might be downfalls. However; if that ratio is too low then the qualification criteria are too thin. Same applies if the win rate is too high, then probably only the "very sure deals" should be qualified. Losses need to be allowed from a sales management perspective.
- **Total cluster TCV target generated by business unit**: This TCV (total contract value) target is important to measure as it determines the business plan over time. It also makes clusters comparable to the next as then the resources imputized per cluster and the yield in terms of TCV can be analysed.
- **Leads generated by business unit**: The number of qualified leads generated by the business unit in terms of number might be a suitable indicator. If the number of leads generated is too low, then business units are likely to rely on only a series of few deals, where the risk of success or failure is then too much attached with too few opportunities. If that comparatively number of

leads is high, then either the business unit might be chasing after too many deals out in the market – meaning – being too much unfocused or unstructured.

- **Client satisfaction of existing clients**: This is a leading and trailing indicator at the same time. As a leading indicator it shows how clients are likely to consider further purchases – if the client satisfaction is too low. As a trailing indicator it shows how a team has performed over time and has generated a certain impression in the market. Companies such as Capgemini measure their client satisfaction using surveys such as OTACE ("On time and above client expectations"). A rating below than four typically will be highlighted within the organisation to the higher-ups and will yield management attention. On the other side, if a client satisfaction rating appears too high, then it might be debated as to whether too much attention and focus have been put towards a client and this amount of effort and care can be reduced from an economic perspective.
- **Brand perception survey result of future clients**: As future or prospective clients do not directly deal with the company, they are often unknown territory. The only thing they might be aware of is a brand name and further mentioning, i.e. in trade and business papers, the internet and in advertisements that might lead them to consider a further evaluation of purchase. If the brand is relatively unknown, the sales team has to put in more effort into advertising than it would if it is already a known factor. Therefore it can be considered as a leading indicator.

7.7.2.2 Financial Focus

Table 7-3: Financial Perspective Measurements shows a suitable target set for a Financial focus. Many books, professions and seminars have been written about the topics on how to account for revenues, expense and its sub-rations – those will not be repeated here. This table however is a good list of indicators to observe for a business unit or cluster to make it comparable. It needs to be noted that merely all financial indicators are trailing indicators:

- **Revenues**: Revenues come from sales and are the "magic source" of all activities in a business. Without revenues, there are no profits. This might be one of the reasons why sales people are eyed on as either crooks or magicians in some companies. As it is known in financial strategy, not everything that goes into the cashier is revenues, and not everything that is revenues are cash-in. However over time this should even out. What is clear is: If there are no revenues, there cannot be any expenses paid, except from the reserves of the shareholders or from previous periods' profits.
- **Signings or bookings**: Typically, the contracted volume of services of a contract is called signigs or bookings. It even can be seen as a leading indicator in that extent as signings eventually generate revenues, thus signings can be seen as the sum of all future revenues of a contract. Large deal makers typi-

cally are measured upon signings, some companies then overweight the revenues that come earlier and discount revenues of later time periods, i.e. by a discount factor.

- **Expense according to business plan**: Expense for a business unit is mostly composed of personnel costs, rent, depreciation or lease for assets and external expense, plus some other expense i.e. for financial expenses. All of this grouped together then takes the total expense which needs to be deducted from the revenues.
- **External expense and personnel expense**: From experience it makes sense to especially look into the sections "external expense" and "personal expense" separately.
- **Lease or depreciation or asset**: Asset purchased needs to be depreciated over time yielding in additional cash flow which can be used as a reserve for the purchase of new asset when the asset is used off. Leases are like expense. Both have their particular advantages and it is widely debated – depending on measurement and ratios whether a lease of an asset is more optimal or a purchase.

Financial Focus	**Target**
Revenues	Number M€
Signings or Bookings	Number M€
Expense	Number M€
External Expense	Number M€
Personnel Expense	Number M€
Lease and/or depreciation for asset	Number M€
Utilisation of personnel of overall time	Percentage
Overhead ratio billable people vs. Non-billable	Percentage%
Profits per business unit	Number M€
Profitability ratio	Percentage%
Accounts receivable days	Days

Table 7-3: Financial Perspective Measurements

- **Utilization of personnel**: The utilization ratio of the personnel employed is also of quite importance to know. If people being employed can be charge at a high ratio into billable projects or tasks, then they the profit per person without overheads is high, as typically the charge mechanism is based ultimately on time and material, i.e. person per day, however the salaries are paid by year. Thus if many days of the year an employee can be billed and the charge-out-rate is appropriate then the person yields a profit.
- **Overhead Ratio:** Typically, there are always people who cannot be billed directly to external clients, they are considered as administrative or management overhead. If that overhead becomes too high a proportion of a business unit, then the business unit in total can become unprofitable even despite the

fact that the billable personnel is utilised to a high degree in billable client projects.

- **The total profits per business units:** They are in essence the subtraction of expense from revenues. This amount should be greater than zero. Some cynics argue that much more than this is not necessary to know about accounting.
- **Profit ratio:** In order to compare one business unit with the next, the profit ratio is a useful vehicle. Definitely at the end the return on capital employed (ROCE) of the overall operation might be more useful to know for the shareholders; however first and foremost the operational profit ratio is the key input for the latter.
- **Accounts receivable days:** As it is mentioned above, revenues are accounted for the moment a product is shipped or a service is performed an invoice is being sent to the client. However, companies can go out of cash quickly if they do not collect their bills and get paid. Therefore it makes a great deal of sense to observe this ratio and make sure that this average days of accounts receivable is low. There are highly country-dependent views on what numbers of days of accounts receivable is tolerable with southern European countries ranging in the 100+ days and Switzerland more being in the 10s of days (Wilson & Summers, 2002).

With revenues being a function of total contract value divided by time, the key is to measure TCVs and a healthy mix of portfolio durations.

7.7.2.3 Innovation and Learning perspective

The following elements are proven to be useful in an innovation and learning perspective and summarised in Table 7-4, most of them can be considered as leading indicators for the future of the business:

- **Budget spent for education**: Money alone will not help people to learn, however if there is no money spent for education then it is very likely that the focus on education does not exist.
- **Skill built up according to plan for new hires**: New hires especially have an increased requirement for training compared to experienced personnel. Besides people working in the organisation and culture, they need to understand particular tools, processes, working practices within their specific environment etc. This falls both into place with professional hires coming from a different, i.e. competitive company as well as young graduates from an educational facility, i.e. University, Fachhochschule or Berufsschule.
- **Ratio of innovative projects within area**: What is clear is that innovation and learning comes along with innovative projects. If that ratio is too low, probably there is a steady-state operation which might have a hard time in taking on new clients or trying out something new. If that ratio is too high, there might be a loss of distinct focus causing a profit distortion. As this ratio

often can be biased and is subject to interpretation, some strict rules need to be applied to make this number or ratio comparable.

- **Average age of deals contracted:** In services businesses especially there is a tendency to do follow-on businesses to an existing deal, as the costs of prolongation of a deal of a specific client, especially a strategic client, is lower than the costs of hunting after new clients. If then the average age of deals is quite old then there is a likelihood that no new deals have been hunted on for the last years and as a result also no new deals might follow. As all deals over time have a tendency to expire it might imply then that a relatively high age of deals is a leading indicator of an aging or dying business unit.
- **Offshore mix as part of a team:** With an international company it shows that working offshore in some parts is a prerequisite for success. If the overall team dedicated to a client has a high offshore ratio, the business mix is then a healthier one than that of a team that might only be on-shore. If the off-shore element is not being utilised then it might be argued as to whether the local team is utilizing the full power of a global company and further investigation might be applied into the capabilities of a team to integrate globally.

Innovation and Learning Perspective	**Target**
Budget spent for education purposes	Target
Skill build-up according to plan for new hires	Number of days spent
Offshore Mix as part of the team	Percentage
Ratio of innovation projects with clients	Ratio%
Average age of deals contracted	Age
Ratio of deals worked cross-divisional	Percentage Ratio%
Employee satisfaction ratio	Target
Employee productivity ratio	Target

Table 7-4: Innovation and Learning Perspective Measurements

- **Ratio of deals worked cross-divisional:** As in a multi-divisional environment it is argued that deals should be worked cross-divisionally, i.e. in Capgemini a deal entailing both Technology Services and Outsourcing Services it might be worth measuring as a learning effect the ratio of those deals that are being executed in more than one division compared to single-divisional deals. If that ratio is very low then it might be argued whether the business area is leveraging the full power of the company or not.
- **Employee satisfaction ratio**: Employee satisfaction might have to do with innovation and learning. Satisfied employees might have a higher tendency to learn than dis-satisfied employees; or the other way round, dis-satisfaction can be a great motivator to move oneself out of this situation by learning. This ratio can be measured by the number of employee feedback talks with managers being held, a further measurement indicator might be an employee

satisfaction index generated by an employee survey, conducted across the whole group or multiple business units.

- **Employee productivity ratio**: The employees should be productive both in performing their tasks but also by the amount of work they can perform for a certain amount of money within a certain timeframe. This ratio needs to be observed by business division and tasks, and it might be subdivided in a tailor-fit manner, i.e. Number of E-Mail accounts managed by Account Manager, Numbers of Servers operated by Server operator, Numbers of Gigabytes of Storage managed by Storage manager etc. The number itself is futile if it is not being compared with both a global but also cross-company level and also has to do with the amount of tools and automation employed. Automation the other way round is also associated with a cost; hence it is not for free.

7.7.2.4 Process Focus

The following elements summarised in Table 7-5 are proven to be useful from a process perspective with most of them being trailing indicators:

- **ISO certification and re-certification**: Nearly all services organisations are now to be certified by standard bodies such as ISO (International Standardisation Organisation) on quality management aspects, security aspects etc. A key certification is ISO 9001 (International Standardisation Organisation, 2010) for overall quality management, and ISO 20000 for Information Technology Service Management, ISO 27000 for security management. It is of key for a business unit to choose and select the right set of standardisations required in order to perform with its clients – it is shown that many clients now especially do consider an ISO 9001 certification as a prerequisite. As these ISO standards can be audited by auditing organizations, the compliance and adherence to these standards can be used as a good indicator for an overall process perspective.
- **Deviation from audits**: Most companies and businesses do perform internal audits. Practically a deviation discovered within an audit has consequences for the management, depending upon the deviation discovered it might even cause the management to be exchanged. Therefore taking this number and observing it – as well as making sure that audit compliance is possible at any time is a good leading and trailing indicator for the health of a company or business organization, overall.
- **SLA compliance**: Service Level Agreements (SLAs) contracted with clients typically foresee a compliance rule, means that the services provider needs to adhere to. Typical compliance ratios are: Numbers of server downtimes per quarter for an IT operation, Percentage resolution of calls fixed first time within a service desk, Percentage of application management tickets resolved within the agreed time etc. An adherence to the process – if the process is good - typically yields into a high ratio of SLA compliance.

- **SLA penalties paid**: Unfortunately, the downside in non-compliance to SLAs is often the contractual obligation to pay penalties which might be as high a one year's revenue or – still not desirable – one year's profits. If that amount exceeds a certain trigger level, definitely corrective action should be enacted.

Process Perspective	Target
ISO certification and re-certification	Timing of Certification, Audit result
Deviation from audits	Number of deviation from Process Audits
SLA compliance per client and overall	Percentage % of SLAs compliant
SLA penalties paid	Amount €

Table 7-5: Process Perspective Measurements

7.8 Summary and Conclusion

Senior Practitioners inside Capgemini see a need for collaboration and cross-selling, however they are being felt impeded by the systemic. The culture itself is less of an impediment than initially thought – Consultants definitely are different than Technologists and those are different than hard-nosed Outsourcers. Nevertheless, they can work together, if the common goal is being set and the change can be implemented, tracked and measured. However in light with all the change proposed, it needs to be said that the author whilst having the role of a researcher is at the same time part of the organisation, implying having a "double-role" which might lead to a bias in the line of the argumentation. Currently, there are strategic gaps inside Capgemini in order to really grow the market share. There are many resources that exist, thus a resource augmentation is not necessarily needed, nevertheless, those resources are not grouped together to generate the capability to cross-sell across different disciplines and to grow.

The current discipline-orientated organisation is good for the execution of a functioning delivery unit, contrary to this, in the market, the unified view of "One Capgemini" needs to be depicted and shown by the people. It is therefore recommended to group the sales processionals together and unblock the systems in a way that they have an easier possibility of working together for the better result of all of the individual disciplines. This unblocking of course needs to be tracked and monitored using a system like a Balanced Scorecard. Here, not only the financial focus counts, it needs to be thought about quality, learning and improvement and other parts. Especially in smaller and more condensed geographies, such as Switzerland, it is of key importance to show a unified face towards the market and to re-group. This change, coming from a discipline based organisation with different areas such as Consulting, Technology Services and Outsourcing Services is more a difficult change which has to overcome middle-management fiefdoms and fears of power loss – as always heavily depends upon personal leadership. However, the expected increased results over time will show that this effort is worth taking it.

8 Thesis-Like Summary

How to choose the right strategy in a marketplace: Here, the resources a company have should first be looked at, what capabilities can be assembled out of it and what the external market wants from a company best. What then is demanded by the external market should be focused on and not necessarily what can be produced right now, no matter whether it is demanded or not.

How to plan accounts: Accounts should be planned both along a proven methodology, i.e. KARMA in order to select the right accounts to target within a territory. The entire team working around this account should be invited to contribute. This planning should then be monitored on a quarterly base and reviewed.

Intercultural work in international accounts: It is heavily recommended to build global integrated teams for globally operating clients, by grouping them after the revenue source, whilst assembling the delivery teams around the production end. Besides the sales leaders local key consultants should be included into this globally operating team. A global knowledge pool, i.e. a groupware database, maintained by an administrator should be set up and maintained.

Configuring organisations: The organisation should be configured in an "octopus-way" with a "local brain" and a "global" strategic apex. The parts in-between, like the operating core, the support staff, and the technostructure should be located where a client – who is always the ultimate arbiter of success – sees the biggest value and therefore is willing to pay a price.

How to measure the business success: Besides the financial trailing indicators, such as order entry and revenues, financial leading indicators should be taken into account to measure success. Early indicators can be: Pipeline of deals to come, but also learning and development indicators, such as checkmarks in integration of a team, certification of sales and consulting leaders, alignment of the team towards the client, numbers of client calls per week or month, numbers of proposals out to the clients etc.

How to orientate towards the client: Every large organisation is different and there is not a "one size fits all" towards a client. However there should be a certain leadership position towards a client who has the authority to act on behalf of the supplying company towards this client on a global scale and knows the client inside-out. It is clear, that this person being longer in the business might be rejective towards new ideas from the supplying organisation; therefore "innovation targets" need to be given towards this key person. The key people working towards one client should at least know each other and meet on a regular basis.

How to win: Winning is not a linear game. Demonstrate to the customer that she is important to the supplier: Know the customer and understand what the customer has as business plan and competitive environment. Build a value proposition around the customer's key business objectives. However, without client access failure is imminent: Understand risk transference of the client towards the supplier and also the different phases of a deal starting from need determination to value proposition to price and towards risk avoidance. The first proposition should knock them off of the customers' seats. Winning is a team game, use the power of the whole global team – of both sides, the client and the own organisation. Winning is everything but the journey is the real experience. Small, highly skilled and motivated teams are better than average armies, know the process, know the journey.

Embrace change, innovate, innovate and innovate: Be pragmatic, winning something creates a platform but be obstinate about the supplier's uniqueness. Include the support teams and Delivery from the outset; bring everyone along the journey with you. Be humble, however, know when to walk away.

Abbreviations

AM	Application Management
BPO	Business Process Outsourcing
CC	Capgemini Consulting
CIO	Chief Information Officer
CEO	Chief Executive Officer
COO	Chief Operating Officer
CRM	Customer Relationship Management
CSO	Chief Sales Officer
CFO	Chief Finance Officer
CS	Capgemini Consulting / Consulting Services
CHF	Swiss Francs
EDS	Electronic Data Systems Corporation
EUR	Euros
GDP	Gross Domestic Product
HP	Hewlett-Packard Company
I3	I-Cubed or Innovation, Industrialisation and Client Intimacy
IDC	International Data Corporation
IBM	International Business Machines Corporation
IT	Information Technology
KARMA	Key Account Relationship Management Analysis
OECD	Organisation for economic Co-Operation and Development
OS	Outsourcing Services
OSEC	Organisation of Swiss Export Companies
OTACE	On Time and Above Client Expectations
SD&M	Software Design & Management, a division of Capgemini
SLA	Service Level Agreement
SSM	Solution Selling Methodology
TCV	Total Contract Value
TS	Technology Services

Table of Figures

Table of Tables

Bibliography

Businessweek, Top Outsourcing places. (2009, 02 09). Retrieved 06 08, 2010, from Businessweek: http://images.businessweek.com/ss/09/02/0203_emerging_outsourcers/7.htm

Dabbawallas, Topnews.IN. (2009, 12 31). Retrieved 08 18, 2010, from Topnews.IN: http://www.topnews.in/dabbawallas-represent-maharashtra-republic-day-parade-2248912

3M. (1997). Lessons in Teamwork: the 3M experience. *Management Development Review, 10*(7), 376-378.

Accenture. (2010, 06 08). *Accenture*. Retrieved 06 08, 2010, from Accenture Annual Report: http://www.accenture.com

Alaganandan, P., Bhowmick, R., & Mohanty, S. (2010, Jan 20). Human capital challenges of M&A transactions in India. *Mercer, http://www.mercer.com/referencecontent.htm?idContent=1351290*.

Apel, K.-O. (1973). *Transformation der Philosophie, 2 Bände,(Bd. I: Sprachanalytik, Semiotik, Hermeneutik; Bd. II: Das Apriori der Kommunikationsgemeinschaft)*. Frankfurt am Main, Germany: Suhrkamp.

Arora, A., Arunachalam, V. S., Asundi, J., & Fernandes, R. (2001, October). The Indian software services industry. *Research Policy, 30*(8), 1267-1287.

ASCO. (2007). *ASCO*. Retrieved 02 04, 2010, from ASCO Award 2007: http://www.asco.ch/award07/teilnehmer.php

Auswärtiges Amt. (2010, 03 01). *Chile, Kultur und Bildungspolitik*. Retrieved 06 06, 2010, from Auswärtiges Amt: http://www.auswaertiges-amt.de/diplo/de/Laenderinformationen/Chile/Kultur-UndBildungspolitik.html

Auswärtiges Amt. (2010, 03 01). *Indien: Kultur- und Bildungspolitik*. Retrieved 06 08, 2010, from Auswärtiges Amt: http://www.auswaertiges-amt.de/ diplo/de/ Laenderinformationen/Indien/Kultur-UndBildungspolitik.html

Barash, M., & Mitchell, D. H. (1998, Summer). Account-based forecasting at Nabisco Biscuit Company. *Journal of Business Forecasting Methods and Systems, 17*(2), 3-7.

Beckett, A. (2009, 07 09). *Systems Failure*. (T. Guardian, Editor) Retrieved 06 19, 2010, from Guardian: http://www.guardian.co.uk/society/2009/jul/09/nhs-computer-programme-failure

Bennett, A. (2002, 12 05). *IBM PWCC Integration is on track*. Retrieved 01 18, 2010, from IT World: http://www.itworld.com/021205ibmpwc

Biotech Cluster Development GmbH. (2010, 07 06). *BIO M*. Retrieved 07 06, 2010, from Münchner Biotech Cluster: http://www.bio-m.org/de/ muenchner _biotech_cluster/index.html

BITKOM. (2009, 10). *BITKOM ITK-Marktzahlen*. Retrieved 01 18, 2010, from BITKOM: http://www.bitkom.org/files/documents/ITK-Marktzahlen_Oktober_2009_Kurzfassung.pdf

Bitner, M., Fisk, R., & Brown, S. (1993). Tracking the Evolution of the Services Marketing Literature. *Journal of Retailing, 1*(69), pp. 61 - 103.

Bölscher, J. (2009). *Business-Knigge für deutsche Manager in Indien: Verhaltensweisen verstehen und Zusammenarbeit erfolgreich gestalten.* Books on Demand GmbH.

Bolten, J. (1991). Fremdsprache Wirtschaftsdeutsch: Bestandsaufnahme und Perspektiven. In B.-D. Müller, *Interkulturelle Wirtschaftskommunikation* (pp. 71-89). München: iudicium.

Bolten, J. (2007). *Einführung in die Interkulturelle Wirtschaftskommunikation.* Göttingen: Vandenhoek & Ruprecht.

Bossidy, L. (2002). *Execution – the discipline of getting things done.* New York, NY: Crown Business.

Bowman, C. (1990). *The Essence of Strategic Management.* London: Prentice-Hall.

Braun, C. (1991). Interkulturelle Barrieren in der Fach- und Berufssprache der Tourismusbranche. In B.-D. Müller, *Interkulturelle Wirtschafts-kommunikation* (pp. 193-202). München: idudicium.

Bryman, A., & Bell, A. (2007). *Business Research Methods.* Oxford, UK: Oxford University Press.

Capgemini . (2007). *Global Readyness Training: India.* Les Fontaines: Capgemini Corp.

Capgemini. (2010, 01 18). *Capgemini Brand Promise*. Retrieved 01 18, 2010, from Capgemini: http://www.uk.capgemini.com/about/

Capgemini S.A. (2007). *Blue Book.* Paris, France: Capgemini S.A.

Capgemini S.A. (2008, 11 13). *Rightshore Fact Sheet.* Retrieved 1 18, 2010, from Capgemini U.S. - Rightshore: http://www.us.capgemini.com/DownloadLibrary/files/factsheets/Capgemini_RightshoreFS.pdf

Capgemini S.A. (2009, 05 18). *Annual Report.* Retrieved 01 17, 2010, from Capgemini : http://annualreport.capgemini.com

Capgemini S.A. (2009, November 04). *Capgemini creates Global Application Lifecycle Business.* Retrieved 01 17, 2010, from Capgemini Press Room: Capgemini, 2009, Press Release "Capgemini creates global Application Lifecycle Services to help its clients get more value from congested application landscapes"; http://www.capgemini.com/news-and-events/news/capgemini-creates-global-application-lifecycl

Capgemini S.A. (2010). *Annual Report 2009.* Paris: Capgemini S.A.

Capgemini S.A. (2010, 08 15). *The Values We Share.* Retrieved 08 15, 2010, from Capgemini S.A.: http://www.capgemini.com/about/capgemini/values/

Carmel, E. (2003). The New Software Exporting nations: Success Factors. *The Electronic Journal of Information Systems in Developing Countries*, V.13.

Carter, J. R. (1994). The impact of interorganizational alliances in improving supplier quality. *International Journal of Physical Distribution and Logistics, 24*(5), 15-24.

Central Intelligence Agency. (2009). *CIA World Fact Book.* Retrieved 1 18, 2010, from CIA: https://www.cia.gov/library/publications/the-world-factbook/

Chen, H. (2001). *Kulturschock China.* Bielefeld: Reise Know-How Verlag Rump.

Christopher, M. G., Payne, A. F., & Ballantyne, D. F. (1991). *Relationship Marketing: Bringing Quality Customer Service and Marketing Together.* Oxford, UK: Butterworth Heinemann.

Claycomb, C. Germain, R., & Dröge, C. (2000). The Effects of Formal Strategic Marketing Planning on the Industrial Firm's Configuration, Structure, Exchange Patterns and Performance. *Industrial Marketing Management,, 29*(3), 219-235.

Clutterbuck, D. (1998). *Coaching the Team at Work.* London, UK: Nicholas Brealey Publishing Ltd.

Conant, J. S., & J., W. C. (1999). Marketing Program Planning, Process Benefits, and store Performance: An Initial Study Among Small Retail Firms. *Journal of Retailing, 75*(4), 525-542.

Cooke, E. (1999, Winter). Control and motivation in sales management through the compsensation plan. *Journal of Marketing Theory and Practice*, 80-83.

Coombs, R., & Hull, R. (1997). *Knowledge-Management Practices and Path-Dependency of Innovation.* Manchester: CRIC.

Corbett, C. J. (1999). Partnerships to improve supply chains. *Sloan Management Review, , 40*(4), 71-83.

Corner, I. a. (2005, May 20). Monitoring qualitative aspects of CRM implementation: the essential dimension of management responsibility for employee involvement and acceptance. J. *ournal of Targeting, Analysis and Measurement in Marketing, 13*(3), 267-274.

Cros, P.-Y. (2007, 03 15). *Capgemini.* Retrieved 12 12, 2009, from Capgemini Day Transformation for Leadership: http://www.fi.capgemini.com/ m/en/doc/ Capgemini_Day_07_Pres_3.pdf

CSC. (2007, 11 20). *CSC.* Retrieved 01 18, 2009, from CSC Names David Booth President of Global sales and Marketing: http://www.csc.com/newsroom/ press_releases/3295-csc_names_david_booth_president_of_global _sales_and_marketing

Dash, A. (2008). Globalization, Knowledge Society and Knowledge (In)Security for the Peripheral Communities. In A. K. Nayak, & M. Jomon, *India in the Emerging Global Order* (pp. 354-366). Dehli: Tata McGraw-Hill.

Davis, D., & Cosenza, R. (1985). *Business Research for Decision Making.* Boston, MA: Kent Publishing.

Davis, D., & Cosenza, R. M. (1993). *Business research for decision making.* Belmont, CA: Wadsworth.

de Liso, N., & Metcalfe, S. (1997, Aprile). Progresso tecnico e sistemi tecnologici. *Economia politica*, pp. 85-120.

Deci, E., & Ryan, R. (1980). The empirical exploration of intrinsic motivational processes. *Advances In Experimental Social Psychology, 10*(1), 39-74.

Desarbo, & Zikmund, W. G. (2009). *Business Research Methods.* South-Western Pub.

Dibb, S. (2002, Summer). Marketing Planning Best Practice. *Marketing Review, 2*(4), 1-4.

Dibb, S. F. (2001). The marketing planning experience: a UK and Portuguese comparison. . *Marketing Intelligence & Planning, 19*(6), 409-417.

Dobbs, R., Leslie, K., & Mendonca, L. T. (2005). Building the healthy corporation. *The McKinsey Quarterly, 3*(62), 62.

Drucker, P. F. (1995). *The Practice of Management.* London: Heron.

Dueck, G. (2002). *Wild Duck – empirische Philosophie der Mensch-Computer-Vernetzung.* Heidelberg, Germany: Springer.

Dueck, G. (2007). *Lean Brain Management.* Heidelberg, Germany: Springer.

Dülfer, E. (1999). *Internationales Management in unterschiedlichen Kulturbereichen (6. Auflage).* München: Oldenburg.

Duncan, T. (2002). *High trust selling – Make more money in less time with less stress.* Nashville, TN: Nelson.

Dwyer, F. R. (1987). Developing Buyer Seller Relationships. *Journal of Marketing, 51*(2), 11-27.

Else, R. A. (1973, May 14). Sales planning by objectives at General Electric. *Sales Management, 62*(8), 47-49.

FAO. (2008). *Questionnaire building*. Retrieved 1 18, 2010, from FAO: http://www.fao.org/docrep/w3241E/w3241e05.htm

Fiocca, R. (1982). Account Portfolio Analysis for Strategy Development. *Industrial Marketing Management, 11*(1), 52-63.

Florida, R. (2002). *The rise of the creative class – and how it's transforming work, leisure, community and everyday life;.* New York, NY: Perseus Books.

Foucault, M. (2005). *Analytik der Macht.* Frankfurt am Main: Suhrkamp.

Gabler Verlag. (2010). *Wirtschaftslexikon*. Retrieved 06 19, 2010, from Gabler Wirtschaftslexikon: http://wirtschaftslexikon.gabler.de/Archiv/54709/outsourcing-v7.html

Gartner Group. (2007, 09 26). *Gartner Says Indian IT Service Providers Increasing Pace of Growth* . Retrieved 8 30, 2010, from http://www.gartner.com/it/page.jsp?id=526008

Gaston-Breton, T. (2007). *The Capgemini Saga.* Paris, France: Capgemini.

Grant, R. M. (1999). *Contemporary Strategy Analysis,.* Malden, MA: Blackwell Business.

Gregory, A. a. (2004, November/December). Take me to your leader. *Sales and Marketing Professional*, 38-39.

Grimwade, N., & Grimwade, N. (1996). *International Trade Policy: A Contemporary Analysis.* New York: Routledge.

Günther, S. (1991). Pi Lao Zheng ("Müdigkeit im Kampf") - Zur Begegnung deutscher und chisischer Gesprächsstile. In B.-D. (. Müller, *Interkulturelle Wirtschaftskommunikation* (pp. 297-324). München: iudicium.

Hall, E. (1976). *Beyond Culture.* New York: Doubleday.

Hamel, G., & Pralahad, C. K. (1994). *Competing for the Future.* Boston, MA: Harvard Business School Press.

Hammer, M. (1996). *Beyond Re-engineering.* . London, UK: HarperCollins Business.

Heckscher, E. (1919, ed 2006). *International Trade and Economic History: Edited by Ronald Findlay, Rolf G.* Dehli: Mit Pr .

Hedin, M. (2009, 03 15). *IDC Worldwide Services 2009-2013 Forecast: Making the Most of Economic Crisis –Doc#217479.* Retrieved 08 19, 2009, from IDC: http.//www.idc.com/research

Henry, J. (2001). *Creativity and Perception in Management.* London: Sage.

Hessler, P. (2009, 05 21). TechnoVision. (Capgemini, Interviewer) http://www.youtube.com/watch?v=-sCKpdS9muk. Youtube.

Hofstede, G. (2001). *Culture's Consequences: comparing values, behaviors, institutions, and organizations across nations (2nd ed.).* Thousand Oaks, CA: SAGE Publications.

Holden International. (2009). *Holden International.* Retrieved 1 18, 2010, from Holden International: http://www.holdenintl.com/

Holt, S. (2003). *The Role of the Global Account Manager: A Boundary Role Perspective.* Cranfield, MA: Cranfield School of Management: PhD thesis.

Homburg, C., & Pflessner, C. (2000, Nov). A Multiple-Layer Model of Market-Oriented Organizational Culture: Measurement Issues and Performance Outcomes. *Journal of Marketing Research, 37*(4), pp. 449-462.

Hout, T., Porter, M., & Rudden, E. (1982, September-October). How Global Companies Win Out. *Harvard Business Review*, pp. 98-108.

Huntington, S. P. (1996). *Der Kampf der Kulturen. Die Neugestaltung der Wirtschaftspolitik im 21. Jahrhundert.* München: Europa-Verlag.

IBM. (2002). *Signature Sellling - Course.* Retrieved 1 18, 2010, from IBM: https://www-304.ibm.com/jct03001c/services/learning/ites.wss/sg/en?pageType=course_description&courseCode=SSMR1SG

IBM. (2009). *Relationship Sales Discipline Overview*. Retrieved 12 29, 2009, from IBM Human Resources: , http://www-05.ibm.com/employment/ europe/ua/roles/roles2.html

IBM Corp. (2010, 06 06). *IBM Corp.* Retrieved 06 06, 2010, from Diverstiy 3.0 at IBM: http://www-03.ibm.com/employment/us/diverse/

IBM Corp, IBV. (2010, 06 05). *IBM Corp.* Retrieved 06 05, 2010, from Component Business Models - Making Spezialisation Real: http://www-935.ibm.com/services/us/imc/pdf/g510-6163-component-business-models.pdf

IBM Corp. (2004). *IBM Insider's Guide to Client Briefings – Practical Advice for Building Relationships.* White Plains, NY: IBM.

IBM Corp. (2010, 01 24). *Jobs at IBM - Major Business Units*. Retrieved 01 24, 2010, from IBM: http://www-03.ibm.com/employment/us/ibm_major_units.shtml

IBM Corporation. (2005). *IBM US Human Resources*. Retrieved 01 15, 2010, from Sales professions: http://www.ibm.com/us/hr

IDC and Hedin, Marianne. (2009, 03 15). *Worldwide Services 2009-2013 Forecast: Making the Most of Economic Crisis –Doc#217479.* Retrieved 08 19, 2009, from IDC: http.//www.idc.com/research

Ihlau, O. (2006). *Weltmacht Indien, Die neue Herausforderung des Westens.* München: Siedler.

Intel Corp. . (n.d.). *Moore's law.* Retrieved 01 27, 2010, from Intel Corp: http://www.intel.com/technology/mooreslaw/

Interbrand. (2010, 06 06). *Best global Brands*. Retrieved 06 06, 2010, from Interbrand Inc.: http://www.interbrand.com/best_global_brands.aspx

International Standardisation Organisation. (2010, 06 06). *ISO.* Retrieved 06 06, 2010, from ISO: http://www.iso.org/iso/home.html

Investorwords. (2011, 02 05). *Investorwords.com*. Retrieved 02 05, 2011, from Investorwords.com: http://www.investorwords.com/6600/offshoring.html

ITIL Organisation. (2010, 06 05). *ITIL.ORG*. Retrieved 06 05, 2010, from ITIL: http://www.itil.org/en/vomkennen/itil/index.php

izreloaded.com. (2007, 09 07). *izreloaded.com*. Retrieved 08 22, 2010, from izreloaded.com: http://izreloaded.blogspot.com/2007/09/starbucks-in-goa-india.html

Jackson D. Jr, H. T. (2006). Examining career development programs for the sales force. *Journal of Business & Industrial Marketing, 21*(5), 291-299.

Jensen, M., & Meckling, W. (1976). Theory of the firm. Managerial behavior, agency costs, and ownership structure. *Journal of Financial Economics, 3*(4), 305-360.

Jones, M. L. (2007). *Hostede - Culturally questionnable.* Wollongong: Wollongong University.

Kalwani, M. U., & Narayandas, N. (1995). Long-term manufacturer-supplier relationships: Do they pay off for supplier firms? *Journal of Marketing, 59*(1), 1-17.

Kaplan, R. S., & Norton, D. P. (2001, 05 08). *The Strategy-Focused Organization.* Boston, MA: Harvard Business School Press.

Kay, J. (2004). *Why Firms succeed.* London: Penguin.

Kay, J. A. (1993). *Foundations of corporate success: how business strategies add value.* Oxford University Press: Oxford.

Kellen, V. (2002). *CRM Measurement Frameworks.* Chicago: Blue Wolf and DePaul University.

Kiran, V. (2009, 09). *September.* Retrieved 08 15, 2010, from Vijaykiran.com: http://www.vijaykiran.com/2009/09/

Knorr-Cetina, K. (1993). *Epistemic Cultures. How the Sciences Make Knowledge.* Cambridge MA: Harvard University Press.

Knox, S. a. (1998). *Competing on Value.* London, UK: Pitman Publishing.

Knox, S., & Maklan, S. (1998). *Competing on Value.* London, UK: Pitman Publishing.

Kotler, P. (2003). *Marketing Management.* London, UK: Prentice Hall.

Kotler, P., Rackham, N., & Krisnavany, S. (2006). Ending the war between sales and Marketing. *Harvard Business Review, 07*, 23-38.

Kumar, S. R. (2008). Reconsiling World Trade Integration and India's Destination. In A. Nayak, & M. G. Jomon, *India in the Emerging Global Order* (pp. 203-216). New Dehli, India: Tata McGraw-Hill.

Küng, T. (2007). *Gebrauchsanweisung für die Schweiz.* München Zürich: Piper.

Lacity, M. C., Willcocks, L. P., & Rottman, J. W. (2008). Global outsourcing of back office services: lessons, trends and enduring challenges. *Strategic Outsourcing: An International Journal*, 13-34.

Lane, S. a. (2000). The implementation of marketing planning: a case study in gaining commitment at 3M (UK) Abrasives. *Journal of Strategic Marketing, 9*(3), 225-239.

Latour, B. (2005). *Analytik der Macht.* Frankfurt am Main: Suhrkamp.

Latour, B. (2005). *Reassembling the Social: An Introduction to Actor-Network-Theory.* Oxford: Oxford.

Lemke, D. (2009). *Shifting Buyer Concerns.* Retrieved 12 28, 2009, from Vision Consulting Group: http://tinyurl.com/riskprice

Lewin, K. (1943). Defining the "Field at a Given Time.". *Psychological Review-Republished in Resolving Social Conflicts & Field Theory in Social Science, Washington, D.C.: American Psychological Association, 1997.*, 292-310.

Lewin, K. (1947). Frontiers of Group Dynamics. *Human Relations*, 5-41.

Lewis, R. (2007, 03). Communicating Successfully across Cultures. *HR Director*, : http://www.crossculture.com

Locke, E. A. (2004, November). Linking goals to monetary incentives. *Academy of Management Executive, 18*(4), 130-134.

MacKenzie, Podsakoff, & Rich. (2007). The effects of service climate and the effective leadership behaviour of supervisors on frontline employee service quality: a multi-level analysis. *Journal of Occupational and Organizational Psychology*.

Manager-Magazin. (2009, 05 20). *Berater-Ranking: McKinsey und Berger weiter vorn*. Retrieved 01 18, 2010, from Manager-Magazin: http://www.manager-magazin.de/unternehmen/artikel/0,2828,626032,00.html

Mandelbrot, B. (2009, 9 15). How Fractals can explain what's wrong with Wall Street. *Scientific American*, pp. http://www.scientificamerican.com/article.cfm?id=multifractals-explain-wall-street.

Maslow, A. (1943). A Theory of Human Motivation. *Psychological Review 50(4) (1943)*, 370-396.

Matthies, H. (2001). *Zwischen Nepotismus und Reflektiven Standards*. Berlin: Wissenschaftszentrums Berlin für Sozialforschung (WZB).

McDonald, M. H. (1998). *Key account management - learning from supplier and customer perspectives*. Oxford, UK: Butterworth Heinemann.

McDonald, M. H. (1999). *Key Account Management - building on supplier and buyer perspectives*. London, UK: Cranfield.

McDonald, M. H. (2000). *Key customers - how to manage them profitably*. Oxford, UK: Butterworth Heinemann.

McDonald, M. H. (2001). Achieving Excellence in Marketing Planning: objectives, barriers and solutions. *Cranfield School of Management: Research report for the Cranfield Strategic Marketing Planning Research Club*. Cranfield, MA.

McDonald, M. H. (2003). *Marketing Plans*. Oxford, UK: Butterworth Heinemann.

McDonald, M. H., Millman, A. F., & Rogers, B. (1996). Key Account Management - learning from supplier and customer perspectives. In C. S. Club (Ed.). Cranfield, MA: Cranfield.

McGovern, G. J. (2004, November). Bringing Customers into the Boardroom,. *Harvard Business Review, 82*(11), 70-80.

Mehta, A., Armenakis, A., Mehta, N., & Irani, F. (2006). Challenges and Opportunities of Business Process Outsourcing in India . *Journal of Labor Research*, 324-338.

Meyer, C.-H. (2005). *Mauern aus Glas, Südafrikanische Narrationen zu Konflikt, Differenz und Identität*. Münster: Waxman.

Millman, A. F. (1994). From key account selling to key account management. *10th Industrial Marketing and Purchasing (IMP) Conference* (p. September). Groningen: University of Groningen.

Minto, B. (1996). *The Minto Pyramid Principle.* London: Minto.

Mintzberg, H. (1999). The structuring of organizations. In S. Segal-Horn, *The Strategy Reader* (pp. 238-265). London: Blackwell Business.

Mises, R. v. (1951). *Positivism: A Study In Human Understanding.* . Cambridge, MA: Harvard University Press.

Moore, F. (2006, March). Strategy, power and negotiation: social control and expatriate managers in a German multinational corporation. *The International Journal of Human Resource Management*(17), pp. 399-413.

Morgan, P. (1986). International Human Resource Management, Fact or Fiction. *Personnel Administrator*, pp. 38-62.

MSSSCB. (2004). *Sales - an occupational map.* Retrieved 10 4, 2008, from Marketing and Sales Standards Setting Body, MSSCB: http://www.msssb.org/documents/SalesOccupationalMapreport.pdf

Müller, B.-D. (. (1993). *Interkulturelle Wirtschaftskommunikation.* München: iudicium.

Murphy, R. P. (2007). *The Politically Incorrect Guide to Capitalism.* Washington, DC: Regnery.

Nayak, A. K., & Jomon, M. (2008). *India in the Emerging GLobal ORder.* New Dehli: Tata McGraw-Hill.

Niklowitz, M. (2009, 12 18). *Handelszeitung.* Retrieved 02 04, 2010, from IT Marktführer:http://www.handelszeitung.ch/artikel/Business-IT-_HP-Schweiz-wird-bedeutend-staerker-wachsen_670125.html

NIST. (2010, 1 20). *Baldridge National Quality Program.* Retrieved 1 27, 2010, from NIST: http://www.baldrige.nist.gov/PDF_files/2009_2010_Business_Nonprofit_Criteria.pdf

Nollen, S. (2008). Software Industry Performance in India and China. In A. K. Nyak, & M. Jomon, *India in the Emerging Global Order* (pp. 67-83). New Dehli: Tata McGraw-Hill.

O'Toole, T. a. (2002, Winter). The strategy to implementation cycle of relationship marketing planning. *The Marketing Review, 3*(2), 195-209.

Ohlin, B. (1933). *Interregional and International Trade.* Cambridge.

Oksaar, E. (1993). Prolematik im interkulturellen Verstehen. In B.-D. Müller, *Interkulturelle Wirtschaftskommunikation* (pp. 13-26). München: idudicium.

OSEC. (2009, 10 16). *Direct investments and Swiss corporations abroad.* Retrieved 01 18, 2010, from OSEC: http://www.osec.ch/internet/osec/en/home/invest/us/handbook/overview_switzerland/international_outlook/direct_investments.html

Ouchi, W. G. (1981). *Theory Z - How American Busienss can meet the Japanese Challenge.* Jackson: Perseus Books.

Palmisano, S. (2006, May/June). The Globally Integrated Enterprise. *Foreign Affairs*, pp. 127 - 136.

Pamp, F. (2004). *Die Entwicklung der Stahlindustrie*. Retrieved 07 06, 2007, from Oberhausen Rheinland: http://www.oberhausen-rheinland.de/industrie/entwicklung/entwicklung.html

Pandey, G. (2010, March 07). *Finishing School for Indian IT Graduates.* Retrieved 08 17, 2010, from BBC News: http://news.bbc.co.uk/2/hi/south_asia/8547327.stm

Permutter, H. (1969, Vol. 4). The tortous evolution of the multinational corporation. *Columbia Journal of World Business*, pp. 9-18.

Peters, T. H., & Waterman, R. (1982). *In Search of Excellene.* Boston, MA: Harper Business.

Phillips, P. A. (2001). The Interactive Effects of Strategic Marketing Planning and Performance: A Neutral Network Analysis. *Journal of Marketing Management, 17*(1/2), 159-182.

Piercy, N. F. (1990). Organisational Context and Behavioural Problems as Determinants of the Effectiveness of the Strategic Marketing Planning Process. *Journal of Marketing Management, 6*(2), 127-143.

Piercy, N. F. (2001). *Market-led Strategic Change: Transforming the Process of Going to Market.* Oxford, UK: Butterworth Heinemann.

Piercy, N. F., & Land, N. (2005). Strategic Imperatives for Transformation in the Conventional Sales Organization. *Journal of Change Management, 5*(3), 249 – 266.

Piercy, N., & Lane, N. (2005). Strategic imperatives for transformation in the conventional sales organization,. *Journal of Marketing Management*, 563-582.

Plath, A. (2001). *International Enterprise.* Milton Keynes: Open University.

Plouffe, C. R., Williams, B., & Wachner, T. (2008). Navigating Difficult Waters: Publishing Trends and Scholarship in Sales Research. *Journal of Personal Selling and Sales Management, 28*(1), 79 - 92.

Pop, P. (2009, 11 26). *PHW.* Retrieved 01 18, 2010, from Strategic Value Creation in Banking: http://www.phw.info/downloads/forum/20/ Peter%20Pop_web.pdf

Porter, M. E. (2008). *Competitive Strategy: Techniques for Analyzing Industries and Competitors.* New York, NY: Simon & Schuster.

Prentice Hall. (1999). *Guide to the Essentials of World History.* New York: Prentice Hall.

Rayner, C., & Adam-Smith, D. (2005). *Managing and Leading People.* London, UK: CIPD.

Reeder, G. a. (2001, Fall). Integration of supply chain with demand planning: Tropicana's journey. *Journal of Business Forecasting Methods and Systems, 2001, 20*(3), 3-7.

Reimann, L. (2009, 07 01). *Schiffe Schweiz*. Retrieved 07 06, 2010, from Schiffe Schweiz: http://www.schiffe-schweiz.ch/

Resourcebridge. (2011, 02 05). *Resourcebridge.com*. Retrieved 02 05, 2011, from Resourcebridge.com: http://www.resourcebridge.de/definition_rightshoring.htm

Reuter, E., Schröder, H., & Tiittula, L. (1993). Zur Erforschung von Kulturunterschieden in der Internationalen Wirtschaftskommunikation. In B.-D. (. Müller, *Interkulturelle Wirtschaftskommunikation* (pp. 93-121). München: iudicium.

Robock, S., & Simmonds, K. (1989). *International Business and Multinational Enterprises*. Homewood, Il.: Irwin.

Rogers, B. (1999, February). The key account manager as leader. *The Journal of Selling and Major Account Management, 1*(3), 60-66.

Rogers, B. (2007). *Rethinking Sales Management, A strategic guide for practitioners*. London, UK: Wiley Publishing.

Rose, S. (1977, August). Why the multinational tide is ebbing. *Fortune Magazine*, pp. 112-123.

Rumelt, R. P. (1995). Inertia and Transformation. In A. Cyntia, *Resources in an Evolutionary Perspective: Towards a Synthesis of Evolutionary and Resource-Based Approaches to Strategy* (pp. 101-132). Norwell, Mass: Kluwer Academic Publishers.

Ryals, L. J., & Rogers, B. (2006). Holding up the mirror: The impact of strategic procurement practices on account management. *Business Horizons, 49*, 41-50.

Ryals, L., & Rogers, B. (2007). "Key account planning, benefits, barriers and best practice. *Journal of Strategic Marketing, 15*(2-3), 209-222.

Salminen, R. T. (2001). Success factors of a reference visit – a single case study. *Journal of Business & Industrial Marketing, 16*(6), 487 - 507.

Santucci, S. (2010). *Technology Buyer Insight Study: Are Salespeople prepared for executive conversations?* Cambridge, MA: Forrester Research.

Schröder, H. (1993). Interkulturelle Fachkommunikationsforschung. Aspekte kulturkontrastiver Untersuchungen schriftlicher Wirtschaftkommunkation. In T. Bungarten, *Fachsprachentheorie Band 1: Fachsprachliche Terminologie, Begriffs- und Sachsysteme, Methodologie* (pp. 517-550). Hamburg: Attikon.

Schröder, H. (1998). Ethnozentrismus, Stereotype und Lakunen Methodologische Überlegungen zur Analyse interkultureller Kontaktsituationen. In U. Hans, H. Völlings, J. Zimmer, & C. Stracke (Hrsg.), *"Soziologie als Krisenwissenschaft" Festschrift zum 65. Geburtstag von Dankwart Danckwerts, Politische Soziologie Band 11* (pp. S. 41-56.). Köln.

Schröder, H. (2008). *Das Lachen der Kulturen.* Lindau im Bodensee: Plenarvortrag im Rahmen der 58. Lindauer Psychotherapiewochen.

Schröder, H., & Rothe, M. (2008). *Stil, Stilbruch, Tabu. Stilerfahrung nach der Rhetorik. Eine Bilanz. (Semiotik der Kultur - Semiotics of Culture, Band 7).* Münster: LIT-Verlag.

Schröder, H., Reuter, E., & Tiittula, L. (1989). Deutsch-finnische Kulturunterschiede in der Wirtschaftskommunikation. Fragestellungen, Methoden und Ergebnisse eines Forschungsprojekts. In *Jahrbuch Deutsch als Fremdsprache 15.* (pp. 237-269). München: iudicium.

Schrüfer, E. (1989). *Einführung in die Messtechnik.* München, Germany: Hanser.

Schulz von Thun, F. (2001). *Miteinander reden 1-3: Störungen und Klärungen. Stile, Werte und Persönlichkeitsentwicklung. Das "Innere Team" und situationsgerechte Kommunikation* . Hamburg: rororo.

Schunk, D. H. (2008). *Learning Theories: An Educational Perspective.* London, UK: Pearson, Merrill Prentice Hall.

Segal-Horn, S. (1993). The Internationalization of Service Firms. *Advances in Strategic Management*, pp. 31-55.

Sharma, A. (1999). Do salespeople and customers understand each other? Surprising results from extant research. *Journal of Selling and Major Account Management, 3*(1), 29-39.

Simkin, L. (2003). Barriers impeding effective implementation of marketing plans - a training agenda. *Journal of Business & Industrial Marketing, 1*(1), 8-17.

Simpkins, R. A. (2004). *The secrets of great sales management.* New York, NY: Amacom.

Slatter, S. (1984). *Corporate recovery: Successful turnaround strategies.* Singapore: Penguin.

Slotegraaf, R. J. (2004). The Paradox of a Marketing Planning Capability. *Journal of the Academy of Marketing Science, 32*(4), 371-386.

Smith, B. (2003). Making marketing happen: How great medical companies make strategic marketing planning work for them. *International Journal of Medical Marketing, 4*(2), 129-142.

Smith, K., E., J., & Blair, E. (2000). Managing salesperson motivation in a territory realignment. *The Journal of Personal Selling and Sales Management*, 215-226.

Stratis, G. a. (2001). The impact of multiple strategic marketing processes on financial performance. *Journal of Strategic Marketing, 9*(3), 165-192.

Swisscom IT Services AG. (2005, 09 13). *Swisscom and Comit join forces.* Retrieved 01 18, 2010, from Swisscom IT Services AG: http://www.swisscom.ch/IT/content/News_Events/IT_News/20050913_MM_SCIS_Comit.htm?lang=en, last accessed 2010-01-17.

SwissICT. (2010, 1 18). *SwissICT.* Retrieved 1 18, 2010, from SwissICT: http://www.swissict.ch/?L=0

Taleb, N. N. (2008). *The Black Swan – The impact of the highly improbable.* London, UK: Penguin Books.

Techterms.com. (2011, 02 05). *Techterms.COM.* Retrieved 02 05, 2011, from Techterms: http://www.techterms.com/definition/technologyservices

Trompenaars, A., & Hampden-Turner, C. (1995). *Riding the waves of culture.* London: Nicholas Brealey Publishers Ltd.

Trompenaars, F., & Hampden-Turner, C. (2001). *21 Leaders for the 21st Century.* London: J. Wiley & Sons.

Turnbull, J. (2010). *Oxford Advanced Learner's Dictionary.* London: Oxford University Press.

Urban Dictionary. (2011, 02 05). *Urbandictionary.com.* Retrieved 02 05, 2011, from urbandictionary.com: http://www.urbandictionary.com/define.php ?term=right-shoring

von Gamm, C. (2001). *IBM - deploying development activity in non-US-countries?* München: GRIN.

von Gamm, C. (2004). *Swisscom IT Services and The Swiss IT Services Market.* München: GRIN.

von Gamm, C. (2009). Durch Industrialisiertes Outsourcing zu mehr Synergien und zur Transformation. In C. Oecking, R. Jahnke, H. Kiehle, & M. Weber, *Industrialisierung im Outsourcing, Welchen Nutzen Outsourcing-Anwender und -Anbieter aus der Industrialisierung ziehen können* (pp. 57-65). München: CMP-WEKA.

von Gamm, C. (2009). *How to win.* Zürich, Switzerland: Capgemini.

von Gamm, C. (2010). *Integrating a multi-disciplined services organisation in front of a client.* Portsmouth: University of Portsmouth.

Ward, J. a. (2002). *Strategic planning for information systems.* Chichester, UK: John Wiley and Sons.

Wardlow, A. (1988). Investment appraisal criteria and the impact of low inflation. In J. Rutterford, *Financial Strategy – Adding Stakeholder Value* (pp. 27-53). Chichester, UK: Wiley.

Weber, M. C. (1904). *Die protestantische Ethik und der 'Geist' des Kapitalismus.* München: http://www.zeno.org/Soziologie/M/Weber,+Max/Schriften+zur+Religionssoziologie/Die+protestantische+Ethik+und+der+Geist+des+Kapitalismus.

Wilson, H. (2003). Towards rigour in action research: a case study in marketing planning. *European Journal of Marketing, 38*(3/4), 378-401.

Wilson, N., & Summers, B. (2002, 05 17). *Trade Credit Terms Offered by Small Firms: Survey Evidence and Empirical Analysis.* Retrieved 06 06, 2010, from SSRN: http://ssrn.com/abstract=312711

Wimmer, A. (2008). *Möglichkeiten der Effizienzssteigerung für die private und gesetzliche Krankenversicherung in Deutschland.* Karlsruhe: Verlag Versicherungswirtschaft.

Woodburn, D. a. (2001). World-leading key account management: identification and development of strategic relationships. *Report for the Cranfield KAM Best Practice Resarch Club.* Cranfield, MA: Cranfield School of Management.

Ziegler, P. A. (2010). *MSM Research Update July 2010 - Swiss IT Industry.* Schaffhausen: MSM Research.

Appendix

Capgemini – Sales Management Survey (November 2009)

1. From which area of Capgemini are you?

X	Technology Services incl. Capgemini SD&M
X	Outsourcing Services
X	Consulting Services
X	Sogeti

2. What primary job role do you cover?

X	Business Development
X	Consulting
X	Technical Services CSD
X	Technical Services AM
X	Outsourcing Services Delivery
X	Corporate Account Management
X	Enabling Function: Finance
X	Enabling Function: HR
X	Enabling Function: Legal

3. In which country organisation of Capgemini are you employed?

X	Austria
X	Germany
X	Poland
X	Switzerland
X	Czech Republic
X	Slovakia
X	Russia
X	Other, if other please indicate ________________

4. Capgemini employees are paid by base salary and a bonus element, which is determined by role and grade level and function. Mainly said, there are non-sales and sales bonus plans. Which bonus model are you being paid on?

X	Sales / Bookings quota
X	Bonus Scheme based upon qualitative and quantitative goals
X	No bonus scheme

5. For how long do you work with Capgemini?

X	**Less than 1 year**
X	1 - 3 years
X	> 3 - 6 years
X	> 6 - 10 years
X	> 10 years

6. Performance Opinion

What is your personal view on the performance of Capgemini?

O Superb	**O Good**		**O Fair**	**O Below average**	**O Bad**	**O Very bad**

| [...] Any comments?

What is your personal view on the performance of your business areas?

O Superb	**O Good**		**O Fair**	**O Below average**	**O Bad**	**O Very bad**

| [...] Any comments?

7. Do you think Capgemini is missing out Business Opportunities in any area?

X	None
X	Sometimes
X	Often
X	Many
X	Virtually all the time

8. How often do you have (external) client contact (all contact counts, like phone calls, face to face visits, e-mail etc)?

X	Every day
X	1- 5 times per week
X	1- 5 times per month
X	less than one times per month

9. Suggestions on improvement

What are your suggestions on how the operating model of the company might be improved in order to have a faster growth?

Text answer

10. Capgemini utilizes Rightshore as a means to promote a distributed delivery model. How do you believe Rightshore helps you to achieve your business goals?

O A lot	O A bit	O Neutral	O Is contrapro-ductive	O Is very contra-productive

| [...] Any comments?

11. Text question: What would you do in order to improve client intimacy for Capgemini?

Text answer

12. Text Question: What would you do in order to improve the innovation inside Capgemini?

Text answer

13. Text Question: What would you do in order to improve the industrialisation of services inside Capgemini?

Text answer

14. Client encounter: In terms of client encounter, is your client encounter rather the same client or different clients

O Always the same	O Mostly the same	O Quite the same	O Some varying clients	O Many different clients

15. In offering a solution, did you ever encounter one of the following?

Text	Choice
Client just wanted to exactly have what my area did offer.	always O O O O O never
Client did not exactly want what my discipline did offer but bought it anyway, as it did fit halfways well	always O O O O O never
Client did not exactly want what my discipline did offer but bought it anyway, as it did fit halfways well, however a competitor brought the price down.	always O O O O O never
Client wanted to have what my area did offer but other competitors were there and pushed the price down.	always O O O O O never

16. Opportunity Development is referred to as developing a client need the client did not really feel before. In terms of this process and within the last twelve months:

Text	Choice
How often do you work together with clients to explore "wild new" ideas?	often O O O O O never
How often do you work with people who did not meet the client before but could add extra value by combining them with you?	often O O O O O never
How often do you take colleagues from other areas (i.e. TS, CC, OS)?	often O O O O O never
How often do you include colleagues from other geographies (i.e. Poland, India) into your opportunity development discussions?	often O O O O O never
How often do you work together with third parties (i.e. partners, suppliers) directly in front of the client to bring complemented/added value?	often O O O O O never

17. In working so, what enablers and inhibitors did you feel inside Capgemini?

Text answer

18. In losing against competition, Did you ever found one of the following reasons?

Text	Choice
We lost on price	Never O O O O O Always O no opinion
We lost because we did not show the full Power of Capgemini as the whole picture (i.e. missing outsourcing piece, consulting piece, technology piece)	Never O O O O O Always O no opinion
We lost because one of our competitors broadened the scope or bundled other product/service elements into his offer we could not match?	Never O O O O O Always O no opinion
We were not able to provide the references desired	Never O O O O O Always O no opinion
We were not able to provide a the industry or domain expertise the client did expect	Never O O O O O Always O no opinion
We were not able to provide the right credible experts who actually would deliver the service	Never O O O O O Always O no opinion
We were not able to understand the client	Never O O O O O Always O no opinion

fully in his commercial behavior	
We were not able to understand the political intimacy of the client buying cycle	Never O O O O O Always O no opinion

19. Did you ever participate in one of the following planning activities:

X	Account planning for one account with your business area (TS/OS/CC)
X	Account planning for one account with more than one business area (TS/OS/CC/Sogeti)
X	Territory planning for a multitude of clients within your area
X	Territory planning for a multitude of clients with multiple business units (TS/OS/CC, Sogeti)
X	Account planning with an external partner (i.e. supplier, other consultancy firm)
X	More than one of those options
X	None of those

20. On the concept of Integrated Account Management / Key account Management / Client Account Management:

X	I heard of it and I think I do use it
X	I heard of it but I cannot apply it
X	I heard of it and I do not believe into it
X	I do not understand what you mean

21. Capgemini is about to install a series of account managers for major clients

Text	**Choice**
Key account management helps coordinate activities for the client across multiple disciplines	disagree O O O O O agree
Key account management does add unnecessary overhead to a client activity	disagree O O O O O agree
Key Account management helps yield additional opportunities for areas not primarily covered otherwise	disagree O O O O O agree
Account Management costs more than it yields for my business unit	disagree O O O O O agree
The biggest challenge is that my business/offering is so specialized no one else but a few and myself understand it, therefore account managers would need to be highly integrated into my business unit.	disagree O O O O O agree

Key account managers are not compensated to help my business unit or area flourish.	disagree O O O O O agree
The skill level of key account managers needs to be improved in order to yield results for my business unit.	disagree O O O O O agree

On the concept of pay to performance, key account managers for businesses do receive a certain "share" of the revenue as their pay, which then overall deducts from the total "piece of cake" a sales community does receive. How do you believe the pay scheme should be organised?

22. This question discusses pay to performance

Text	Choice
The variable element of the pay is to be associated with the overall success of the business units or area the key account manager is serving.	disagree O O O O O agree O no opinion
The variable element of the pay (bonus) is to be paid according to the individual contribution of the sales person, only.	disagree O O O O O agree O no opinion
The contribution and pay of the key account manager should be decided upon the revenues from the different business units and pre-agreed at the beginning of the quota period, i.e. year.	disagree O O O O O agree O no opinion
Specialist business area leaders (i.e. TS, OS, CC) should determine the pay of the key account managers, individually.	disagree O O O O O agree O no opinion
On a large deal, a pool bonus should be defined and be decided by the business unit leader how to distribute the deal bonus to ALL members according to contribution.	disagree O O O O O agree O no opinion
Key account managers should simply see a certain percentage of revenues of the accounts they are working on, no matter what their individual contribution was.	disagree O O O O O agree O no opinion

23. On account planning:

Text	Choice
A coordinated plan across all divisions on how to work best with a client and to tap the potential will yield additional revenues.	unlikely O O O O O very likely

The account plans I have participated on have helped grow the business.	unlikely O O O O O very likely
The account plans I have worked did involve all disciplines (CC, TS, OS).	unlikely O O O O O very likely

24. Territory planning is a process that inspects a sales territory (industry- geographywise) and plans the signings and revenue opportunities accordingly.

Text	Choice
Do you think territory planning should be done as a team or rather through individuals?	disagree O O O O O agree
Should a territory planning involve participants from other business units in order to integrate views?	disagree O O O O O agree

25. Other comments you would like to leave? Text answer.

Text answer

Cross-Reference

Nordeuropäische Beiträge aus den Human- und Gesellschaftswissenschaften

Scandinavian University Studies in the Humanities and Social Sciences

Herausgegeben von / Edited by
Hartmut Schröder

Band 1 Riitta Korhonen / Martin Kusch / Hartmut Schröder (toimittajat): Lopussa teksti. 1992.

Band 2 Marianne Nordman (Hrsg.): Fachsprachliche Miniaturen. Festschrift für Christer Laurén. 1992.

Band 3 Mariann Skog-Södersved: Wortschatz und Syntax des außenpolitischen Leitartikels. Quantitative Analysen der Tageszeitungen „Neues Deutschland", „Neue Zürcher Zeitung", „Die Presse" und „Süddeutsche Zeitung". 1993.

Band 4 Anna Mauranen: Cultural Differences in Academic Rhetoric. A Textlinguistic Study. 1993.

Band 5 Peder Skyum-Nielsen / Hartmut Schröder (eds.): Rhetoric and Stylistics Today. An International Anthology. 1994.

Band 6 Jouko Jokisalo: Vom Bockmist zur geschichtsmäßigen Kraft. Determinanten und Wirkung der Heilsversprechen des „deutschen Sozialismus" (1933-1939). 1994.

Band 7 Jarmo Pulkkinen: The Threat of Logical Mathematism. A Study on the Critique of Mathematical Logic in Germany at the Turn of the 20th Century. 1994.

Band 8 Eero J. Laine: Learning Second National Languages. A Research Report. 1995.

Band 9 Vesa Oittinen: Der Akt als Fundament des Bewußtseins? Zur Differenz zwischen G.I. Hartman und nachkantischer Transzendentalphilosophie. 1996.

Band 10 Christer Laurén / Marianne Nordman: Wissenschaftliche Technolekte. 1996.

Band 12 Harry Anttila: Prädikate und Satzmodelle in Zeitungstexten. Ein Beitrag zur historischen Syntax des Deutschen, gezeigt an der Leipziger Zeitung 1660-1914. 1997.

Band 13 Hannele Kohvakka: Ironie und Text. Zur Ergründung von Ironie auf der Ebene des sprachlichen Textes. 1997.

Band 14 Pertti Ahonen / Ari Salminen: Metamorphosis of the Administrative Welfare State. From Depoliticisation to Political Rationality. 1997.

Band 15 Gerhard Schmitt: Zyklus und Kompensation. Zur Denkfigur bei Nietzsche und Jung. 1998.

Band 16 Yves Gambier (éd.): Discours Professionnels en Français. 1998.

Band 17 Irmeli Helin: Vom Brodverein zur co op. Terminigeschichte der deutschen Genossenschaftssprache. Ein Beitrag zur Terminologieforschung. 1998.

Band 18 Pekka Kujamäki: Deutsche Stimmen der *Sieben Brüder*. Ideologie, Poetik und Funktionen literarischer Übersetzung. 1998.

Band 19 Jürgen Gercken: Kultur, Sprache und Text als Aspekte von Original und Übersetzung. Theoretische Grundlagen und Exemplifizierung eines Vergleichs kulturspezifischer Textinhalte. 1999.

Band 20 Christer Påhlsson: Decision-Making and Limited Resources. Studies in Interlanguage Vocabulary Space of Learners of English for Special Purposes. 1999.

Band 21 Urpo Kovala: Anchorages of Meaning. The Consequences of Contextualist Approaches to Literary Meaning Production. 2001.

Band 22 Eckhard Höfner / Hartmut Schröder / Roland Wittmann (Hrsg.): Valami más. Beiträge des Finnisch-Ungarischen Kultursemiotischen Symposiums *Zeichenhafte Aspekte der Veränderung* (25.-28.11.1998 Berlin – Frankfurt (Oder) – Slubice). 2002.

Band 23 Ewald Reuter / Marja-Leena Piitulainen (Hrsg.): Internationale Wirtschaftskommunikation auf Deutsch. Die deutsche Sprache im Handel zwischen den nordischen und den deutschsprachigen Ländern. 2003.

Band 24 Irmeli Helin (Hrsg.): Dialektübersetzung und Dialekte in Multimedia. 2004.

Band 25 Irmeli Helin: ... *so der Wetterbericht.* Evidentialität und Redewiedergabe in deutschen und finnischen Medientexten und Übersetzungen. 2004.

Band 26 Ingrid Simonnæs: Verstehensprobleme bei Fachtexten. Zu Begriffssystemen und Paraphrasen als Visualisierungs- bzw. Verbalisierungsinstrumente in der Kommunikation zwischen Fachmann und Laien. Eine Untersuchung anhand gerichtlicher Entscheidungen. 2005.

Band 27 Heikki J. Koskinen / Sami Pihlström / Risto Vilkko (eds.): Science – A Challenge to Philosophy? 2006.

Band 28 Lars Wollin / Dagmar Neuendorff / Michael Szurawitzki (Hrsg.): Deutsch im Norden. Akten 18.-19. Mai 2007. 2009.

Band 29 Jasmin Cornelius: Mediation und systemische Therapie. Überlegungen zu einer Adaptierung des Mediationsverfahrens auf die speziellen Bedürfnisse von Paaren. 2010.

Band 30 Jonathan Knowles / Henrik Rydenfelt (eds.): Pragmatism, Science and Naturalism. 2011.

Band 31 Christoph Freiherr von Gamm: Multi-national and intercultural services organisations and the integration in front of global clients. 2011.

www.peterlang.de

Kolibri 360 GmbH
Ferdinand-Jühlke-Straße 7
99095 Erfurt, Deutschland
produktsicherheit@kolibri360.de